Chicken Soup for the Soul®

Empty Nesters

Chicken Soup for the Soul®:
Empty Nesters; 101 Stories about Surviving and Thriving When the Kids Leave Home
by Jack Canfield, Mark Victor Hansen, Carol McAdoo Rehme, and Patricia Cena Evans

Published by Chicken Soup for the Soul Publishing, LLC   www.chickensoup.com

The publisher gratefully acknowledges the many publishers and individuals who
granted Chicken Soup for the Soul permission to reprint the cited material.

Cover photos courtesy of Jupiter Images/Botanica and photos.com.
Interior photo by iStockPhoto.com/filonmar

Cover and Interior Design & Layout by Pneuma Books, LLC
For more info on Pneuma Books, visit www.pneumabooks.com

Distributed to the booktrade by Simon & Schuster. SAN: 200-2442

Publisher's Cataloging-in-Publication Data
(Prepared by The Donohue Group)

Chicken soup for the soul : empty nesters : 101 stories about surviving and thriving
   when the kids leave home / [compiled by] Jack Canfield ... [et al.].

   p. ; cm.

ISBN-13: 978-1-935096-22-1
ISBN-10: 1-935096-22-2

1. Empty nesters--Literary collections. 2. Empty nesters--Conduct of life--Anecdotes.
3. Empty nesters--Family relationships--Anecdotes. 4. Adult children--Family relation-
ships--Anecdotes. I. Canfield, Jack, 1944- II. Title: Empty nesters

PN6071.P28 C485 2008
810.8/03520431   2008934198

PRINTED IN THE UNITED STATES OF AMERICA
on acid∞free paper
16 15 14 13 12 11   02 03 04 05 06 07 08

Chicken Soup for the Soul. Empty Nesters

101 Stories about
Surviving and Thriving
When the Kids Leave Home

Jack Canfield
Mark Victor Hansen
Carol McAdoo Rehme
Patricia Cena Evans

Chicken Soup for the Soul Publishing, LLC
Cos Cob, CT

Chicken Soup for the Soul

Dedication

We dedicate this book to our children:
Kyle Rehme, Katrina Hatch, Kayla Crockett, and Koy Rehme;
Dustin Hankins, Ryan Hankins, Meredith Hankins Bloxham,
and Kristin and Jonathan Evans.

Thanks for the memories...
and the (almost) empty bedrooms you left behind.

Chicken Soup
for the Soul

Contents

❶

~First Flights~

❷

~Under Our Wings and In Our Hearts~

❸

~Out on a Limb~

❹

~Ruffled Feathers~

❺

~Wings and Wisdom~

❻
~Left Behind~

❼
~Branching Out~

8

~Home Sweet Nest~

Chicken Soup for the Soul

Foreword

From the moment children enter our lives, whether by birth or by bonding, they become an extension of our selves. When she sings, we sing. When he hurts, we hurt. In a whisper, we plant seeds that say, "You will always be my baby. Forever and ever."

And we gladly pour heart and soul—not to mention paychecks and stamina—into raising these precious beings. We become nurturers, teachers, advocates, and private booster clubs. We champion and chastise, shape and sustain, comfort... and complain. Complain that they're unreasonable. Immature. That they need to grow up.

Then, at mach-speed, they do grow up.

One unexpected day, we awake to mortarboards, college tuition, and wedding toasts. And we discover that in building the boy, we molded the man; in growing the girl, we fashioned the woman. Those beautiful eyes that once locked into ours for protection and delight—that melted our hearts and pried open our wallets—now focus on the future, in pursuit of Bright Hopes and Big Dreams.

It matters not that we did this to our parents, who planted the same whispered seeds on our birth day. It matters not that leaving home is a rite of passage for all generations. The house heaves a sigh of relief yet echoes our footsteps in miserable loneliness. The washing machine spits out the last missing sock and hiccups to hold back its tears. The car belches, pats its unaccustomed girth of a never-empty tank, and naps in the drive, utterly bored. All because millions of our sons and daughters graduated or got married this year, moved out and moved on. And where are the middle-aged, Baby Boomer parents they've left behind?

Judging from the hundreds of stories submitted on this topic, they're trying to focus on their own—newly or nearly child-less—futures. Daring to dream new dreams or patching together the pieces of old ones they left strewn along the parenting pathway. They are mourning the years passed and past. Then, squaring their shoulders and lifting their heads, they are discovering exciting new ways to be part of their children's lives.

The stories these Empty Nesters share will encourage, validate, and nourish those of us approaching or adjusting to this new season, those whose family defines them. After all, it is a rite of passage for us, as well. Just as we want our children to blossom, so must we.

And so we serve them up, these candid stories that portray an often over-looked and under-realized stage of life: The Empty Nest. Whether tender or humorous, tearful or tongue-in-cheek, these episodes and essays offer the wisdom of experience and the hope of example.

In the creases of these pages, may you discover solace and joy, courage and liberation—and the tools to forge ahead in the pursuit of your own Bright Hopes and Big Dreams.

~Carol McAdoo Rehme and Patricia Cena Evans

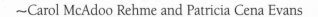

Empty Nesters

First Flights

How do you know when a fruit is ripe?
When it leaves the bunch.
~André Gide

Trading Spaces

A wise man hears one word and understands two.
~Yiddish Proverb

She's leaving for college in just a few weeks and we've made all the preparations. Went to the dentist and had her teeth cleaned. Bought contacts. Checked off lists of things to take. Cleaned out her closet. Purchased tickets so she could come home at Thanksgiving.

And all the while, I mentally prepared a separate list: a calculated rearrangement of the furniture and trinkets crowding her bedroom to create a new space. A study. A place to call my own. A place where I can spread out. Room for everything. A file cabinet for my files. A bookshelf for my books. After years of squeezing in here and there, of sharing space with our son's disks labeled X-Wing Fighter and my husband's marked *Orthopedic Review*, I'm dreaming of a desk all to myself. My own space.

Everything seemed to be going along as planned—until today. Just before she left for work, we had a confrontation. Our voices were raised; our emotions ran deep.

"I can't believe you want to pack all my things into boxes and store them in the basement. This is still my home. I live here. I'm just going away to college."

"Honey," I reasoned, "you'll only be here for holidays."

"And all summer!" She tossed her head and I caught a look in her eye. A look that said, "I'm really excited about this, but I'm scared too. I want to leave and grow up, but don't you want to beg me to stay?"

Last night she curled up next to me on the couch.

"Scratch my head," she purred. "Now my back. You won't get to do this much." Her declarations of independence tinged with pity puzzled me. But maybe I'm beginning to hear what she's saying. She's asking for reassurance that life won't be quite as special once she's gone. She needs a place to come back to—just in case.

And maybe I need to acknowledge that her departure is ripping a hole in my heart.

When I look at her, I glimpse the child she was. I can feel the press of her tiny fingers as they wrapped around mine a moment after her birth. I can smell her fresh new baby skin and feel her fuzzy head against my cheek. I can all but hear her toddler's plea of, "Mom-mom, hold me-me."

Perhaps she needs to be sure that no one could ever take her place, and that I'll miss her more than she'll ever know. Maybe she wants to see me ache—just a little—and to know I mourn losing her. Instead of being eager to turn her room into a study, perhaps she longs for me to melt into a puddle of tears. To exhibit the hurt that tells her she is irreplaceable.

Maybe she's right.

Instead of putting up this brave front—this shield of reorganization and continuance of life—I need to allow the pain of parting to sweep over me. To taste the grief. To acknowledge that our family is changing and will never be the same. To accept the young woman replacing my little girl. To admit that, while I'm very proud of her, I long for the days when she needed me in so many ways.

Maybe she knows that in the coming months it will be better for me to have access to her old familiar bedroom. Maybe she recognizes my need to grab her favorite stuffed polar bear, bury my face in its soft fur, and cry because my baby grew up too fast. Maybe she understands that if I pack away all her knickknacks and keepsakes, my fingers will have nothing to grasp when my arms ache to hold her.

Maybe... just maybe... she knows I'm not ready for a study yet and losing her is harder than I want to admit. And that the only space needing to be rearranged is the empty one in my heart.

~Susan M. Cameron

"Have fun at College! I'll miss you...and, by the way... I'll be turning your room into a yoga studio!"

Forty Weeks

I walk into my teenage daughter's room to find—once again—her bed, floor, desk, and most other surfaces covered with papers, books, projects, or clothes. I offer to help clean her room and reorganize her closets and drawers.

With a sly grin, Tara replies, "No need to, Mom. I'll be leaving soon."

"Oh, where are you going?" I ask, trying to remember if she has soccer or piano that evening.

"You know, Mom, to college. I'll be leaving in about ten months. Only forty more weeks. It's not worth reorganizing my room since I'll be going so soon."

I blink, startled. She's serious.

An hour later, I walk into her twin brother's room to check his progress with college applications. My effort is far from appreciated.

"Mom, you need to stop nagging me," Jake says. "I'll be leaving for college soon. In only forty more weeks, you won't know what I'll be doing or where I'll be."

My heart skips a beat. Can it be true they'll both be off to college so soon? I suddenly remember countless mothers peering into my twins' stroller commenting on how fast the years would go. They were right. But it feels surreal.

Who could have known our inquisitive daughter would grow into a beautiful young woman with plans to study psychology and neuroscience? Likewise our toddler son, who beat table tops and toy drums with an array of silverware and sticks, will soon enter a conservatory to pursue his passion for composing and performing classical percussion music.

Only forty more weeks. Although I have spent their life-times teaching, loving and encouraging them, somehow—at this moment—it doesn't seem enough. So much left to be said and done. Myriad bits of advice dance and tumble in my head like loose buttons in a spinning dryer.

I feel an urgent need to ensure that Tara and Jake will have the skills necessary to manage the multiple demands placed on them. Practicalities like opening checking accounts and the art of monthly balancing must still be taught. I want to emphasize the importance of relishing each day while setting limits in an unbounded environment. I feel the need to talk more about dating, relationships, marriage. And what about daily exercise and sleep? I want to reinforce how important it is to follow their dreams and passions, work hard and play hard, and do ordinary things in an extraordinary way.

Further, we need more time together. Time for picnic breakfasts by meandering streams. Time for more bike rides encircled by beautiful mountains.

I find it difficult to acknowledge that our daily interactions over these past eighteen years will come to an abrupt end. Although I'm elated that their departure will open new doors for all of us, I also feel my heart breaking. I picture myself peeking into their silent bed-rooms before I leave for work only to see dust particles floating in rays of early morning sunlight. But I vow to follow my own advice and relish all the surprises and opportunities that await us in this next phase of family life.

Recently, Tara argued about her curfew. "Give me one good rea-son I should be home that early!"

Without a moment's hesitation, her dad grinned and replied, "Because you'll be leaving soon. In less than forty weeks. And we want to see a lot of you before you go."

She returned his grin, hugged him and headed quickly out the door.

~Marian Gormley

Baby Steps

I woke my son David for school for the last time ever yesterday. Not a big deal, really. I wouldn't have even thought of it if he hadn't reminded, "Don't wake me tomorrow, Mom. I'm going in late for a final." Then he added, "In fact, you won't have to wake me from now on."

And that's when it hit me. He's done with high school. Again, not a big deal, really. Except that it is. He's my baby, this 6' 4" man.

Twenty-seven years ago, I managed my firstborn the best I could with my entry-level maternity skills. My second child, four years later, was easier, because I knew what to expect. Then, after the heartbreak of a miscarriage, there was David. He was it, my last baby. That awareness made me savor every moment of his babyhood in a way I hadn't with the others.

I rocked him to sleep, and then continued rocking, feeling his warm weight on my shoulder, instead of plopping him in his crib to "get something done" as I'd done before. On walks, I didn't hurry him past the storm drain when he knelt to plop pebbles into the water. I didn't hurry David on to the next step. I let him unfold like the leaves in spring, sometimes early, sometimes not.

Now my final fledgling is ready to fly and I'm ready to let him go. Life is unfolding as it should. I raised David to stand on his own two feet, find his path in the world, and be productive in a way that matters.

He is my baby, but I didn't baby him. I shortened my pace for him. I walked slowly with his small hand grasping mine. I stepped lively along as he wobbled on his first bike. I sat stiffly and pushed my foot on an imaginary brake as he learned to drive. Now, I just wave out the window as he heads off somewhere. I let him test his wings. I know he'll soar.

I'll miss him. I'll look forward to having him come home to roost now and then. Meanwhile, I'll set my own pace. There's a new life waiting. For both of us.

~Ruth Douillette

Giving Birth

Two children born eighteen months apart. The years zippity-doo-dah by and suddenly it's time for our darlings to choose a wider life.

In 1986, Greg sprints to Oregon and college. The following year, Kaaren scoots to a university on the Washington coast. With each departure, my husband John and I snuffle and feel bereft. For about a month. After all, the kids will be home for holidays and we will make occasional weekend treks in their directions.

Three years pass. Greg falls in love. He and our daughter-in-law to-be make a surprise visit proclaiming a summer wedding. We are thrilled. In tandem, Kaaren learns she will spend her fall term as a study abroad student in Tanzania. We are elated.

August 17, a sweet wedding in Eugene, Oregon. Our family expands. I ignore the lump in my throat. August 18, en route to Sea-Tac Airport to send our "baby" to Africa I am unsettled. But why? Such joyful times, such opportunities, such a short separation.

An hour before we arrive at the airport, I sniff. John asks if I'm getting a cold. Unable to deny any longer that our precious quartet has changed forever, my mother-water breaks. I wail, as out of control as the Cowardly Lion.

When we pause at traffic lights, I notice Kaaren stretched across the back seat. She's hiding because people are staring as I flail about the passenger seat. What neither John nor Kaaren understand is that a birth is in process—get me to a delivery room.

_ the airport, I tone it down to an occasional gasp with a ₒn chaser. My nose burnt sienna, my eyes swollen slits. Kaaren ₒorwards a half mile ahead of us. John vaults beyond my grasp. . here is the doula?

When it's time to say goodbye, Kaaren appears relieved I am not gripping her ankle and shrieking her name. We hug. It's not enough. I desperately need to forge a link before she leaves.

"Darling, remember to find the last star on the handle of the Big Dipper—and know that we are looking at it with you. There are a few oceans between us, but we'll be with you every step."

On our return trip to Spokane, like a stuck record I weep out a sound track of aborted grief for 267.9 miles. My twenty-two-year pregnancy of holding on has come to an end. This birth is about letting go.

After many evenings of Dipper-spotting, January finally arrives and we return to Seattle to collect our changed-forever daughter. I cry grateful tears.

"We looked at the Big Dipper nearly every night the stars came out. Did you?" I muse to my daughter.

Kaaren stalls. "Um, no, Mom. I considered writing you about this, but it didn't seem like such a great idea. Actually," she cleared her throat, "the Big Dipper doesn't appear in the African sky."

And then, we all give birth... to laughter.

~Gail Goeller

At the Close of the Day

*W*e should have been asleep, but we weren't. David because he's eighteen, and me, because I lose track of time when I'm at my computer.

I'm usually in bed long before he is, reading or maybe curled with the cat. Sometimes David stops outside my door and says good-night. Other times, he comes in, pats the cat, and gives me a kiss. If I'm really lucky, he stretches out beside me and shares his day, making the scenes alive with his talent for imitation.

He's already in charge of his own time and activities—up to a point. But he's still my baby, so when I heard him whisper, "'Night, Mom," on my way down the hall, I pushed open his door, and sat on the edge of the bed to give him a kiss.

"Remember when you used to fall asleep on the floor beside my bed?" he asked.

I do remember. It eased him through his nightmare stage. I'd lie on my back, so tired I'd often wake hours later to crawl into my own bed. If he woke in the middle of the night, he'd come and sleep on the floor beside me.

I was glad when that stage passed. I was glad when he'd go upstairs by himself to wash his face, brush his teeth, and put on his pajamas.

"'Night, Mom," he'd yell from bed. "Will you come up and tuck me in?"

I was glad when the bed-to-living-room conversations ended,

too. Just when I settled with a cup of tea and a book, he'd yell down, "Mom?"

"What?"

"Who do you think would win in a fight? Tyrannosaurus Rex or Spider-Man?"

"Tyrannosaurus. Go to sleep."

"Mom?"

"What?"

"What was your favorite thing to do when you were little?"

"Read. Now go to sleep."

By the time my tea was finished, my patience was drained as well. To his "Mom?" I'd shout back, "WHAT!" It was a horrible sound, a shriek that escaped my throat with the force of a sneeze.

After a pause he'd say in an aggrieved tone, "I was just going to say, 'I love you.'"

"I love you, too, David. Now go to sleep."

Who knew that I would miss those days? Who knew they would seem so sweet in retrospect? Soon he'll be sleeping in a college dorm, the first tentative steps toward a life on his own. But I'll still whisper, "'Night, Dave," when I turn off my light each night.

~Ruth Douillette

6

A Close-Up Shot

A daughter may outgrow your lap, but she will never outgrow your heart.
~Anonymous

I plopped in my easy chair after lugging the last piece of equipment back to storage. It had been a grueling day—another day of chasing a bride. That's what we call it in the photography business. You play tag with the bride as she flits from the make-up table to hugs; from flowers to dresses; from the aisle to the cake; from reception to a limo.

All while you try to capture memorable photos.

It is demanding physically and emotionally. Months of detailed planning and preparation precede each wedding and everyone's feelings float warily on the surface. For many, weddings mile-mark the beginning of an empty nest. Someone's son and someone's daughter are leaving home and parents behind in anticipation of forging a future and a home of their own. Because it's the event of a lifetime, everything must be perfect. After all, there are no second chances for the photography—it must be done right. And it must be done right the first time.

Everyone seems to know of a sad photographic experience at a wedding. That is why I triple check everything, have backup equipment, and force myself to keep a level head. My clients and even my wife compliment me on my ability to go with the flow and not get stressed during these highly stressful occasions.

Satisfied with the day's results, I balked at the thought of the next bride, surprised to acknowledge that, after thirty years of honing my craft, I felt insecure.

This sitting would be tougher than most. It was a bridal portrait and the final image would be large and displayed on an easel at the wedding reception. Mothers-of-the-brides are infamous for their demanding reputations, distress over letting go of their daughters, and angst at the thought of the holes left in their lives. This particular MOB carried the added burden of being a relative.

Yes, a relative. They are always the most difficult. Relatives expect more. They expect perfect work. And they expect perfect work for free. Many photographers refuse to photograph family events. But I am a pro and pride myself on keeping all those tensions in check. Once I commit there's no turning back.

Shouldering the responsibility, I load my car and drive to the site the bride chose. A glance upward confirms a cooperative sky as I hunch to inspect the gear packed into my trunk. I load film first—sure don't want to make that simple mistake. Then I double-check the lighting systems, set up the tripod, and make test shots. All is well; all is calm. And I'm ready just as the bride arrives.

She looks so young. Too young to get married. "Are you sure you're old enough to be legal?" I deadpan.

She looks startled, then grins. "Almost twenty-two," she insists. "Legal and beyond!"

My brows shoot up and I shake my head doubtfully.

"Don't you feel some guilt for leaving your parents?"

She shakes her head and giggles.

She's giddy—just like all the rest. She's in wispy white—just like all the rest. She's accompanied by her faithful entourage—just like all the rest. It's her final picture as daughter, her first as a bride. And I can see by the expression on her face that she's ready to grasp the kite-tail of her dreams and fly into her future.

I am fully prepared to make a beautiful portrait. I know the procedure so well—place her feet just so, shift her weight, angle her shoulders, tilt her head, position her hand into graceful "Barbie doll fingers" …and then be ready for the perfect expression she and this picky MOB hope for.

Both of them have planned this image all their lives. They're expecting that Cinderella look-and-feel they always envisioned. Well, this bride is drop-dead gorgeous. I nod in approval. It's going to be a piece of cake.

I bend my head to look through the viewfinder. Something is dreadfully wrong with this picture. It's out of focus. The bride looks odd, she looks too... young. I check the settings and try again. Now the bride is fuzzy.

"What's going on?" I mutter.

Once more, I examine the camera. All is in order.

No, wait. The lens is fogged.

My heart flutters and I steady myself. Yet, no matter how hard I try to call on my years of professional training, I can't seem to make this picture clear. A jagged breath catches in my throat and I suddenly understand the problem.

With a rueful sigh, I turn away and swipe roughly at the mist of tears blurring my optics. No pro worth his salt would let them be discovered.

I corral my emotions. "Turn a little. And, lean in," I hear myself say in a surprisingly normal tone. "Now, a sweet smile, Sweetie," I swallow hard. "A special smile just for your old... er... for your groom." I force myself to separate my personal feelings from the image in the lens. "That's it. That's it. Yes... wow!"

Click.

Click, click, click.

I clear my throat and manage a broad beam in spite of myself. "What a beautiful, blushing bride."

Another daughter leaving the nest to find her future. I shake my head ruefully. My daughter. This daddy's little girl.

~Norman L. Rehme as told to Carol McAdoo Rehme

Condo-lences

"**B**y the way, Mom, I won't be home for dinner tomorrow night."

Those words, "by the way, Mom," make me shudder with fear and dread of unimaginable proportions ever since my son, Jeff, first began to utter that phrase.

He used it innumerable times during his early school years, usually at bedtime. "By the way, Mom, my report is due tomorrow."

As he grew older, the subject changed, but never the phraseology and never, never the method. "By the way, Mom, tomorrow's the prom, and I didn't order any flowers."

For some reason, his use of the phrase this time caught my attention. "Why will you miss dinner, Jeff?"

"I've got an appointment to go see a condo."

Condo? Jeff moving out?

Thoughts tumbled in, out, and around my head. I knew, deep in the depths of my heart, that a parent's goal is to prepare her child for an independent, productive life to prepare him to spread his wings and soar. I was all for that. But in pursuit of that goal, I hadn't prepared myself for that moment.

Jeff put in a bid for the condo the next day and we waited for a response. As the evening drew to a close and I still hadn't heard from him, I had a sinking feeling his bid wasn't accepted. Setting aside my sadness and angst, I felt concern for Jeff's disappointment. First,

I worried about Jeff getting the condo; then I worried about him not getting it. Even I could sense the irony in the situation.

"She accepted my offer." Jeff's cryptic text message suddenly appeared on my screen. I called him immediately and congratulated him.

As soon as he got home, I questioned him. "When will you close?"

"Either thirty or sixty days, I'm not sure."

Grappling with the impact of this information, I gasped. "But, that's not enough time!"

"Mom, it's okay. That's plenty of time to get a mortgage."

"Sure, that's plenty of time for a mortgage and for you to get ready to move; it's just not enough time for me to prepare." Then I smiled to signal I was half joking—the half that wasn't serious.

I didn't want to stop him, not really. It's just that Jeff and I have always been close. I thought back, remembering when, as a four-year-old, he took it upon himself to become my coach before, during, and after physical therapy sessions during the dark weeks that followed my two spinal cord surgeries.

At day camp that summer, Jeffrey had approached a counselor who led the camp in exercises. "My mom's having trouble moving her fingers," he said. "Can you show me some exercises to help fix her hands?"

The counselor obliged by demonstrating a simple technique.

When Jeff came home, he promptly closed my hands into fists. "Look what my counselor showed me." Jeff pressed his small fingers against mine for resistance. "Now, try to open them, Mom."

He worked with me over and over that summer, helping me to regain gradual mobility until I could use my hands and stretch my fingers wide. His determination and effort bonded us in a way that nothing else could.

Now, witnessing Jeff purchase his first home was, I understood, a joyous time in spite of my sadness and nostalgia.

I knew I must let him stretch and spread his wings—because he once helped me do the same.

~Donna Lowich

My Nice Surprise

S imon came to live at our house when my daughter was three. I had promised Jessica that when we went shopping for clothes for her new baby brother, I would buy a nice surprise for her, too.

We walked among the toy aisles searching for just the right thing. I pointed out Birthday Barbie, Silly Putty, and Polly Pocket. Judiciously, she looked each item over, then carefully slid it back onto the shelf.

"No," she said thoughtfully. "I'll know it when I see it."

I was about to give up that she would ever see it, when suddenly she stopped—eyes fixed on a shelf above her head—and clapped her hands together. "Mommy, there it is! There's my nice surprise!"

I could see nothing that might appeal to a three-year-old girl. It was definitely the "boy side" of the aisle, filled with Legos, Hot Wheels, and forty-nine renditions of Batman action figures.

She stood on her tiptoes. "There! Right by you. My nice surprise."

A rubber snake hung suspended, halfway off his perch, on a shelf that was my eye level. I reached for him and Jessica bounced with glee.

"This?" I asked, sure I was mistaken, and that there must be a silver-swirled My Little Pony hidden at an angle I just couldn't see.

"Yes!" She reached up to take the snake, a look of pure adoration in her brown eyes. "Oh, yes, Mommy. Isn't he cute?"

"Uh… yeah. He's cute." I bit my lip. Now, I was worried. Not only did my little angel show a total lack of interest in girl toys today, she chose something so hideously ugly I would hope even a boy would pass over.

"I'm going to name him Simon. Simon the Rubber Snake."

Oh, brother. There was no turning back now. But I had to try, anyway.

"Wouldn't you rather have some Play-Doh?"

"No. You said it's too messy, remember?"

Yes I had said that—it's really hard to get out of carpet.

"How about a box of crayons? A really big box."

She held Simon the Rubber Snake close. "Can I have the crayons, too?"

I was about to say no, but something stopped me. Simon was beyond ugly, and I had never been a fan of reptiles, but...

"Mommy, no one will love him if we don't buy him. He was all alone up there on the shelf." She looked at the snake again, then back up at me. "Please?"

I hugged her, my eyes filling with tears. Tears for a rubber snake. Simon, the Rubber Snake.

"You're such a good girl, Jessi."

"An' Simon's a good snake, too."

I nodded. "Yes. Let's take Simon home with us. But first, we'll go pick out that box of crayons."

I couldn't understand her fascination with Simon. She had a room full of Beanie Babies and baby dolls, but Simon the Rubber Snake got to sleep under her pillow every night.

Simon roamed the house. At times, he found his way under my pillow or into the clothes hamper. I'd always be properly startled, squealing in mock fright. "Oh, Simon," I'd laugh. "You really got me that time."

Because this game delighted Jessica so much, I began hiding Simon in her room for her to find. I always knew when she made the discovery. I'd hear her infectious giggle, followed by, "Oh, Simon. You really got me that time!"

Eventually, Simon was relegated to the toy shelf, then the top of the closet. But suggestions to pack him away were met with stern opposition.

Jessica's high school graduation day came and went. In the blink of an eye, she was headed to college. Even though she would be only an hour's drive away, I felt the hole in my heart as surely as if she were moving across the country. Becoming a college girl marked a new phase of her life, a new level of independence.

With mixed emotions, I waved goodbye as she pulled out of the driveway, car radio blaring. She rolled the window down and shouted something I couldn't hear above the roar.

"What?"

"Look in your bedroom!"

I nodded, and waved again. I reminded myself that I had known this day was coming, but it didn't help. I waited until she drove around the corner. Then, I went inside and opened my bedroom door. Nothing was different. I must have misunderstood what she was telling me. I sat down on the bed, then lay full length.

But when I put my head down, I felt something odd. I pulled the spread back. There was Simon the Rubber Snake staring up at me from hellish orange-red eye sockets, his fangs still intact after all those years.

"Isn't he cute? Simon's a good snake," a childish voice from the past echoed in my head.

A yellow sticky note wrapped his body. I unfastened it, reading slowly.

Take care of Simon the Rubber Snake for me, Mom.
I'll see you this weekend.
Love, Jess

I hugged Simon to me, remembering that long-ago day when he'd come to live with us—and all the years in between. You're such a good girl, Jessi, I thought. "Oh, Simon," I whispered. "You really got me that time."

~Cheryl Pierson

Send Cookies

*Y*es, I'll admit it. I cried when my daughter went to college. A mother-in-mourning, I curled on her bed hugging one of her little pink teddy bears. When she finally called to say—in a voice radiating sheer joy—that she was unpacked and settled, I got up, baked her some cookies, and moved on with life.

Two years later, the scenario replayed itself when our older son packed his car and headed to college. I felt like my heart was broken. Like a good mother, I carefully researched and wrote out a list of every possible place along the route where he could find friends and refuge. I even called people and told them he might show up on their doorstep. He, too, phoned to say he had arrived safely and was excited about his new beginnings. I got up, baked him some cookies, and moved on with life.

Then our younger son turned seventeen and announced he intended to enlist in the Marines. Nothing—and I do mean nothing—could have prepared me for that bombshell, no pun intended. A huge lump of steel dropped straight into my stomach and lodged itself there.

"No," I gasped. "You're just a boy."

"Mom, I'm almost out of high school," he argued. "Besides, I've already talked to the recruiter."

I waited for my husband to say something like: "No, not only no, but NO!" Instead, all I saw was a father's beaming grin.

Granted, no wars were going on at the time, a fact the boy made certain I knew. But why had my quiet, tender-hearted son decided to be a Marine? This time I didn't wait until he drove off into the sunset. I broke down and cried right there on the spot.

Fortunately, a calmer head prevailed. My husband, an Army veteran, took it upon himself to educate our son in the whys and wherefores of military service—including the fantasies and realities of boot camp as well as the loneliness of being far from home and family. When our son grinned with anticipation, I knew I had lost not only the battle, but the war.

In the end, we did sign the early enlistment form—after he fully investigated all branches of the military, finally choosing the Air Force. With utmost care, he studied the calendar and made certain he could finish boot camp and be home for up-coming events, like his sister's wedding in October, and all important holidays.

At the end of summer, he boarded a plane for Texas.

"Mom," he informed me, "Don't be sending me stuff, okay? And don't be writing. It will make me look like a wimp."

I gulped and nodded, all of my motherly instincts squashed. When he left, I bawled like a baby. He did not call to say he arrived safely. That would not have been soldierly, I guess. A week crept by before he rang.

"Hey, Mom. I'm here. I'm fine. I hate boot camp!"

My heart soared. He wanted to come home. Not.

"Send cookies," he begged. "And write letters. Lots of letters. Everybody is getting mail but me!"

I baked and mailed cookies before day's end.

When boot camp ended, our son prepared to come home as planned. Instead, our phone rang and, while a horn honked in the background, he told us he was being transferred.

In the wee hours of the morning, he called again. His voice cracked with uncertainty. "Mom, I'm somewhere in Florida and I don't know what I'm supposed to do. I only have $10 and I haven't eaten since morning. I'm starved."

Now large and in charge, I gave instructions on "how to survive far away from Mommy" and told him to call me from the new base as soon as he could.

Suffice it to say, in the weeks following, he missed his sister's wedding, his birthday celebration, Halloween parties, Thanksgiving, and—yes—Christmas with the family. Our holidays were significantly subdued.

In January, his training completed, our son came home to visit. He stepped from the car dressed in crisp blue, his long blond hair replaced by a crew cut, his slouched shoulders replaced by a straight, proud stance. I admit it, I cried again. My little boy had come home a man.

Here I offer simple words of inspiration to other parents. Be brave. Cry a little or cry a lot. Above all, hitch your resolve to the future—for that's the direction your kids are headed.

Send cookies… and move on with life.

~Jean Davidson

Gone Packing

My son is upstairs packing;
He's clearing out his room.
He's moving and I should be sad
And filled with lots of gloom.
Oh sure, I'm going to miss him
But I cannot hide my glee—
I have not seen his carpet
Since 1993.

~Vie Stallings Herlocker

11

Give Me a Sign

"How can we tell which graduate is Betsy?" I asked my husband as I sat in the balcony of the auditorium and surveyed the long procession of college students below. Dressed in black caps and gowns, they all looked alike from behind as they entered to the strains of "Pomp and Circumstance."

"Knowing Bets, she'll make sure you can find her," Jim assured me.

While my eyes searched, I visualized Betsy as a five-year-old, showing her love with tight hugs, sweet kisses — and by raising her index finger, thumb, and little finger to form the American Sign Language symbol she'd learned for "I love you."

I pictured Betsy as a teenager, clutching a paint brush and climbing a ladder to paint above the front porch of our weathered farmhouse. When she finished, she showed me her completed job. On the green shingles of the porch roof, scrawled in large, white letters were the words "I love you," followed by a painted hand positioned in ASL.

"I still can't find her in the procession!" I clutched my camera in frustration.

"You'll find her," replied Jim.

Suddenly, I noticed a decorated mortarboard perched above a mane of long blond hair. Outlined in white tape on the square top, was the shape of a hand forming the "I love you." The mortarboard turned and I saw my daughter's beautiful face as she searched the balcony. When she spotted us, she beamed, raised both arms, and flashed the sign. Later, she walked to the stage and received her degree in electrical engineering. Her college days were over and her new job would take her farther from home.

Two years later, Betsy was a radiant bride as she walked down the aisle on her father's arm. When her eyes met mine she smiled, winked, and signed, reassuring me even though there was a new love in her life.

Time passed, and Betsy and her husband were the proud parents of five-year-old Amy. When they flew home for a visit, I searched for them in the crowded airport. Suddenly, I heard Amy scream in delight as she ran into my arms. She gave me a tight hug, a sweet kiss, and then raised her thumb, pointer, and pinkie.

"Look, Gram. My hand is saying 'I love you!'"

As I walked—hand-in-hand—with Betsy and Amy, I realized my nest wasn't empty at all. The signs were there all along. The signs of love.

~Miriam Hill

12

A Matter of Time

I have noticed that the people who are late are often so much jollier
than the people who have to wait for them.
~Anonymous

Our four children first appeared in a six-year span. No wonder their parents found themselves happily crazed with the hullabaloo a house full of little ones entailed. Yet those same parents never gave thought to the possibility their children would depart at the identical mach-speed in which they'd arrived.

College applications, scholarship forms, senior years, baccalaureate services, graduation ceremonies, bag-packings, and leave-takings crowded both the calendar and our emotions. Each of our children — with unique personalities, plans, and dreams — vied for our time and attention.

But the one who concerned us the most was Katrina.

Second in seniority, our dominantly right-brained daughter was sweet, bright, and intuitive. She was focused. She was creative. She was artistic. In fact, her talent for painting and drawing evidenced itself at an early age and she shared it generously. Home, church, school, family, friends... extra-curricular activities. Katrina found many opportunities to tap into her flair for the imaginative. We delighted in her developing skills and successes.

What Katrina wasn't, however, was punctual.

Time — or rather being on time — didn't matter a whit to this more global-thinking girl of ours. And it affected the entire family.

In fact, we all chanted the same refrain: "Katrina, you're making us late!"

No matter what the family outing, or its rank of importance, Katrina kept us from arriving in a timely manner. Especially Sunday morning church services.

"I'm going to warm up the car," her dad would holler up the stairs.

"We're getting our coats on," her brothers and sister advised.

"It's 8:55, past time to leave," I announced, the toe of my shoe tapping an impatient tattoo on the entryway tile.

With her long wet tresses saronged in a towel, Katrina appeared at the top of the stairs. Fresh from the shower. Wrapped in her bathrobe.

"What's the rush?" she asked. "Church doesn't start for five more minutes."

We groaned in dismay. And, as parents, we certainly wondered how Katrina would cope at college where she would have to rely on her alarm clock and the good graces of her roommates. When we waved goodbye to the forlorn figure silhouetted against the bleak college skyline, my breath caught in consternation.

Even so, those of us left at home heaved a collective—and not so imperceptible—sigh of relief. No longer must we all traipse to the front for the only pew seats available. Nor would we be shushed by a concert usher as we stumbled to our dark seats during the second cantata. Or slip into a wedding reception just in time to catch the garter. From now on, we would always be on time, we vowed to each other.

As it turned out, dorm living wasn't a simple or easy adjustment for Katrina. Homesick, dealing with "impossible" roommates, our teary daughter called one Sunday morning, a mere two weeks into the semester.

I listened… and soothed… and counseled as she hiccupped her fears and sniffled her concerns into the phone. But the rest of the family wasn't as empathetic.

"I can't believe it," her dad shook his head woefully and heaved a huge sigh. "She's a thousand miles from home," he pointed to the kitchen clock, "and still making us late to church!"

~Carol McAdoo Rehme

13

And Suddenly He Was Gone

*W*ell, it happened. Our nest just emptied. Now he's gone.

Andrew got off last Tuesday morning, right on schedule. He had all his odds and ends sorted and ready to go, early by a good half hour, neatly packed and loaded into his Saturn. Of course he already had his schedule carefully prepared; he's that kind of person. And it was right there in bold print; he showed me: "Pull out at nine."

He had everything nicely laid out in bullets:

- *Lunch in Jacksonville, 1:00.*
- *Supper in Fayetteville.*
- *Check into the Fayetteville Best Western right after supper.*
- *Get to sleep by midnight.*
- *Get on the road again 9:00 Wednesday morning.*
- *Get off Interstate 95 at Emporia (Virginia) and take Highway 58 to Virginia Beach.*
- *Arrive at Aunt Rachel's house in time for supper.*
- *Play for a couple of days.*
- *Cross 58 to pick up I-95.*
- *Richmond, Fredericksburg, the Potomac, Dale City, Woodbridge.*

Independence—dutifully organized, precisely penned in neat bullet points. New job, new digs, a new schedule at a new college. A new life. And there he went, out the door. One carefully planned road trip an awfully long way up I-95.

To be honest, I didn't think it would be like this. I didn't think it would be so easy to execute, so cut and dried. I didn't think it would be so darned hard.

And I had been doing really well, too. Until, that is, I leaned into his room Monday evening to say goodnight. This time it stuck in my throat. I realized—suddenly and overwhelmingly—for twenty-one years I'd been saying, "Goodnight, Andrew," to the lump in the bed, often leaning over to kiss his forehead, or touching his shoulder to pray.

Twenty-one years is a very long time. I considered that reality in an unexpected rush of emotion and I broke down.

Don't misunderstand me; this is not a bad thing. My wife Rebekah and I are honestly excited for him. We are happy, pleased that our son has it in him to set up this whole adventure and then to follow through. He'll be taking on new responsibilities, pushing his envelope a little beyond the comfort zone, making his way in the world under his own head of steam.

But he definitely is gone, cruising at seventy-five miles per hour up I-95 even as I write, piloting his small car stuffed with everything he really needs. Everything, that is, except his parents.

But that isn't our job, not anymore. Somewhere, recently, I read: "The simple goal of being a family, of parenting our children, doesn't really look any more complicated than this: Raise them well equipped to leave home and to establish faithful lives that are both fulfilling and self-sufficient."

So we wonder about how well we have done with this twenty-one-year raising thing. All parents do. We wonder about their confidence, we wonder if our children believe in themselves the way that we believe in them. We wonder about their faith, about how well-equipped they are to deal with the realities and hostilities beyond our doors.

And we wonder about ourselves, about how our own hearts are bound so deeply and tenderly into the substance of these wonderful young people whom we have released into the world.

There are words for days like this, words not only for our children, but for us, too. They are words we can all hold onto; they are the words I have for Andrew. "The Lord bless you and keep you; the Lord make his face to shine upon you and be gracious unto you; the Lord lift up his countenance upon you and give you peace." (Numbers 6:24-26)

Travel well, my child.

~Derek Maul

Chapter 2

Empty Nesters

Under Our Wings and In Our Hearts

*As a mother, my job is to take care of the possible
and trust God with the impossible.*
~Ruth Bell Graham

14

A Time to Keep

J 'm a memory keeper. I keep all kinds of memories in boxes, drawers and totes. It started with the wrist band that identified him as mine. A ring of plastic with a smudged last name and the first name all newborns receive at delivery: Baby.

Our first day home, I snipped the bracelet off his tiny wrist and put it away for safe keeping. Within days his first mail arrived, bursting with blessings from family and friends. I tied a satin ribbon around the stack.

By the time his face was smeared with chocolate frosting one year later, an assortment of items filled the container: A newborn sleeper, strands of gold clipped at his first haircut, a flattened birthday hat, and one wished-upon candle. All treasures tucked into a cardboard box marked "Rickie" and much too valuable to ever throw away.

Mementos of his life. Reminders of what my boy was like before he became a man. Sometimes the item was small — a feather or a note left on the refrigerator. Bulky keepsakes joined the loot — artwork, baseball glove, and the basketball signed by his senior teammates. Twelve years of report cards were kept there. Last into the makeshift time capsule, his mortarboard and tassel, a sign that life would never be the same.

Childhood was finished. Mothering was, too. Every savored tid-bit outlined the making of an individual that I nurtured, prayed for, and wept over. Hope in hiding, touchable remnants stored away for a time when we would need to remember days swiftly stolen.

Eventually, the question surfaced. When does a grown son become the keeper of his own memories? I decided the time would not be right until he had clipped off a hospital bracelet, understood the softness of baby locks, and had taped more than one toddler masterpiece to his refrigerator door. Meanwhile, I protected them. They were my comfort when the basketballs stopped bouncing.

His years between twenty and thirty were stormy. My nest was empty but my bird wasn't taking to flight as I'd coached. Drugs and alcohol captured his attention. A couple of silent years passed when he was too proud to visit or call. He didn't want a mom right now. Didn't need one. So I waited and left the porch light on.

By his mid-twenties, Rickie had a son of his own. Still, there was an uncomfortable breach in our relationship. Disappointments, failures, and angry words had taken a toll. There didn't seem to be a way to bridge the chasm.

We each had a lot to learn about holding on to what's most important—each other. Stowed memories reminded me that at one time we hugged often, laughed out loud and dreamed about the future. Hope lay buried in the box. Deep within, I knew the tie between us was not severed forever. We had shared almost all of his life together and that's a deep reservoir.

Then it was time. I'd warehoused the mementos for thirty years, protecting them from weather, address changes, garage sales, and divorce divisions. When his birthday was one week away, I went treasure chest shopping.

I bought a weathered wooden trunk, rounded on the top. From the booty I'd saved, I selected priceless pieces sure to deliver the biggest smile, the loudest, "You saved this?" and even a nostalgic tear.

Last of all, I added an extensive letter about what it was like to raise a son as a teenage mom. I reminisced about how we parented each other and learned our Bible verses together. What it felt like to go to his graduation and what I experienced when as a two-month-old he attended mine. I recounted funny stories only he and I shared. And I told him that I loved him, that I would always love him, no matter what.

I licked the tear-stained envelope, placed it amid the treasures, and lowered the lid.

Conversation was awkward at the restaurant. After a quiet rendition of "Happy Birthday," he walked me to my car. I opened the hatch-back and presented his gift. My adult first-born bawled like a baby when he peeked inside. And there it was—his wide smile, the one missing for so many years. In the darkness of the parking lot, a prayer was answered: He hugged me.

Sometime after midnight, he called. "Mom, I've been reading your letter for hours." His sobs were muffled. "We really did grow up together, didn't we? I love you, Mom."

Wise King Solomon wrote that "there are times… and seasons for every activity under heaven… a time to keep and a time to give away." Relationships are preserved in the keeping and in the giving away. It turns out, three decades of birthdays was exactly the right amount of time to hold on to silly things.

~Leslie Yeaton Koepke

15

Friends and Feathers

*Any transition serious enough to alter your definition of self
will require not just small adjustments in your way of living and thinking
but a full-on metamorphosis.*
~Martha Beck

Many of my friends belong to a club I will never join. They meet every other month to commiserate and also celebrate the unexpected joys and sorrows of empty nesting. They discuss the changing landscape of their days, with children gone and husbands coming home following retirement.

"I don't know what I'm going to do with my husband home all day," said a friend to me recently.

"The house feels so empty now," shared another whose last child recently moved out.

This past week, another friend excitedly announced, "My husband and I are taking a ten-day trip to the Bahamas."

As I listen to my friends, I feel a sense of loss, knowing I may never share these experiences. My nest may never be completely empty. My three adult children are challenged by Fragile X Syndrome, a genetic abnormality that causes developmental delays, severe learning disabilities, and emotional problems. For now, they have chosen to continue living with my husband and me.

A few years ago, we built a new home with an attached garden-level apartment to allow them a larger measure of independence. They cook their meals, buy groceries, do laundry, and manage countless other things that occur with day-to-day living. Their space is open to ours, and they frequently pop up to visit, share a movie or a meal, or just hang out. We are rarely totally alone.

I could spend my days grieving the difference of our life—and sometimes I do. But I've come to realize that being different isn't necessarily bad, it's just different. I could foolishly waste my time lamenting things that cannot be changed, but when I do so, I fail to savor the blessings of our uncommon life.

Instead of emptying my nest, I am feathering it with the rich and unexpected joys that come with parenting those with special needs.

My nest is feathered with humor. My children have grown into delightful people. Each has a wacky sense of humor that lifts us, makes us smile, and provides great comic relief.

During a recent road trip from our home in Colorado to visit family in Utah, my two large, adult sons began performing a segment from the movie *Shrek*.

"Are we there yet?" one son asked in a perfect donkey voice.

"No, donkey," replied our thirty-year-old Shrek.

As they continued through the entire dialogue mimicking to perfection the voices, we laughed away the miles.

I'm feathering my nest with gratitude. All of my children participated in high school graduation. My daughter attended classes at a local community college. They have jobs within our community working with caring, supportive people.

My nest is feathered with faith—knowing that a caring, compassionate God loves my children as I do and that He understands when I want to scream at the uniqueness of our life.

And finally, I'm feathering my nest with learned perspective. I have been allowed to look at life through different eyes, to see small achievements as reasons for large celebrations, to embrace simple pleasures. This nest of mine that may never be completely empty is warm and good—feathered with love and joy.

~Jeannie Lancaster

Read and Right

The life I touch for good or ill will touch another life,
and that in turn another, until who knows where the trembling stops
or in what far place my touch will be felt.
~Frederick Buechner

is name is David. I know his name because nearly every day he sits across from my desk at the middle school, waiting to be seen by the principal.

At fourteen, David should be in high school; instead, he is struggling through eighth grade. He's loud and troublesome in every class. And, he's in danger of being suspended for the rest of the school year.

A teacher walks past him. Then a student. Both ask the same question, "What did you do now?"

David simply tosses his shaggy blond mane, glares at them with big blue eyes, and sinks a little lower in his chair.

Another teacher passes by and orders, "David, sit up!"

Again, the glare. But seconds later, I see David swipe his eyes on the back of his sleeve.

I edge around the corner of my desk and sit down on the hard plastic chair next to him. "What's wrong?" I whisper.

"I'm stupid." He rubs away the moisture on his cheek. "You know, I can't even read."

Hmm, I don't know that. "Have you asked your teacher for help?"

"No," he shakes his head and sobs, "I'm just stupid."

My heart aches for this boy. I reach to take his hand and—in that instant — I'm no longer the busy school secretary. Even though my own son is now grown and on his own and I haven't felt needed as a mother in way too long, I simply do what a mother does: I pull David into my arms… and cry right along with him.

Later, with the help of the school counselor, David's schedule is rearranged to include a remedial reading class. And I watch his progress throughout the remainder of the year. I encourage him. I praise him. I brag about him to others. By the end of the year, he's reading, this boy of mine.

Oh, I know David is someone else's son, but he's still a child.

And I am an empty nester, but I am, above all else, still a mother. And I have a mother's love to share and a heart willing to share it.

~Robin Crain

The Christmas Rose

I am thankful that thorns have roses.
~Alphonse Karr

t's been several days since he left. The rose on the kitchen windowsill continues to remind me of his visit. The softly curled petals, like scarlet velvet, are still fresh.

"Which hand do you want, Mama," he had said, impishly hiding his gift behind his back.

The note propped against the bud vase brings a smile to my heart as I read, "I love you, Mom. Keith." The whimsical smiley-face drawn under his name brings another smile. My thoughts return to the phone call just a few weeks before.

"I'll be home for Christmas, Mom. This time I'm going to make it. This time it isn't going to be 'if only in my dreams!'"

It has been five years since Keith was able to come home for the holidays. Each was a dream unfulfilled. Each year I sent his gift to a different address but the same destination: a county jail. Like thorns on a rose, his costly mistakes pricked my heart. This year, it was different. This year, he made it home. And—this year—I sensed a difference in Keith.

"Here I am!" he yelled, waving us over as our car swung into the airport pick-up area. Wrapping his arms around me in a bear hug, he squeezed as tight as he could. It had been so long and it felt it so good. As we embraced, we both sensed this week would go by much too fast.

Keith's peels of laughter rang through the house, lifting my spirits each time I heard them. He welcomed his childhood holiday traditions. Eager to apply his artistic talents to the annual cookie baking, he taught his nephews the creative art of cutting out original designs. Licking icing from his fingers, he hummed to Christmas carols.

There was also a tenderness about Keith that I hadn't seen before, a genuine desire to please others rather than wanting others to please him. "I don't need any presents, just your p-r-e-s-e-n-c-e." His grin was infectious as he spelled out the word.

"Let me cook for everyone before I leave," Keith insisted one evening, to the amazement of all. His brother and sister quickly agreed that it would, indeed, be a treat. Encouraged by the affirmation, Keith and I enjoyed shopping together for his gourmet dinner.

Anxious to talk about God, Keith and I read the Bible and prayed together. I could hardly believe it was really happening. I had often pictured it in my mind.

One evening, as we sat by the warmth of the hearth, Keith talked about his mistakes. "I haven't gone through everything for nothing. There's a reason for it; I want to help kids avoid making the same mistakes I've made."

Sharing his hope to provide a place for kids to turn their lives around, Keith envisioned a haven where music, art, and God would be a positive influence in their transformation. It felt good to be warmed by his dreams.

Too soon, our week was over. Bags packed, it was time to catch his flight back to Georgia. Wrapping his arms around me one last time, Keith whispered, "Pray for me, Mom. I still have some bad habits to kick."

"One step at a time," I replied. "One step at a time."

Once again, I find myself drawn to the rose on the windowsill. Could it be that my prodigal son has really come home this time?

~Karen R. Kilby

Coming Home

He who never made a mistake, never made a discovery.
~Samuel Smiles

could tell by my mother's voice that she wanted me home for Christmas. It felt good knowing that—despite my past mistakes—I was still welcome. There was so much to catch up on; so much can happen in five years.

As the plane descended into the Houston airport, I wondered if my mother would even recognize me; I had gone through so many changes. But, at the passenger pick-up area, I heard her familiar voice calling my name. It felt so good to wrap my arms around her; I didn't want to let her go. I wondered if the rest of the family would be as welcoming. As we pulled into the driveway, the old phrase, "home sweet home," rang true. Everyone graciously welcomed me back to the fold. How grateful I was that the love in our family was firm and unchangeable.

I knew I wasn't an ideal son. As a teen, I explored avenues other than I'd been taught, ignoring any promptings I might have felt from God. Despite other artistic talents, my ultimate goal was to sing in a hard-rock metal band. It offered a life of sex, drugs, and rock and roll that was too hard for me to resist and eventually landed me in jail again and again.

I found it hard to understand why my family refused to help with my legal problems. I knew they were praying for me, but I felt that they were being stubborn and selfish. I know now, in reality, it was me.

I didn't want to just come home for Christmas. Like the Prodigal Son, I was ready to return to my relationship with God. It felt good to be home, back in their loving arms, back to the loving arms of my Heavenly Father.

As I finished some last minute shopping, I noticed a display of beautiful red roses and immediately thought of my mother. I needed to somehow show her I really wanted to change. That I was changing. I wanted her to know how much I appreciate her for always being there for me.

The soft, velvety petals of the roses reminded me of the tenderness of her love. And the thorns reminded me of the painful lessons I had learned.

I couldn't think of a more fitting gift to give.

~Keith Kilby as told to Karen R. Kilby

Adam's Place

*Too often we give children answers to remember
rather than problems to solve.*
~ Roger Lewin

Giving my children their independence was never easy. I was the mother who deposited her child at kindergarten and then hung around the door, getting funny looks from the teacher.

By the time they left home, I was older and braver, accustomed to them flying in different directions and leaving me behind. Besides, my husband was with me, and I could not convince him to sleep in the car outside the university or wait while I peeked through the window of their new nests. He gently touched my leg as we drove away in silence.

But then there was Adam. He wasn't able to fly on his own, although I had spent many hours teaching him. At twenty-four, Adam had the mind of a young child. How do you put a six-year-old in his own place and wave goodbye?

Years ago, I was advised to put Adam on a waiting list for an adult group home, but knew it would take years before a spot became available. So, I visited another house of twelve adults who all needed help with their daily living. Required to follow strict zoning rules, the facility could not be in a family neighborhood and sat on a large piece of land at the edge of town.

The residents appeared happy. They didn't seem to mind the

donated, mismatched furniture. Even their clothes were not important, comfort coming before fashion. Reluctantly, I put my son's name on the waiting list, and pushed it to the back of my mind; at twelve, Adam was years away from adulthood.

By the time he was twenty-four, Adam worked in a sheltered environment. My husband dropped him off each morning and Adam rode the bus home. He had to use his own judgment when crossing roads. If he missed the bus stop, he would be completely lost. In winter, I worried Adam would walk in the road to avoid slipping on sidewalks. But he loved this independence and I could not take it from him.

I was in the midst of moving our elder son, along with most of our furniture, and packing our daughter, along with most of our money, off to the university, when a letter came: A new group home was opening. They had a room for Adam.

Not now, I thought, he's too young.

Yet the timing was perfect. Perhaps Adam would view it as a natural sequence, to move from home along with his brother and sister. I went to the proposed meeting to find out more.

Group homes had progressed over the past dozen years. Several houses, now in family neighborhoods, accommodated four or five adults with special needs and had live-in managers who helped with daily living.

Adam's was a lovely five-bedroom near us. He would have his own room, and he knew the three others who would share the house. We understood that many others still waited for openings, necessitating a quick decision.

But Adam's too young to be without a mother and father, my whirling thoughts insisted.

Finally, I faced the truth—no matter how many birthdays he had, Adam would never be old enough. Parents get old and some even die. Adam could not stay with us forever, and the longer he stayed the harder it would be for him to adjust to a new life. Although my heart ached, I knew the time was right.

"Adam, how would you like to share a house with some of your friends?" I asked, laying his next day's clothes on the chair, and worrying how he would dress without my help. "It's time for you to move out, too."

Adam looked bewildered. "Can I take my movies?"

"Yes, you can take everything in your room."

"Can I take my television?" He still looked concerned.

"Yes, Adam, you can take anything you want."

Adam smiled.

Adam is now a regular Sunday visitor at our house and comes to stay every holiday. He loves to come home, but at the end of each visit, he returns happily to his own home. He is content with his routine. He has a girlfriend and is busy with bowling, church group, movie night, and other outings.

There are times when Adam isn't dressed the way I'd like. Some days he hasn't shaved. Other times he needs a haircut. And yes, it bothers me. But it doesn't bother Adam.

Each time I return him there, I feel a pang of guilt along with an undeniable urge to keep Adam home, in our achingly empty nest. Yet, I am truly thankful for the wonderful people who make it possible for my son to have a life independent of his parents. His own place in the community.

~Jean Padgett

Fallen Nests

One swallow does not make a summer.
~Aristotle

A majestic blue spruce shades our front yard. Its mighty crown stretches higher each year. The feathery branches of that green giant are like gentle arms cradling countless birds and squirrels. I know animals feel welcome and safe in the comfort of the thick warm tree.

One day, my husband was doing yard work near the big blue spruce when something caught his eye. An empty bird's nest had fallen to the ground and next to it were broken pieces of a robin's egg.

A little bird had developed inside that egg, cracked the shell, and worked his way out into the world. We knew the mama and papa birds had kept him nourished with worms. As he grew, they'd taught him to fly and one day he flew off to live life on his own.

As we looked at the emptiness of the woven twigs, it seemed so much like our own home.

Both our sons were adopted. The older married on Memorial Day and graduated from high school the following Saturday. His beautiful daughter was born six months later. The younger began running away when he was thirteen years old. Not just once, but time after time.

My nest was empty when it should have been full. My heart felt the same way.

I knew the mother robin would lay eggs in another nest next

spring. She would dig more worms and raise more baby birds, teaching me that life goes on. I faced the choice of wallowing in depression or moving on with life. I needed to trust that I had done my best to teach my boys to fly. I knew God's "eye was on the sparrow" and He would care for my sons no matter where they went or what they did. It was time to let Him be in control and provide.

But I also knew I needed a reminder to strengthen me.

I took the empty bird nest and propped it on a twig. Inside it I positioned a broken eggshell and a tiny "blue bird of happiness" from the local craft store. I topped it all with a glass dome to become my symbol of hope.

God did provide. In unbelievable ways. Both sons are now married to beautiful Christian women and have filled my home and my heart with six grandchildren. Like the blue spruce, my arms stretch out to cradle and keep them all.

~Alice M. McGhee

A Different Vision

Life does not have to be perfect to be wonderful.
~Annette Funicello

Puddles of rain water glistened under the street lights around midnight. The ambulance sat unmoving along the curb. We watched the back door, mystified by the vehicle's idling, wondering why it didn't race to the hospital. That brief remembered moment marks a threshold I'll never forget.

Mere minutes earlier, nineteen-year-old Laura had raced gleefully across the street to our hotel in Munich, Germany. But her miscalculations catapulted her into the path of a speeding car. Now, this ambulance ride would be followed by six weeks of coma—interrupted midway by a flight home—and rehabilitation that would result in a life drastically altered.

Not only was our daughter's body seriously injured, but the wholeness of our family was broken. Laura had accompanied us on a student tour of Europe as part of a teaching assignment for my husband. For our younger sons back home with relatives, their world became scarier and less predictable. My husband and I felt adrift in a foreign land with unfamiliar language and customs.

Will she live? How long must we stay here? How will we get her home? And, where will she go then? These unanswered questions hung heavy between us those first few days.

Slowly and doggedly, we made call after call and accepted the help of all who offered, amazed that our prayers were answered even when we didn't know what we prayed for. Angels appeared everywhere. New German friends helped us navigate the unfamiliar territory of a foreign land. Stateside friends knew how to get us home and where to hospitalize Laura and set those arrangements in motion. Others launched a fundraiser to pay for the medical transport. Neighbors entertained our sons and allayed their concerns. And when we finally did return, church friends brought us dinner every night for two weeks.

We didn't know if Laura would wake from the coma. That pivotal issue would dictate our future. In the meantime, we learned about the complex world of traumatic brain injury (TBI) where no two injuries are exactly alike and major complications were normal. Her recovery was figured not in days or weeks or months; a year was the unit of reckoning for TBI. We discovered both her personality and body were affected, and Laura's recovery would involve multiple types of treatment and therapies.

Fortunately, Laura did awaken—but not the Laura we had known for nineteen years. The shy sweet girl was replaced by a young woman unable to walk, talk, dress, feed, or care for herself. What followed were three years of rehabilitation that would return her to a world where she would never be able to drive a car or hold down a fulltime job. A world where living independently, so crucial for growing up, was tempered with our awareness of her limitations.

Laura's new reality altered ours. My husband re-committed himself to his teaching career since we depended on it for income, insurance benefits, and family stability. I had just completed my Ph.D. but had to lay aside a new career, planned for when the kids were older, to give full attention to the family's needs.

Prior to Laura's accident, my husband and I talked a lot about what it would be like when the kids were gone. Our conversations swung between remembering the sweet times and imagining how it would be when... when she graduates from college, when he begins his first real job, when one brings home that special someone. At the same time, we tried to picture ourselves finally having time for all we'd postponed.

What we didn't imagine was a whole different life vision.

So while Laura recovered, we faced our own grieving process. My husband strengthened himself through his work. I rented a studio, not to work at my career, but to have a safe place to mourn our losses and create a new vision. Three days a week, I hired a home health aide and went to the studio to paint and write and shape clay to hold my grief and transform it. This became my sanity, my way of surviving.

Almost twenty years have passed since that fateful night. My husband is nearing retirement. I have practiced psychotherapy for over ten years. The boys are grown and pursuing their own careers and marriages. Laura completed her B.S. in Social Work and lives almost-independently in a nearby town. She volunteers, is a spokesperson for the disabled, and has a boyfriend.

My husband and I continue to walk that fine line between holding-on and letting-go of an adult child with disabilities. We have put as many safeguards in place as we can, including a living trust for when we are gone.

I do not have the life I'd envisioned as Laura's mother, but that vision has been replaced by a new one, especially when I view the world through Laura's eyes. I see her fight for her place in the world, to demand it when others don't want to recognize it, and to use her unfailing sense of humor to put her challenges in perspective.

My daughter is one of my most profound teachers and when I witness her, I am humbled by her courage, proud of her accomplishments, and thankful for the compassion she has fostered in me toward all who live a different kind of life.

~Nancy Burnett with Carolyn Miller

Left Behind

Mother's love grows by giving.
~Charles Lamb

My mom and I left my brother Oscar in college while we moved across the world to reunite with my dad at his job relocation. It was 1994. I was fifteen and leaving a school I hated. My mother left behind the frustrations of living in a third-world country but she also left Oscar—her elder son and longtime confidant.

Ten years my senior, Oscar is my half-brother. But he's bailed me out of more trouble than I care to remember, and that's a real brother in my book. He's an even better son. Oscar and Mom have always been there for each other.

Although we left Chile in the heat of summer, the gray February skies of Seattle matched the mood that fell upon my usually cheerful mother. Pictures of Oscar inundated the coffee table, Mom's nightstand, and my room.

I still remember how she cried when his first letters arrived. With no job or money, Oscar tried to sound strong. He wrote how the teddy bears she had left made him feel "like the house was full." Although she knew he was struggling, she could do nothing about it.

But as my mom says, "When God closes a door, he always opens a window." During one of our English lessons at the local library, she met another Chilean, a lanky forty-two-year-old electrician named Ramon, who had just arrived from Santiago, like us.

Who was feeling lonely, like us. And who played chess—well, like me.

As we played, he told us about his family in Chile, how he hated leaving them behind, and how I reminded him of his oldest son... all the while winning game after game of chess. I didn't like losing, so played less and less often with him. Still, Ramon visited our house. It wasn't me who invited him, nor my dad, although we both liked him.

"Ask Ramon if he wants to come for dinner," my mom offered.

"Ask Ramon if he wants to come for tea," she urged.

"Ask Ramon if he wants to come for donuts," she insisted.

Her invitations were endless, and since Ramon was the only friend I had in America, I happily obliged. Besides, we had switched to checkers.

During Ramon's visits, conversation invariably touched on my absent brother, and Mom seemed a great deal happier. Gone was her quivering lip; she seemed cheerful and optimistic. And she always insisted Ramon stay a little longer and eat a little more.

Her emphasis on eating caught my attention. Always health-conscious, always watching her waistline (and mine) closely, she went out of her way to feed Ramon. Even the foods she always avoided weren't off-limits anymore. For Ramon, that is.

A darker-minded person might have suspected something, but I knew anything dishonorable was out of the question. Why Ramon? Why all this attention for someone she met less than three months ago? And why, wondered this hungry teenage boy, so much food?

Her answer hit me hard.

"Because," she said, "Ramon is here alone, and our Oscar is in Chile alone. And if there's somebody here feeding Ramon, I believe there's somebody down there feeding Oscar."

Mom wasn't just feeding Ramon because he was too skinny; she was patching the tear in her heart, one spoonful at a time.

~Sebastian Moraga

23

Let It Snow!

Family isn't about whose blood you have. It's about who you care about.
~Trey Parker and Matt Stone

Our Christmas tree stands in the living room, a lifetime of memories and accumulated snowflakes dripping from its branches.

It's true what they say—no two snowflakes are alike. At first glance, these three-inch flakes appear to be identical. In color, in size, in composition. But, on closer inspection, their quarter-size nucleus reveals the unique soul of each one. For in that space is displayed a picture of every foster child who has touched our lives. Every year sees more snowflakes than the last and every snowflake has a story to tell.

There's Tamika*, the nine-year-old African-American girl in the white and red candy cane nightgown, holding a karaoke microphone and singing the blues for her mama. Hanging nearby is Timothy, her seven-year-old brother who called me "mama" the first day he came to our home. And here's Jerry and Michael, two little guys with reindeer antlers perched on their heads, reminding me of the silliness we shared... and the heartbreak when they left our home more than two years later.

Amid popsicle-stick reindeer and pom-pom angels hangs Carrie, a blond-haired, brown-eyed beauty who came to our home a scared teenager and left as a confident young woman. She poses between the sibling group of four we adopted and precious, three-year-old Sarah whom we discovered hidden inside her autism. Over here is Pablo, an eleven-year-old whose once terrified eyes now smile without reservation.

My husband and I began foster parenting in the summer of 1999, naïve to the life-altering journey we were embarking upon. The younger of our two biological children was about to leave for college that fall. Perhaps our fear of an empty house persuaded us to become foster parents, but, whatever the reason and despite questions like, "Are you nuts?" and "Why now when your own kids are grown?" we followed our hearts and made this our life. A life that was quickly and irrevocably changed the day two little boys walked through our front door.

Over the years, we gained insight into the complexities of these children who enter our home. We became professional parents, making decisions that established our commitment to them. I went back to school, and my husband chose early retirement so he could devote his attention to their special needs.

The rewards far outweigh the challenges of parenting previously traumatized children. Certainly, at times I may question my sanity. And, yes, I wonder where in the world I might have traveled had I not opened my home to these kids—until a little one's arms tenderly tug me back to reality.

Then I realize that my world is right here. With them. At home.

As I hang each cherished face on the tree, I see those who entered our lives briefly and those who became a permanent part of our family. Each snowflake has melted into my heart, forever a part of me. I have learned some of life's greatest lessons from them: perseverance, compassion, courage, and hope for the future.

Together, our accumulated snowflakes create a magnificent snow sculpture.

A family. Each member a unique work of art.

No two alike.

~Karen Heywood

* All the children's names have been changed.

24

Linked Together

Pray for a good harvest, but keep on plowing.
~Nancy Otto

It was a brilliant early-summer day in the Midwest. Full of sunshine and life and expectation.

Sharon, a new nursing school graduate, was about to leave home to start her first professional job as a neo-natal nurse at Stanford University's children's hospital. My husband and I helped pack her belongings into her new car, a two-door Plymouth that almost matched the color of the sunlight. There were happy hugs and sad kisses as warm tears slid down my face.

Sharon got into her car, rolled slowly down the driveway and into the cul-de-sac. Then the brake lights flashed and she bolted out, ran back to hurl herself into our arms, sobbing. There we stood, rocking back and forth, six hands patting three backs.

"Please stay well," she choked out. "And don't even think about dying."

"Sweetie," I smiled gently, "we all are born to die."

She tightened her arms around us. "Yes, but could you just wait until I finish growing up?" She tore herself away, scurried back to the car, and drove right out of our everyday lives.

My husband and I dragged ourselves back into the house. There were no voices. No music. No life. The silence seemed to wrap itself around us.

I started up the stairs. Her room was vacant. The closet stood hollow. I pulled out the top dresser drawer. It, too, was empty… except for something gleaming on the bottom. Startled, I looked closer.

A silver chain gleamed up at me.

Sharon had left behind her Star of David necklace! A sacred Jewish token, the six-cornered star symbolized a shield, a protector. We had given it to Sharon years earlier as a gift to celebrate her confirmation at Temple.

Yet now I stared at the necklace, abandoned in the drawer.

My heart sank. I knew immediately that the deserted chain represented our daughter's rejection of her faith, a denial of her heritage. My husband and I were devastated, even though we accepted that it was Sharon's choice to make. Just as surely, we knew it was our job as parents to accept that choice.

We had adopted our Sharon when she was only seven days old, feeling like a higher power had handed us a precious gift of new life. And she had brought us nothing but pure joy, fulfilling all our expectations. Until now.

Still, we had hope. Meanwhile, no matter what, Sharon was our daughter. Our beloved daughter.

Some thirty years marched by. During that time, Sharon worked at her nursing career. She also married, had three children, divorced, and became a grandmother. Through it all, we stayed in close contact and she came home often.

During a recent visit, I reminded her of an upcoming birthday. "Sweetie, Dad and I would like to get something you really want," I said. "Can you think of anything special?"

"Yes." Sharon reached over and patted my hand. "I am all grown up now," her voice was confident and firm, "and what I really want is a Star of David. On a silver chain."

I felt a smile slide across my face as I remembered an abandoned necklace gleaming from the bottom of a dresser drawer many years ago. I turned and looked out the window. It was a brilliant early-summer day, full of sunshine and life… and expectation.

~Beverly Ginsberg

25

The Truth
of Consequences

No bird soars too high if he soars with his own wings.
~William Blake

I should have been thrilled. The journey was long and the path was bumpy, but having my daughter accepted to college was a goal worthy of the biggest sacrifices. I didn't anticipate the journey would teach me that the shortest distance between two points isn't always a straight line.

My oldest daughter, Kori, was diagnosed at age seven with severe Attention Deficit Disorder (ADD). Information on the disability was hard to come by because ADD was not well-known in 1984. Fortunately, we had a superb pediatric neuro-psychologist who guided us every rocky step of the way and helped us understand the dysfunctions she faced.

Kori's ability to prioritize was virtually nonfunctional. Put simply, everything got equal focus no matter its importance. In addition, the cause and effect processing center of her brain did not work efficiently. Punishment for a crime was never justified, because in her mind, the cause was never attached to the effect.

"Enroll her in gymnastics," the doctor suggested. "She'll experience immediate consequences for her actions."

Gymnastics was perfect. Kori excelled beyond all expectations.

As a senior, she was even offered a scholarship. But the college would take her nearly three thousand miles from home.

The thought of living on her own exhilarated Kori. But fear and anxiety consumed me. Would she be able to manage her disability on her own? Who would remind her to get her paper written for English, to get her bills paid on time, and to take her medicine regularly? The Internet was brand new; we didn't own a computer or even a cell phone. Daily reminders would be out of the question.

Nevertheless, Dave and I celebrated our daughter's achievement. We knew she was old enough to live independently, and she was intellectually capable of collegiate studies. Traveling to competitions had made her street smart and socially savvy. With gymnastics as her anchor, she would have a sense of continuity and belonging that would be essential for her to thrive. Satisfied with our reasoning, we dropped our daughter at campus with a pat on her back and a reminder to call home.

After her first few weeks of school, I asked Kori if she was having any trouble with her assignments. She resented the inquiry and insisted she was doing fine. Midterm grades proved otherwise, so she promised to meet with her professors. The cause and effect of not competing in gymnastics if she received bad grades had to be emphatically repeated to her.

I sent Kori spending money to fill in the necessities, but my funds were limited. She promptly signed up for several credit cards that were much too easy to get. I had given her a prepaid card for emergencies only, but with easy access to as many credit cards as she wanted, she quickly overspent on things she deemed necessary.

The most frustrating situation I tried to deal with from across the country was her medical situation. I sent her prescription refills—along with reminders to prioritize her health concerns—and happy-face sticky notes that urged her to take her medicine. Then I discovered she hadn't been taking her medication often enough.

Concerned, I called the gymnastics coach to see if she could intervene on my behalf. She politely recommended that I leave Kori alone; it was her experience that these things tend to work themselves out.

"Let's bring her home, Dave," I begged. "She can finish college here where we can keep a watchful eye on her."

"You're pulling up the flower to inspect the roots," he countered. "Give her some space and trust the experts."

I reluctantly agreed to let her neuro-psychologist have the final say in the matter. "Let her try her wings," he advised. "She'll learn to cope on her own — or she'll completely fail on her own. Either one is better than bailing her out."

A suffocating lump crowded my throat when I hung up the phone. I felt as though I had thrown my firstborn to the hungry vultures. Over the next few years, I nearly wore out my knees with prayers on her behalf.

Kori soared. Her senior year, she was elected captain of her gymnastics team. After graduation, she performed with Siegfried & Roy in Las Vegas. Kori adapted to the world with a remarkable strength and independence.

Today, she has her Masters of Education and is teaching fourth grade. She has a unique understanding of children who learn in ways that are outside the norm. Her classroom is lively and full of innovative experiences for her students.

When her journey from home took her spiraling downward, it took all the courage I could muster to stand back and do nothing. But it was the best thing I did for Kori. I trusted she would learn to succeed on her own, and learn she did.

With ADD as a constant companion, her path isn't always straight, but she reaches her destination in her own way. And all of us are better for the journey.

~Nancy Ann Erskine

It's in the Mail

You don't just luck into things... You build step by step.
~Barbara Bush

The card arrived two days before Mother's Day, bearing a Seattle postmark. It was from my stepson, Chase, a freshman at Seattle University.

I wondered about the contents, since each previous Mother's Day, my stepchildren had dutifully given me a homemade card created by my stepdaughter Chelsea. Although younger than Chase, she'd always been the one who kept track of special occasions, made the cards, and then cajoled Chase to sign them.

They'd signed those cards with kind words—words that, when the kids were six and eight and we had all just become a family, their biological mother probably helped them write. I loved those cards, but always suspected they were more of an exercise in politeness than an expression of feeling.

This card was different—unless Chelsea had made it, sent it to Chase, and ordered him to sign and send it to me. Although I wouldn't put it past my sometimes imperious stepdaughter to do that, I knew Chase would no longer tolerate her control.

We had visited him at school the previous November, and he had seemed so self-assured, so mature. I felt better after seeing him. Not because I had worried about him living so far away, but because

I hadn't. Chase was the second child in our family to leave home for college, and I hadn't worried as much when he left.

It may be normal to fret less about your second fledgling, but I felt guilty. The first to leave had been my biological son, Brandon. So, I convinced myself there was a good reason for the discrepancy in the intensity of my worrying. Chase was more self-confident and independent than Brandon. He wanted to cut the strings, ties that to him were binding. He would prefer I worry less.

Now I was holding a card from him, with his spidery writing on the envelope. Chelsea could not have made it. Chase had to have made it himself, or actually gone to the store to buy it.

My fingers trembled slightly as I opened the envelope. He had gone to the trouble of buying me a card. The thought that practical, efficient Chase had probably bought the same one for his own mother crossed my mind, but I swept it away. So what?

I read the front and the printed verse. Nice, Hallmark-approved.

Then I read his inscription. In the most honest, caring words I've ever read, he thanked me. This young man who had always been polite, caring, and kind — but just a bit distant — thanked me with a flourish, and signed the card, "Love, Chase."

He'd written that signature before, but this time, I knew without a doubt he meant it. All those years of butting heads because we were too much alike (we're both rather cerebral and introspective) or butting heads because we were total opposites (he has a quick, sometimes callous wit, while I can't even remember knock-knock jokes) — all those years melted away.

I cried. I read and reread that card. I had plenty of time to do so, because it was the only one I got. In the poignant world of step-parenting, you accept the joys, and leave the hurts behind. Although I found it a bit ironic that both my always-reliable Chelsea and my ever-forgetful Brandon did not send me cards, it didn't hurt. Chase had filled my heart to overflowing.

Now, as another Mother's Day approaches, I wonder what will happen. It cannot compare, so I won't make comparisons. I know in my heart that my independent, confident, and fairly well-adjusted children love me, and they know I love them.

That's all we need.

~Lisa Coalwell

Empty Nesters

Out on a Limb

*You're braver than you believe,
and stronger than you seem,
and smarter than you think.*
~Christopher Robin to Pooh

27

Heavens to Betsey!

You're only given a little spark of madness. You mustn't lose it.
~Robin Williams

Miriam and I loved to shop. My husband, bless him, accepted that it was perfectly normal for his lovely daughter to have trendy outfits, shoes (oh, those shoes) and purses, although he did express some alarm when she outgrew her bedroom closet and took over the guest room closet as well.

It was a lovely life—shopping together each week, going out for lunch afterwards to discuss our purchases, school, and the latest boyfriend. But Miriam cut me to the quick; she moved to New York to go to school.

I panicked. Without my daughter, how could I justify sprees at Guess, H&M, or Bebe? Or Betsey Johnson? Oh, no. Betsey, my Betsey. No one would believe this overweight fifty-five-year-old bought clothes in any of those high fashion stores. It was bad enough that my baby deserted and left me lonely, but must I be denied the shopping sprees, too? Life was cruel.

Then it came to me in a flash, an epiphany, really. I could send my daughter Care Packages.

The first one was tentative: some of her favorite Halloween candy—miniature pumpkins and candy corn—a warm sweater from Ireland, oatmeal, and a blanket to keep her warm. Then, I found a cute skirt at Guess to match the sweater. And I added red shoes. Miriam loved them.

Validated, I could hold my head high in the stores again instead of lurking in the shadows.

"I'm making a Care Package for my daughter," I crowed to the clerks at the counters. Life was good.

I filled the second box with adorable Thanksgiving chocolates that looked like tiny turkeys, two perfect little-black-dress outfits, stunning pumps, and long strands of pearls from Betsey Johnson.

About this time, my son Ben decided he needed a makeover and asked me to shop with him for new clothes. Well, hello Hugo Boss. An entire new world of shopping opened up. Not Betsey, but most impressive and satisfying.

As I had with his sister, I treated Ben to lunch. That's when he dropped the bomb.

"Mom, I applied to the Berklee School of Music, in Boston. It's why I need the clothes. I have an audition coming up."

"That's wonderful, Honey." I tried to sound excited when in actuality my heart sank. "I hope you get in. It's what you've always wanted."

Meantime, I set to work on another Care Package for Miriam. Godiva chocolates with a sweet, stuffed teddy bear. And, of course, a new outfit for a Christmas party. Good ol' Betsey provided not one, but two dresses that were absolute must-haves.

Okay, here's the thing. To send each package across the Canadian border into New York, I'm required to itemize the contents and list their value. A small glitch, teensy tiny. Nonetheless, my darling husband offered to mail the New Year's Eve package—with another Betsey outfit, shoes, and matching coat. To be honest, I really didn't think anything of it until he returned home.

"You spent $849.00 on clothes?" he roared. "What were you thinking? We already pay her tuition and rent and food… and a cell phone bill that's outrageous!"

"But she needs clothes," I protested in a voice that sounded lame even to me.

After that, my husband and I came to an... understanding: I can only send one care package a month to Miriam. If there is a valid reason. And if it costs well, well under $500.

It's as if someone cut out my liver and threw it to the dogs. I look longingly at the stores in the mall, but I no longer enter them. There's no point. I'm desolate.

To make matters worse, Ben just announced his acceptance to Berklee and will head for Boston in the fall. Another one leaving so soon? How can this be? I'm not even used to Miriam being gone. How will I cope with two children out of the house?

Ben smiles at me with an adorably mischievous grin. "Chin up, Mom. You're not losing a son. You're gaining an opportunity—another Care Package to send each month. The clerks at Hugo will love you."

Sweet, wonderful Hugo Boss. I'd forgotten about him. Victory and validity are mine once more. I will rise from my lamentable woe and loneliness and joyously shop, shop, shop. It's my duty as a mother. Hugo and Betsey, here I come!

Um, but only once a month.

~Pamela Goldstein

28

Wheel of Choices

Speak when you are angry and you will
make the best speech you will ever regret.
~Ambrose Bierce

t had been five years since the younger of our two daughters left home. Both moved to southern California, while we lived in Phoenix a good five-hour drive away.

Doug and I were actually enjoying an empty nest. The house stayed clean longer, we ate out more often, and we didn't have that constant sense of worrying that comes with parenting.

When Chris called to say she was coming to Phoenix on Friday for a business meeting, I was thrilled.

"I'll be there Labor Day weekend, Mom."

In a nanosecond, I had the entire weekend planned out. I'll take her to that cute Italian restaurant, I thought. And she's never seen the new mall. Oh, and she'll love just being home and relaxing on the couch. We'll make memories.

Chris's business meeting was over early on Friday, and the three of us hung out at the house having a great time. At dinner, she shared stories about her job and we laughed about silly, goofy things only families with wonderful memories understand.

And then she said it. Casually. Without any hesitation. As though words couldn't possibly sting.

"Some of my church friends are having a holiday get-together," she mentioned. "If it's okay with you guys, I think I'd like to go home tomorrow."

Home? Tomorrow?

The room sank into grayness, and my thoughts spun like the giant wheel on a TV game show. The kind where the contestant either wins an exciting prize or lands on the wrong slot—and goes bankrupt.

She wants to go home tomorrow. Isn't this home?

My feeling-wheel kept spinning in a rush of unexpected emotions. I had no idea where it was going to land.

My first instinct was to stop at the slot marked "Angry: How could you grow up and leave me?" I could halt the spinning right there and be content in my anger.

Chris stared at me. Could she see the spinning wheel, too?

It kept turning, to pause on "Hurt: I've worked hard to make this your home."

Keep going, keep going, my inner audience urged. "Attitude: I'm gonna clam up and punish you for ruining the wonderful, weekend plans I had for us."

The wheel kept going. I didn't feel in control of it and feared this wonderful evening could dissolve into a bad memory, if it landed in the wrong spot.

"Pity: I've gotten old and there is no more purpose for my life."

"Detach: Act like you don't care."

"Guilt: No explanation needed here...."

Chris waited for a response.

And as I gazed at her through a maze of confusion, I saw this beautiful young woman. A person of faith, value, and integrity. Hardworking, funny, and likable. I was privileged to be her mom.

And her life was in southern California.

I felt the wheel slow down. I had control of it, after all, and searched for the one slot that had been blurred by the others. The one marked "Acceptance: It will be okay, let her go, she still loves you."

Easy? No. Worth it? Absolutely.

Chris and I spent the rest of Friday evening eating too much ice cream and sharing too much gossip. Me and my beautiful daughter, my friend, creating a new memory. In fact, Chris had so much fun—she stayed until Sunday.

I had won the prize, after all.

~Jean Bobb

29

Curtains for Mary

I finally realized I was grown up when I had to buy my own salt.
~Lori Kay Watkins

"Hi, Mom. Guess where I'm calling from? My new apartment!"

Living alone her senior year of college, Mary would only have to clean up her own messes. She could decorate according to her taste, and not have a living room filled with four ugly, unmatching, used couches—each purchased by a different housemate.

"But, Mom, this is the bad part. I went to Wal-Mart and got a few things—wastebasket, dish soap, milk, bananas—and it cost me forty dollars. Forty dollars! Can you believe it?"

"I certainly can," I said, smiling at my child's initiation into the world of independent living.

"The management says I have a month to hang blinds or something. They don't want renters putting up blankets. I priced curtains for my three windows and can't find anything I can afford."

At that moment I was torn. The mother in me wanted to help. That's what mothers do. But then I remembered how many times Mary had called home, broke, asking for loans. She'd spent money on concerts and CDs, leaving nothing for shampoo and other necessities. Even though she always repaid me, I'd resolved not to give her an easy way out. She wouldn't learn life's lessons if I always caved in.

I gritted my teeth. I mustn't help—unless, of course, I could do it without money.

"Mary, I have some sheets," I mentioned, thinking on my feet. "Grandma Panerio made them before she married and came over from Italy. They're heavy hemp cloth and never used. I could make them into curtains for your living room, if you'd like. They're beautiful, hand-monogrammed with an M... perfect for you."

And perfect for me, I thought. I coveted the idea of helping decorate her apartment.

"But don't you want to keep them?"

"I'll never use them as sheets—they're too heavy. And beautiful things are no good left in a drawer."

"You'd do that for me, Mom?"

"Absolutely."

I went to work, measuring and re-measuring the fabric, once, twice, three times. Both panels must be exactly forty-three inches long. I certainly didn't want to cut the material and have the hems hang crooked. When I put the scissors to the cloth, I closed my eyes, took a deep breath, and steadied my hand. After the cuts, the rest was effortless. I hemmed the bottom and made tabs for the top. I spaced and pinned the tabs evenly between the curtain front and the facing.

Only then did I realize it would require an upholsterer with an industrial strength machine to sew through so many heavy layers of cloth.

I called every upholsterer in the yellow pages to find one who could finish the curtains quickly. Tomorrow, if possible. My older daughter, Ann, would be traveling across the state to attend her husband's family reunion. I wanted her to take them to Mary, watch her hang them, and give me Mary's reaction.

The only upholsterer available was forty-five miles away. I told him to schedule me and didn't even ask what he charged. Gas prices were at a record high, but I didn't balk at the drive and barely flinched at his twenty-dollar fee for a half hour's work. Somehow I'd forgotten my resolve to hang onto my wallet for Mary's sake.

My first reward came when I got Ann's report: Mary was thrilled with the curtains. Better yet were Mary's words when she called. "They're beautiful, Mom. So different. I love them. Thank you."

Had Mary learned any "life lessons?" Maybe not. But the joy I took in the project was priceless. Besides, I cherish the idea of Grandma's namesake enjoying her sheets. It's like a thread, tying the family together.

~Carol Panerio

30

Holding Down the Fort

Promise you won't forget me,
because if I thought you would, I'll never leave.
~Winnie the Pooh

After my divorce, I wanted to wait until my kids grew up before moving on with my own life. But when I fell in love with a man who lived in another state, the wait felt particularly long. As my younger son neared his eighteenth birthday and graduation, I started making plans of my own.

But I felt conflicted. When were kids really grown up? And even if they've left the nest, don't they need to know it's still there? Shouldn't I hold down the fort?

I imagined myself doing just that, holding down the fort. But for how long? How many days, weeks, or years would I spend waiting, just in case they needed me?

My twenty-year-old daughter was in her own apartment, and I saw her only when her laundry piled up. Our relationship had survived a volatile adolescence, but Emily was still fiercely protective of her newfound independence. We hadn't yet advanced to the stage of "doing lunch," and she hadn't asked even once for advice on how to remove a stain or cook a family recipe.

Eric, who theoretically lived with me, was often little more than a blur in my peripheral vision as he zoomed out the door to be with friends. With college on the horizon, I knew I'd be lucky to get even a few hours with him during school breaks. Should I keep my life on hold indefinitely for those scattered moments when my children were available?

On the other hand, if I moved from our hometown, how would I ever get even those few minutes with them? And would they feel abandoned, deserted, set adrift in the world with no home base? What if I were 700 miles away when Emily finally wanted to do lunch?

In spite of my worries and years of finely-tuned mother guilt, I decided to claim my own life. After four years of a long-distance romance — and only a few weeks after Eric graduated from high school — I remarried. While my son packed for college, I packed for a move two states away.

That was a year ago. While I suspect my move did create a bit of insecurity for my kids to face and conquer, it hasn't been the trauma I worried about. With several strategically timed trips back to visit (Christmas, birthdays), along with e-mail, instant messaging, and the best way I seem to have of getting my son's attention — text messaging — I think we're more connected now than before I left. Emily and I chat briefly online almost daily. Although it's still hard to keep him pinned down long enough for a complete conversation, I did manage to confine Eric to a six-hour car ride when I drove him and his laundry to his dad's house for summer break.

But probably the most reassuring moment came when I was Emily's houseguest for a few days this summer. We hung out together, not only doing lunches, but breakfasts and dinners as well. I didn't even mind sleeping on the lumpy futon in her living room.

As I was getting ready to leave for home, she enthusiastically asked, "Hey, Mom, when you come back, will you bring some recipes?"

"Recipes?" I asked, not believing my ears.

"Yeah, I want to learn how to make that tuna noodle casserole you used to fix."

"Sure, sweetheart. Of course. I'll be happy to."

~Marjorie Woodall

31

Teen Angles

Laughter leads us, kneads us, and sometimes helps
bleed us of torments and woes.
~Bob Talbert

When Kristine was a baby, I pitied my friends who waved their children off to college. I could never survive without my only child! Fortunately, Kristine's teen years helped me get over that one. I even prepared her for living away from home.

"Someday you'll be out of earshot when she yells, 'Dad! Come quick!'" I told my husband. "She'll need to learn to do her own plunging and killing."

"Then I'll never teach her," he vowed. But, eventually he did show her how to plunge a toilet and kill a spider.

When it was finally our turn to drop Kristine off at the college dorm, a wave of joy swept over me, mixed with sweet sorrow.

Once we were alone, my husband broke the silence with, "Now we can chase each other around the house..."

"Yippee!" I said. "But should we feel so jazzed?"

This question jarred a bunch of memories that bopped me on the head. On the drive home, I took a detour down memory lane.

Of course we love Kristine more than life itself—but living with a teenager can be like lugging a ball-and-complain. (Especially if they're hungry.) For example, from the time she was thirteen, there were strict rules that Kristine tried to enforce—like not being seen with her parents in public. She was terrified we'd humiliate her (an ironic twist) in front of the highly critical junior high crowd.

Now we'll relax, since we don't have to keep close tabs on her at college. I remember the tracking device—a handy pager—we bought fourteen-year-old Kristine. (Like tagging an endangered species in the big jungle.) But there was a glitch. I'd page her and she'd promptly call me from "the library." I was none the wiser; neither was she—because instead of studying, she'd be… well, one can only guess.

Then there was the Dark Age of fifteen. Kristine was learning to drive and wanted to chauffeur me everywhere. We made a truce. She had to listen to my sound advice, such as: "The rearview mirror is not for grooming." And, I had to use a pleasant voice—a hard promise to keep while shrieking, "We're going to die!"

She also insisted I refrain from slamming on an imaginary brake. I assured her it was really an accelerator. She liked that. But after one close call, she made the mistake of mumbling, "I'd be more careful if I was driving my own truck."

Yes, Kristine learned to drive (me crazy) and I learned to be more articulate. For example, at a drive-through, I said, "Go slow, there's a red post." Very slowly she scraped along the post, leaving a long red streak on the car door. A lively discussion ensued. She pointed out, "You didn't say don't hit it, only 'go slow!'"

I then learned to say: "Do not hit the red post." "Do not hit the pedestrian." Whatever it took.

By age sixteen, Kristine was a fairly good driver and an excellent student. She did so well she decided to study the art of forgery. When caught cutting classes, the vice principal wanted to suspend her. I pointed out the punishment should fit the crime, not be the crime. That landed her in Saturday school, where she had time to contemplate her bright future. This could have been a great source of pride for us doting parents, proving we'd instilled correct values. However, her first goal was to get a tattoo and her first career choice was tending bar, not to be confused with taking the bar exam.

When Kristine turned seventeen, she was wonderful. Wonder of wonders, we scarcely saw her. This made us wonder what she was up to. I finally figured a foolproof way to spend time with her. The formula was: invite the boyfriend, bring my credit card, go shopping and out to eat. When the bills came, my husband's comment was, "Kristine's first word wasn't 'mommy,' it was 'money.'"

Naturally, we miss Kristine—but not the daily mess. I had to insist she keep her bedroom door closed to keep the clutter from climbing out in an escape attempt. Although in her defense, I discovered the carpet in her room was utterly spotless when she moved out. Those heaps of strewn clothes provided guaranteed carpet protection.

Throughout the teen years, as expected, there was unexpected yelling. Once, Kristine reported she had partied with Justin Timberlake's entourage and bodyguard. I jotted down his name, since she made him sound so noteworthy. As I wrote, I spelled out loud, "K-i-m..."

Without warning, Kristine went berserk. "T!" she shouted, "T-I-M-berlake!" Convinced I was the most ill-informed person on the planet, she counseled, "You really need to read magazines and watch more TV."

Maybe having all that excitement away from home won't be as stressful as anticipated. Besides, college agreed with Kristine, especially dorm life. I asked if she ever felt homesick.

"No," she replied, "but I get dormsick if I am home too long."

Now it's hard to entice her home for outings like getting her teeth cleaned and having her cholesterol rechecked. On her last visit, Kaiser happened to offer a cholesterol class. Now what are the odds of that? Evidently, better than the odds that she'd attend it.

"I'm not going to just sit there for two hours and let my cholesterol simmer," she refused. "Not when I could be actively shopping the mall!"

We've discovered college life is a blessing, but steaming with influences. The gang(sters) on her floor even pooled their money to buy her a rose tattoo. When I first saw it, I felt sick. Not just because some tattooed-wonder stuck a bunch of needles in my darling daughter, but because the tattoo should have said, "I Love Mom."

And love each other, we do. Immensely. Sometimes even more so when we're not crowding each other in the same nest!

~Ruth Magan

32

The Last Load

Great necessities call out great virtues.
~Abigail Adams

I love doing laundry. Loads of laundry. Many call me crazy. And raising five kids in a blended family provided an endless fix for my laundry addiction.

Maybe I was afraid they would ruin their clothes by mixing colors with whites. Like the time my husband and I tried to enjoy a weekend away and our daughter called sobbing that her best white pants were now a putrid pink; she'd washed them with her favorite red shirt. Possibly, I worried they'd mimic the *I Love Lucy* episode where Lucille Ball wanted to get the laundry done quickly and did four loads at once. Suds spewed over the top of the machine like Niagara Falls.

Perhaps I craved the peace I found as I meticulously folded their clothes—with the laundry room to myself. No one dared venture in for fear they'd have to—horrors—fold someone else's underwear. Or, conceivably, it's what kept me home in the busyness of my empty-nest-wannabe life, doing laundry while writing so I got up and moved every so often, musing as I loaded, unloaded, and folded.

Even so, I came to my senses and realized if my youngsters didn't learn to do their own laundry, one day I might be doing it for their spouses as well!

I'd managed to keep our faithful washer and dryer churning out an average of twenty loads per week for twelve years. But within six months of the kids doing their own wash, the repairman graced my once serene laundry room twice. Then it happened: The week before Christmas, my reliable old machine washed—but failed to rinse—her last load.

So Santa brought me a new washer. And he brought the kids laundry baskets filled with detergent... and quarters for the Laundromat.

The old dryer lasted another year and the new washing machine until the Christmas after that. To no avail, I left "Overload and get grounded" notes on the machine. It seemed our kids preferred doing laundry at home and they had only two systems: wash one solitary item or, like Lucy, an entire month's worth at once just to be done.

However, we raised smart children. After a spell of doing their own laundry, they began asking favors like, "Mom, can you turn my laundry over? I have to go to work." Or, "Mom, are you doing a load of whites? Can you just add these few things to it?" And the one they knew I would always succumb to, "Mom, this is my favorite blouse-pants-skirt-shirt-sweater and I don't know how to wash it. Can you pleeease wash it for me?" And they ran out the door, both of us knowing that, although they were fully capable, I could and would wash for them.

By the time the older four moved out, I was in recovery from my laundry addiction. However, my daughters were appalled that I still did their nineteen-year-old brother's laundry. But this youngest and last child, with problems unique to him, had been the hardest to push out of the house. As I stood in the laundry room feeling pangs of anger that I actually was still doing his laundry, I heard a tranquil, small voice say, "Take care of my child."

Knowing God had a special plan for our youngest and wanting to obey Him, I suddenly found myself washing everything in my son's room. I even rewashed clothes he'd left in the dryer for days. This time, I removed and hung them immediately so never a wrinkle could form.

Our son started college later than his siblings had. After finally completing his fourth year at the local junior college, he found me in the laundry room one day.

"I've done it," he exulted. "And I accumulated 110 units along the way."

A whopping 110? I thought with a measure of dryness. Just shy of enough units for a bachelor's degree had he been at the university!

"The good news, Mom, is that I was accepted to Concordia University. And because I'm turning twenty-four, I can get my own school loans and you and Jack won't have to pay for my college."

As I stood there folding his clothes, I felt a twinge of relief. Not because we wouldn't be adding another loan to our already monstrous college tuition debt, but because I was sure I heard that same, tranquil voice whisper, "Well done, good and faithful servant."

I hugged my son. Then, I reached into the dryer, pulled out the rest of his clothes and piled them in his arms. And I smilingly congratulated the both of us—him for his acceptance and me for doing his last load!

~Patricia Cena Evans

33

Aligned in Time

*Squeeze the tube slowly, because once the toothpaste is out,
it's hard to get it back in.*
~Unknown

So there we sat, four couples at a restaurant table. Eight people thoroughly enjoying one another's company.

I wish I could say such a scene is typical, but the truth is gathering together our three daughters, two sons-in-law and one Significant Other is anything but typical. The logistics involved are enough to stop us in our tracks now that our adult children (the ultimate oxymoron!) are scattered.

Time was when we would gather in the dining room of our old house, at the quirky antique table we kept threatening to use for firewood, to celebrate family occasions of state. Who knew those wonderful, crowded years—when we thought we'd love a less cluttered life in both real and metaphoric ways—would creep up on us while our backs were turned? Who knew we would find ourselves wishing our daughters back just for the pleasure of their company, only to find they simply couldn't make it?

On our first attempt to celebrate several family milestones, Jill and Jeff had to be in Pittsburgh, Nancy and Mike had a long overdue reunion with college friends, and Amy and her David were on their way to a biking trip in Vermont.

The family dinner was put on hold for six weeks.

But when those six weeks were over and the targeted date rolled around, a new subset of complications arose. So we pushed the date back... again.

It was nothing short of amazing that a mere three months after the milestone birthday and major anniversary, we managed to assemble at a funky restaurant—their choice—in the mad, mad town of Manhattan.

Nancy and Michael arrived early. No surprise.

Jill and Jeff were, of course, late. Again, no surprise.

Amy and David left a trail of cell phone messages, their M.O. Nothing is ever simple with those two.

But miraculously, we found ourselves breaking bread together—and catching up on the simple pleasure of being in the same place at the same time. United as a family once again.

Our daughters lead peripatetic lives. Their men also do. And in one of the ironies of life, it's we empty nesters who have more time for family now than we ever did when that family was around. So, while a celebratory family dinner shouldn't be such a big deal, it has become just that. It's also a chance to rediscover who we are as we all march through time, a chance to view one another beyond the old barriers of grown-ups and kids.

Which was the wonderful astonishment of this Saturday night dinner.

Our children are, of course, no longer children. They are people with lives, ideas, values, goals, and dreams. They are smarter, in some ways, than we ever were. They are also capable of being infuriatingly stubborn, foolish, and unreasonable.

Exactly like us.

It was wonderful to share not just everyone's food (we're a family that can't seem to stick to our own plates) but also to share ideas about politics, about work and about whether the Internet is enhancing or ruining our lives.

It was marvelous to argue, to ponder, to debate. We are decidedly not a family that agrees about very much because all of us have stubborn genes, which tends to make life interesting. And challenging.

But there are no people with whom I'd rather linger, laugh, reminisce, and share world views.

I suspect that we overstayed our welcome at the Manhattan restaurant where tables are at a premium on a Saturday night, but, somehow, no one could make the first move to get us up and out. Each time, there was one more joke, one more memory, one more spirited argument to settle.

Finally, when the restaurant was emptying out around us, we surrendered to the clock, our fatigue, and the prospect of our long rides home.

But just before we broke our lovely circle of connectedness, I looked around the table and realized the people I love most in the world were within my reach—literally and figuratively. And in that instant, I wanted to freeze time, to stop the world right there, right then, when the planets were in perfect alignment and I could seize the sweet, sweet pleasure of the company of my own kin.

Instead, I stumbled to my feet, locked my loved ones in hugs, and made them promise we'd do this again soon.

We swore we would. And for that moment, we meant it.

But we all knew our Saturday night family party would be hard to replicate, impossible to repeat. Maybe some future milestone would make it happen. Or a holiday. Or the rare chance that somehow, someday, we'd actually manage the intergenerational family vacation we keep talking about.

But even though we rejoice in their independence, we miss them a lot more than we'd expected to. And we understand that we will have to settle for these rare and fleeting times when we celebrate nothing more—or less—than the incredible pleasure of their company.

~Sally Friedman

34

A Second Chance

Keep your face to the sunshine and you cannot see the shadows.
~Helen Keller

For the fifth time in an hour, I part the mini blinds and peer out, hoping to see my daughter's rusted Beetle in our parking spot. Still no sign of her, although she should be home from work by now. The smell of lasagna fills the apartment and reminds me to take dinner from the oven. I sigh and let the blinds snap back into place.

I put the lasagna on the counter and take two plates from the cupboard. I hesitate, chewing the inside of my cheek and wincing at how sore it's become from that constant habit. My self-confidence and certainty died with my husband a year ago next month. Gone, too, is my ability to say and do the right thing—especially when it comes to my daughter.

Maybe Stephanie will get irritated if she sees the table set and knows I waited for her to come home. She has a life, after all, as she continuously reminds me. Maybe she'll think I'm treating her like a child. I put one of the plates back, and sit down at the flimsy card table, feeling a pang of longing for my beautiful dining room furniture. It went, as did most of my things, when the house was sold after Tom died.

I admire the cake in the glass-domed plate sitting on the table. I made Stephanie's favorite—cherry chip with cream cheese frosting. My social security check arrived early, and cake mixes were half-price, so I splurged. I find myself biting my cheek instead of the lasagna. Cherry chip used to be her favorite, but lately she watches what she eats, complaining when I don't buy organic.

The big cake plate on the little table looks silly to me now; the cake I baked and frosted so carefully seems too humble for the fancy dish. Maybe I shouldn't have bothered. I look around for a place to put it. The apartment-sized fridge? The tiny pantry? Oh, well. There's the jingle of her key in the lock.

"You're late. Big dinner rush?" I squeeze my lips together to keep the words in, but not fast enough.

Much to my surprise, she doesn't shoot back at me, angry and defensive. She just slumps into a chair and shrugs off the black jacket that says Filbert Winery and Café in gold embroidery on the front. She looks too old and too tired for her age.

"No. We closed early for the party, but I stayed to help set tables and decorate."

"Oh? What party?"

"You know all the summer kids, the ones who work part-time at the winery? Well, lots of them are going off to college. The staff threw a party for them."

"Why didn't you stay?" They all love Stephanie, so I know she must have been invited.

She rolls her eyes. "No, thanks. All the parents would be there, whining about how their babies are leaving the nest, or else complaining about the fortune it's costing them, which is really just bragging. I'm tired of hearing about it."

I nod and get up to wash my plate and the few dishes in the sink. Now I understand. I've seen her looking at college course catalogs, and then I've found those same catalogs in the trash, torn in half. I wish I could gather her to me and say how sorry I am that instead of a college acceptance letter, she got a middle-of-the-night call telling her that her father was dead. I want to tell her I'm sorry that instead of a giddy roommate and a college dorm, she got a destitute mother and a low-income apartment.

I wish I could remind her that she's as smart as any of those kids. Smarter. But she knows that, and anyway she doesn't care about being smart. She wants to be educated. There's a difference.

It's quiet, except for the running water and the clank of dishes. If I don't say something now, she'll turn inward and I will lose my chance. So I take a deep breath and jump in.

"Yes, well, I feel sorry for those parents. They may never be as lucky as I am."

She's never said it, of course, but I know Stephanie doesn't think I have the right to feel sorry for anyone, pathetic as I've become. I know she doesn't think there's anything remotely lucky about my life.

Finally she says, "What do you mean by that?"

"Well, when you were a baby I couldn't wait for you to go to school so I could have a break. When you were a teenager, I counted the days until you were out of the house and I could spend time with your dad, get our life back. Selfish of me, I know, and I regret it."

Without a pause, I rush on. "When Dad died and you suggested we move in together, I was grateful—not only because I needed help making ends meet, but for a second chance to be the worrying, over-protective, cake-baking mother I should have been."

I look around the apartment while she looks at her hands and add, "Don't worry, you'll get your chance to leave the nest, too. Sooner than I hope, I'm sure."

She's quiet for a long time. Then she smiles, a weak and watery smile, but a smile all the same. "I'm not really in such a hurry, Mom."

I let out the breath I've been holding. "Why don't you go out with your friends? It's Friday." It's a hard thing to suggest when I just want her here safe with me.

She goes to the cupboard and takes down two plates, retrieves two forks from the drawer. "Nah," she says and cuts two huge slabs of cake. "I think I'd rather stay home."

~Tiffany O'Neill

35

A New Route

No more delays. We wriggled into the family car, arranging assorted arms and legs around the belongings of our older son Ian, the almost-college student. He placed one last bag on my lap, crammed himself into an impossibly small space in the back seat next to his brother Tom, and the four of us were off.

We had triumphed over the challenge many parents face at the beginning of a college school year: fitting an infinite number of items into the finite space of an automobile. We got creative. If it weren't for the microwave ("Mom, a man, a microwave—a meal.") and the mini-fridge ("Mom, leftovers for the microwave.") we might have pulled it off. Instead, we cheated a little by borrowing a neighbor's car-top luggage carrier.

Although we all felt achy by the end of the trip, Ian was so thrilled to be starting his new life, he never complained. Tom, realizing he wouldn't have to share a darn thing until Ian came home for Thanksgiving, was equally cheerful during the six-hour ride.

So much for lingering farewells at the dorm. It was obvious Ian itched for us to leave. We gave him a big hug and left.

I was stoic on the trip home. But I dissolved at the sight of Ian's quilt, left in the hallway. My firstborn was gone.

For several weeks, I busied myself with my job and family affairs. November came and Ian arrived for his first vacation. It was a joy until he left, and then my blues started again. Nothing anyone said made me feel better.

I sent packages almost weekly. Sometimes just a small packet with news clippings or cookies, but occasionally I'd send clothes or other necessities. They were the therapy that got me through that first year.

It was only when we cleaned out Ian's dorm room at the end of the school year that I faced reality: Neatly stacked in one corner, from ceiling to floor, were all the empty boxes from the goodies I had sent. The sculpture testified to a mom's love—and provided an on-going source of amusement to Ian and his friends. Some placed bets on how high the stack would reach. Ian had told me to phone whenever I wanted, but I always hesitated to interrupt his life. The sheer height of the boxes made me glad I'd only sent packages.

Each semester grew easier, and I sent fewer boxes.

Four years later, Tom left for college. I knew women who collapsed into emotional downslides after their last child left home and worried I'd be among them.

Even before we deposited Tom, I felt numb. But something happened after we left the dorm. My husband and I got out the map to decide the return route we'd take. And then it hit me: It didn't matter how long we took getting home. There was no one to check on, no one who needed anything. Amazingly, we were free to take our delicious time, stopping whenever and wherever we wanted.

It took us three days to drive the six-hour trip!

We took long walks, woke up when we felt like it, and ate at nice restaurants. I lazed in the morning wearing only a nightgown, no longer concerned about who would see me. Why hadn't I been told it could be like this?

Of course I miss my sons. They are the biggest blessings in my life. But this new chapter must be embraced, not dreaded. I see a path filled with opportunities I never imagined. A menu overflowing with choices.

Now, what should I do first?

~Kathleen McNamara

36

Birthday Blues

We don't see things as they are. We see them as we are.
~Anais Nin

yawned as I kneaded the dough for my daughter's birthday bread. It was a tradition begun years before, and I looked forward to it—even though it meant getting up at 6 A.M. We had adopted our daughter, and we tried to make every occasion extra special so she'd know how much she meant to us.

Three hours later, I heard her door open. She padded into the bathroom and turned on the shower.

She deserves to take her time today, I thought. I stirred pancake mix for a special breakfast and readied the table with a laminated placemat made from her old birthday cards and a huge cup of steaming chocolate capped with a head of whipped cream.

When she emerged, I turned to see her wearing head-to-toe black. Thick make-up caked her face. "Happy eighteenth! Here are your birthday pancakes," I offered, though I was beginning to feel uneasy. Suddenly recalling her new conversion to vegetarianism, I ate the sausage behind her back, standing at the sink. She ate in silence.

"What would you like to do for your special day?" I asked.

"I have plans," she said tersely.

"Oh. Well… tell me what time you'll be home for dinner and gifts. The bread's already rising."

"Actually," she said, putting down her fork, wiping her mouth, "I'm moving out. He's going to be here in about an hour."

My throat closed. That Young Man was older, and she knew we disapproved of him. He'd been in the picture for some time, but we mostly tried to ignore him.

After she left, I drove to my husband's workplace. Several times I had to pull over to wipe my eyes, blow my nose, and compose myself.

"We weren't perfect, but we tried so hard!" My shoulders shook from the sobs. "Maybe we were too strict?"

"Honey," he comforted, "we did our best. She's eighteen now. This is her choice."

My smile was bitter. "Remember when she was little? She was so thrilled she'd finally found a 'forever home.' She always said she would never leave us."

"And you used to tell her she didn't have to worry about leaving, because you wouldn't survive if she did."

The light bulb went on. Was that what this was about? "We've got to call her."

Thankfully, she answered.

"Honey, it's Mom."

"Yes?" Her voice sounded distant, cold.

"I just want to apologize." I paused. "Remember when I used to say I couldn't survive if you ever left me? I'm sorry. I should never have said that. If you feel it's time to move on, I will respect that. We'll always be here, though, if you ever need us."

There was silence on the other end, then racking sobs. "Can we have dinner at six?" she asked.

"Absolutely," I said. I swallowed. Hard. "Be sure to bring that young man, you hear?"

Eventually, we had to get used to the fact she'd moved out. Knowing she wasn't just behind her bedroom door hurt so badly that we decided to move. But—by accepting and releasing our daughter—we managed to maintain a positive relationship with her.

Now, she's married to That Young Man and, you know what? He's not as bad as we originally thought. In fact, he's rather nice. And we've adjusted and are happy, too.

We learned that nests of Super Glue make horrible launch pads. Our job was to raise our daughter to not need us. Mission accomplished.

If only we didn't need her so much!

~Drema Drudge

37

The Apple of My Eye

It's only money.
~American Proverb

"I don't care where Miriam lives, a $3,000 phone bill for one month is ridiculous!" shouted my husband William, a prominent lawyer in our fair town. I hated to admit it, but he had a point.

Here was the problem. Our nineteen-year-old daughter, the only other female in a house of towering testosterone and the baby of the family, had been accepted at an acting school in Manhattan, New York. And although it was the dream of a lifetime for her, it was a nightmare for me. My baby, a sweet, sheltered girl from a small Canadian town, who possessed no common sense whatsoever, was going to live all by herself in the Big Apple. We knew no one she could call if she ran into trouble. She was about to fly solo without a safety net in the biggest city in North America.

When we brought her to New York to set up her apartment, we quickly discovered that getting her a phone was impossible. Being Canadian, we did not possess the required golden ticket—an American social security card. Nor could she get Internet access for the same reason.

What was a desperate and frantic mother to do?

It was one thing for her to move away for a year, I may have been able to cope with that. But to be unable to phone her, or worse, for Miriam to call me if she had an emergency? It was too much to ask.

So, I upgraded Miriam's Canadian cell phone plan. My blood pressure dropped dramatically when she dutifully called every night after returning from her class. I was still nervous about her safety, well okay, anxious... okay, okay, slightly hysterical, but I could cope if I heard her voice.

Slight glitch—roaming charges. Hence, the $3,000 bill. Who knew? A middle-aged mother from Canada sure didn't.

"There is no excuse for this!" bellowed my husband. "We can't afford it."

"But she's a baby," I wailed. "Just the other day the newscaster reported that girls are less likely to be mugged while walking if they are on a cell phone."

It was a sound argument. My husband paused in his diatribe about the virtues of thrift. Who could argue against a daughter's safety?

"That I understand," said William in a thoroughly patient, yet thoroughly furious voice. "It's the other forty hours that don't make sense. Who can even talk that long? How did she get any school work done?"

That's the problem with being married to a good lawyer. They do know how to get their points across and win the argument.

"Give me a month," I muttered. "We'll work on it."

During the next few weeks, Miriam was invited to a movie premiere. Of course she called her mother for wardrobe advice. She attended a Halloween parade in Greenwich Village. She caught a bad cold. She met a boy. And she saw Kevin Bacon in a restaurant.

That month's bill was a mere $1,100. We'd done better.

"If you two do this again, I'm taking the cell phone away when she comes home for Christmas," announced William.

November came and went. There was her bout of flu, and my directions for homemade chicken soup with matzo balls. American Thanksgiving and instructions on how to make a turkey required an hour-long discussion. Come on. It was her first time making American turkey! Macy's Thanksgiving Day Parade, another hour. Oh, dear. Four Christmas parties, two Broadway shows, a break-up with her boyfriend, and gosh, I had to hear about the new boyfriend.

December? $745.

"That's it, the phone goes," said William in his most lawyer-like authoritative voice.

"But it's my lifeline," I cried. "A Jewish mother needs to talk to her children every day. It's what we live for!"

William sighed. "All right. One more month," he said.

Well, I am happy to announce that January's phone bill was only marginally over the base price. Still, William is not happy. He really is trying hard to understand why I need to hear from my daughter at least two or three times a week. I've explained that the phone calls are vital for my sanity. Much to my relief, I hear other empty nest mothers have the same problem with their phone bills. I also hear that as time moves on, the incredible ache in my heart and the pangs of missing my daughter will fade and become tolerable.

Miriam's roommate has since installed Internet access in the apartment. I think of it as a belated Hanukah present from the dear Lord above. I just knew He wouldn't let me down in my hour of need.

Will my phone bill ever be normal as long as my daughter lives in Manhattan? Perhaps.

Oops—Miriam just called. She's on her way to dinner with her newest boyfriend. In Connecticut.

Wait a minute. Connecticut? Where it's snowing? Aaaagh! "Be sure to call me when you get there!"

~Pamela Goldstein

Bring Her Home

Treat the other man's faith gently;
it is all he has to believe with.
His mind was created for his own thoughts, not yours or mine.
~Henry S. Haskins

The sudden stillness sent a chill down my spine. "What just happened?" I asked myself over and over. I hadn't been unreasonable.

"If she were underage then I could've stopped her from leaving. But she's nineteen." I wanted only the best for my daughter, but her perspective on that issue differed from mine "How will she survive? I shouldn't have yelled," I muttered.

Night fell, but I couldn't seem to move, even to turn on the light. I shivered. I knew someday my kids would leave home. But not this way. I had dreamed of Linda going to college or getting married. I'd anticipated sharing those special moments and watching her mature into a woman.

"Oh God, what am I going to do?" I cried to the empty room. "Linda left with a backpack and a boy I hardly know. Have I failed as a mother because I didn't want to be taken advantage of? Please, please keep her safe. Bring her home soon."

My heart and mind struggled to unravel the reasons why Linda decided to leave. She had been hurt and angry after her dad left us years ago. I understood that her present actions were another way of acting out that anger.

At the beginning of summer, her brother had entered the Job Corps and Linda asked if one of her friends could move into his bedroom. "He's responsible and can help with the rent."

We'd struggled financially and Linda's suggestion seemed sound. I liked her friend and agreed to the win-win idea. But he moved in, ate our food, and three months later had only paid one month's rent. When he ran up my phone bill up and couldn't pay it, I asked him to leave.

"Mom, I'm so sorry. I thought because he worked he'd be responsible," Linda apologized.

"I guess we've both learned a lesson," I replied.

We moved forward with our lives—until Linda came home with another friend and asked if he could move in. When I refused, Linda went to her room. A short time later she appeared with a backpack and defiantly declared, "Then I'm leaving."

The walls in my apartment closed in, and I felt a suffocating panic when she walked out. Hours passed with no word. After making several calls, I learned that none of her friends had seen her. Helpless and exhausted, I fell across my bed. "Please, Lord," I prayed. "Keep her safe. Bring Linda home."

The next day, the call I'd been waiting and praying for finally came. "Mom, Greg and I are living with one of his friends in Newport Beach."

That night I went to plead with her. "Linda, how are you going to manage? Come home where you can finish school."

"No, Mom. My life is none of your business."

Wow! What had I done to deserve this? I drove home in tears.

When I learned about a promising therapist, I called Linda. "I know you are hurting and that's behind your anger. I learned about a counselor who will talk with us in her home. She'll listen and make suggestions that might help."

"Is she expensive?" Linda asked.

"She'll see us once without any charge. I called and she can see us this week."

"Okay. Can you pick me up? "

"Of course. I'll be there."

A couple of days later, not sure that Linda would actually go, I drove to her apartment where she surprised me by being ready. At the appointment, Dr. Lindsay talked with both of us, spent a long time alone with Linda, then invited me back in.

"Linda wants to tell you something."

"Mom, I'm sorry about the ugly things I said to you." She swallowed back tears. "But I want you to let me struggle if I have to. I want to figure out what I'm going to do with the rest of my life. If I make mistakes, I want you to let me handle it. I love you, but I have to do this by myself."

I fought to control my emotions. "Okay, Linda, but I want you to know that I am here for you and I love you."

Six weeks passed before I heard from her again. I'd just gotten home from work when the phone rang.

"Mom, I wanted to tell you we are living in Palm Springs. Now I understand how difficult it is to pay rent, bills, and be responsible. I've learned to appreciate how hard you worked to take care of us. I love you."

"I love you, too, Linda. And the door is always open."

I continued to pray for my daughter. I knew her struggles were many, especially after she invited me to Palm Springs, where I found them living in a friend's vacation home with no furniture and little else except sleeping bags.

Even under those circumstances, a new loving relationship developed between us. I knew if I rejected her the cycle of anger would continue. I had to learn to love her without condoning her choices. She took a job as a waitress and worked long hard hours. I began to see a more mature, compassionate young lady. Yes, I still wanted her home, but I also wanted her to become the woman I knew she could be.

Two years passed, and the day arrived I'd been waiting for: Linda called. "Mom, I'm coming home." I helped her get a job at the hospital where I worked and joy returned.

One year later, at Linda's wedding—the day I dreamed

about—our laughter and tears flowed freely. My beautiful twenty-two-year-old filled my heart to overflowing as she exchanged wedding vows with the man she loved.

At a Christian retreat, Linda and I expressed how blessed we'd been. We both understood that through all the adversity in our lives we'd become women of faith, women of strength who embraced life with love, not anger.

I also realized I'd never been alone in wanting the best for my daughter. God did, too.

~Karen Kosman

"The nest may be empty...
but the storage room's full!"

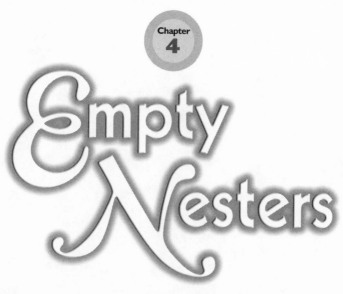

Chapter
4

Empty Nesters

Ruffled Feathers

All the art of living lies in a fine mingling of letting go and holding on.
~Havelock Ellis

Ode to the (Almost) Empty Nest

Alone, alone,
A place just our own,
With all of our children finally grown.

Come see, come see,
We're free as can be.
A bathroom for him and a bathroom for me!

There's space, real space
All over the place.
In bedrooms and closets they've left not a trace.

Mirage, mirage,
It's just camouflage.
They left—but they've left it all in the garage!

~Bonnie Compton Hanson

Remember Me?

Dear Saint Peter,
        I know you're terribly busy at the pearly gates. Believe me when I say I've been to others first. I tried Saint Christopher but my letter came back as addressee unknown. So I tried Saint Anthony but learned I had the wrong department; he only works on lost items. Although I did plead my case for "loss of mind" and "loss of youth."

I'm told you are in charge of customer service and since I hate to bring my issue of dissatisfaction directly to the Big Guy, I thought perhaps you could shed some light on my situation.

I'm the one who asked your help thirty years ago when I wanted a baby. You must have a lot of pull; we received five within seven years. Remember me now? I was the one who kept saying, "Enough already!"

We raised those five boys and kept them out of jail — most of the time, anyway. But here's the situation: They have found other women, other lives, other homes. You had a Jewish mom, so you know how it is: They don't call; they don't write.

The problem is I'm lonesome. So I was thinking...

The second Tuesday of each month, could my home be filled again with those little boys running around wildly, jumping from couch to chair to footstool? To fill my life with their noise and music and fighting?

Oh. I forgot about the fighting.

Hmmm. Make that one day every other month. One day when they laugh and play and get in trouble at school or dent the car.

Oh, wait. Let's catch our breath. Perhaps we should trim that back to two days a year. Just two little old days, days when they ask for money to buy…

Hold your horses there. How could I be so selfish? I forgot how busy you are and I'd hate to impose.

How 'bout we just leave things as they are? I'll simply learn to accept my quiet and clean house, my new car without dents. Instead, I'll just focus on my poor wonderful life of peace and serenity. Meanwhile Pete, keep up the good work. And, God Bless.

~Kathryn A. Begnaud

Help! The Mothers Are Coming

With what price we pay for the glory of motherhood.
~Isadora Duncan

The Mothers—mine and my husband's—are cruising in for a landing to attend my twin daughters' graduation and I haven't dusted since last year.

Philosophies of cleaning are generational. When these Best Generation moms were young, cleanliness was placed on the mantel right next to godliness. With my Baby Boomer reasoning, I consider stirring up dust a disturbance in the force. I need a compelling reason to clean—like just before 2000 when I scrubbed the bathtub so I could fill it with drinking water in case the millennial prophecies came true. The fact The Mothers are coming might be as compelling a reason to clean. Since the twins are about to go to college, I suppose I can't use them as my excuse any longer.

Neither of The Mothers wears white gloves or sees all that well. Still, women of their vintage sniff out dirt quicker than a hound dog smells a criminal. They will know I haven't cleaned under the bathroom heater with a toothbrush and they'll note my kitchen lacks sparkle. I'll hide the stacks of books, papers, movies, and CDs smearing every surface, but my moms will detect the faint dirt outlines that divulge where things were left neglected. I pray they can forgive the dog hairs and parakeet feathers floating around the dining room—and hope none land on their plates.

The Mothers are from the Northwest, where water falls, free-of-charge, right from the sky. They won't understand why, here in the Southwest, I have a drought-stricken patch of weeds, dirt, sage, and prickly pear where my backyard should be. If I showed them my water bill, they'd think it was a lame excuse.

I could blame the alternately overgrown and exhausted state of my yard on my puppy, a Bigfoot of a brute who, like his ancestor Babe the Blue Ox, is an expert at landscape demolition. He pulls whole boards off the fence and drags them, complete with four-inch nails, through the struggling daisies. I tried removing his lumber toys one day but he toppled the plastic Adirondack chairs and chewed up the garden hose in retaliation. He's out there now, calculating how many boards to pull off the fence before he can escape.

My curtain dilemma cannot be blamed on the dog. When we moved in, we found three sets of ugly shutters for four windows. I reconfigured them for two years before I realized the math didn't work. Finally, I removed one shutter—the one prone to falling apart on the floor—and put up cheap rods for curtains I made from an old tablecloth. I meant to replace them with better rods when I got to town, but what with work and kids and puppies, the curtains stayed. An old ketchup stain on one side grows darker every year.

Before The Mothers arrive, I've got to fix the dining room chairs, the ones with holes in the caning and the ones with crosspieces that pop out, those that are slivery and those that scratch the tile. Oh, and I'll need that chair the logger dog dismantled out back.

The clock is ticking (that would be the one with batteries), and lists of chores jitterbug in my brain. I think Buddhists call this monkey-mind, mentally swinging from one branch to another without ever getting a grip.

Maybe what's really going on is I don't want to think about two babies that grew up when I wasn't looking, about children leaving home and taking their fun, creativity, and energy with them. I can't protect them from plane hijackings, disastrous dates, cafeteria food, and computer viruses, not to mention loan sharks and used car sales-men. Who will worry about lightning strikes and broken femurs? Who will make them cocoa when it is cold? And how will their tow-els ever get washed?

But the mother of all questions, lurking like the Loch Ness Monster under my rowboat, is: How, oh, how will I get through sup-pertime without them?

The Mothers better get here soon because while I wouldn't relish a reality-TV look at the state of my nest, I could use tips on what to do when it is empty.

~Carol Mell

The Last Summer

Anxiety is the beginning of conscience,
which is the parent of the soul but is not compatible with innocence.
~Angela Carter

"The last thing on my mind is food!" This reprimand came from my eighteen-year-old daughter as she stood in front of the open refrigerator, studying its contents. I had made the mistake of helpfully explaining what we had in there, as some items were concealed in plastic containers.

I had always said that the person I admired most was my own daughter. But now my fantastic award-winning daughter, who had been an angel throughout high school, had turned into my worst critic. I had lived through this with my son two years earlier, and I knew all about the messy process by which kids and parents separate during the last summer before college. I really didn't mind. It was almost comical.

We mothers share the blame. We hover over our kids, trying to be helpful, and storing up every last moment of togetherness before our children leave. We are on the verge of tears many times during those last summers. So we cling, while our kids try to wriggle away.

All summer, my daughter found me incredibly irritating. I just soldiered on, imparting unwanted nuggets of wisdom during my last few weeks of fulltime mothering. My friends reported the same behavior from their daughters.

My twenty-year-old son watched his sister in amusement. One day, she asked him, "Hasn't Mom changed? She is so much more annoying than she used to be." He responded that I was no more annoying than usual... and that she was the one who had changed.

My son had been worse the summer before he left. I had always believed that the stupidity of teenage boys was perfectly timed to peak at age sixteen, just when they received their learner's permits here in Connecticut. But no... it turns out that the summer after graduating from high school represents a second, even higher, peak of dumb behavior. All the mothers were complaining about their recently graduated sons—the beer, the late nights, the general insolence and lack of judgment.

My own son's awful summer had climaxed with a car accident just one week before he was to set off for his first semester of college, at a university in Spain. His father had allowed him to drive his very expensive BMW, and my son ended up taking a turn too fast and hitting a tree.

Unfortunately, an overzealous police officer had arrested him for leaving the scene of the accident, which as it turned out, was a completely legal thing to do. In our state, you are allowed to leave the scene of an accident to find help, or in this case, to call your father and confess, as long as no one is hurt and there is no damage to anyone else's property.

We begged for an early court date, and the day before my son was to leave for Spain, we spent six hours waiting to see the judge, who reduced the charges to a ticket for unsafe movement. There were several other eighteen-year-old young men at the courthouse that day, looking uncomfortable in jackets and ties, accompanied by unhappy parents. They were leaving for college the next day or shortly thereafter, and they were all taking care of whatever messes they had made that summer!

My son and I had a couple of rather vigorous conversations (okay... there was yelling) during those final days. Nevertheless, as he got into his father's (other) car for the drive to Kennedy Airport, I cried. But five minutes later, I realized that I was feeling something new, something that I hadn't felt in a while—relief. Of course, I resumed crying and missing my son a few days later, and couldn't wait to visit him midway through the fall semester.

Two years later, my son was a true pleasure—mature, independent, and back to his brilliant well-behaved self—and it was my daughter's turn! By the end of the summer, I was accustomed to my daughter's reprimands and let them slide right off me.

Coincidentally, she too was involved in a terrible car accident just one week before she left for college. A dump truck hit her Mini, sending it on a terrifying 200-foot odyssey across two lanes of traffic, through a hedge taller than the car, across sidewalks and another road and into the side of a building. The Mini, the dump truck, and another vehicle parked nearby were totaled, and she and the four landscapers who were illegally squeezed into the dump truck all ended up in the hospital. Miraculously, no one was seriously hurt, and the police found the other driver wholly responsible for the accident.

The destruction of her beloved car and her near-death experience provided for a brief respite from the Rites of Separation, but as I drove my daughter to college, she resumed her recitation of each thing that I did wrong during the 265-mile journey. I have to admit that the tears I expected to shed as I left her dormitory were not forthcoming. In fact, I felt rather light on my feet and I almost skipped back to the car. I drove the five hours home without stopping, despite my fifty-year-old bladder, eager to start my new life as an empty nester with my husband.

The bubble burst about a week later. My daughter called me full of news on her courses and as friendly as could be. She was back! My perfect wonderful daughter was back! So now I miss her terribly, but we "talk" online almost every day, and even on the phone occasionally, but not so much that I could be deemed a Stalker Mom.

I learned that you just have to live through that last summer and view it as a necessary and often humorous exercise in learning to separate. And as soon as the kids are gone, you will have them "back" again, in a way. They will be as wonderful as ever… they just won't be home.

~Amy Newmark

43

The Whiz Kid

"It takes a village to raise a child," they say.

But if you lived in my village you might wonder—as I often did—where the villagers were each time my son's tuition payments became due. The cost to raise a child from birth through college, according to experts, easily exceeds $650K. That's a lot of money. And, few of us will openly admit, even in discrete company that—deep down—we secretly wonder about our investment.

"Will this child, who has cost me more money than I ever imagined, help feather my nest when I am old?"

One strategy, however clandestine, is to exercise raw creativity to steer, direct, and sculpt the careers of our children to increase the probability of our ROPI—Return On Parental Investment.

Throughout high school, my son hoped to pursue a degree in business, then law. Because we lived in southern New Jersey, with access to innumerable institutions, his plans were practical and affordable; he could live at home, we reasoned. By his senior year, we anticipated graduation, followed by his attendance at a university in Philadelphia that September.

Just weeks before commencement, he summoned me for a private discussion. "Mom, I have something to tell you."

I remained silent, my heart at my throat.

"I don't want to be a lawyer. I want to be a chef."

His announcement caught my breath. When I finally inhaled, I took in his handsome countenance, dark eyes searching mine for approval, and I softened to his decision. In the end, we chose one of the top three culinary schools in the country and soon he was off to Rhode Island.

He was exuberant. I, on the other hand, had a new plan.

If this was how my nest was going to be feathered, I wanted fine feathers. Soft, luscious, and — gourmet. Then, in my golden years, when my shaky, arthritic hand raises the diet-restricted soup spoon to my lips, it will be elegant fare. It could be vichyssoise.

At that time, I did not know an aioli from a Zuppa Inglese. My foray into cooking was nebulous, troglodytic. I shamefully admit that I saw nothing wrong with wine that came in screw cap bottles; I was a culinary dilettante in need of an epicure.

While he was away acquiring culinary skill, I frequented gourmet restaurants in Philadelphia. Locust, Walnut, Chestnut, Lombard, and South streets revealed the vast world of the epicurean and the tasty benefits I could claim as mother-of-the-chef. I was a vested quick-study acquiring the language as I honed a more refined palate.

I knew it would take time to craft a professional, and I had supreme confidence in the institution to which I wrote sizeable checks. In his last year of culinary school, the final leg of my financial obligatoriness, I received an invitation to Parent's Day, an event designed to show off his soon-to-be lucrative skills. It was a clarion milestone toward the bounty I was ready to reap.

My son and his fellow chefs lived in a rented house off campus. Four talented young men under one roof proved too much for my imagination.

"Come up for the weekend and stay with us," invited my son.

My taste buds danced. By now, I knew the difference between a gnache and a mousse, between a noodle udon and a noodle soba, between a semifreddo and a dacquoise, between a flan and a crème brulee.

"I'm going up for Parent's Day," I bragged to a friend, "staying with my son, and his roommates." I nodded. "They will be cooking the entire time."

I dreamed of eggs carbonaro with basil and parmesan cheese for breakfast, mugs of rich coffee and steamed milk, hot bouillabaisse and puff pastry with chocolate filling for dessert—a fitting larder for apprentice chefs.

My son picked me up at the airport, and escorted me to the exhibitions of culinary flash: impressive ice sculptures, elegant hors d'oeuvres, towering cakes too beautiful to eat, numberless preparations fit for kings, queens, and check-writing parents. I nibbled while engaging in small talk, but my primary thoughts were of the privately prepared dishes I would soon consume.

I was dizzy with anticipation.

At the end of the event, our group returned to the house. The other parents opted to stay at local hotels for the weekend. I, being the only single parent, felt slightly smug. I deposited my suitcase in the bedroom and meandered innocently to the kitchen.

At the refrigerator, I extended my arm, curled my fingers around the door handle, and pulled. The whoosh of the rubber seal releasing its hold readied me for the jackpot. My mouth went wet and salty—a Pavlovian reflex.

But, my eyes betrayed me. It couldn't be true. Yet, there it was in stark reality—an eighteen-cubic-foot refrigerator completely empty except for one industrial-sized can of Cheese Whiz!

"I thought we'd all go out for pizza," said a voice across the room. "How about it, Mom?"

~Beatrice E. Brown

44

They Come Home Again

Call it a clan, call it a network, call it a tribe, call it a family.
Whatever you call it, whoever you are, you need one.
~Jane Howard

When Thomas Wolfe titled his novel *You Can't Go Home Again*, he wasn't talking about children.

After six years we would finally have all our adult children at the same Christmas table again, and we were delighted to host the event. Nothing fancy, mind you. The usual fare—turkey and trimmings—in family tradition with the host (us) cooking the meat and the attendees (our children) simply providing side dishes.

Elizabeth was assigned her specialty, "Grammy's Salad," (named after Grammy who made it every holiday until her death). Jack signed up for "Papa's Mix." (Okay, so it's the usual party mix made from cereal; the kids long believed it originated with their beloved Papa.) Because Robert's wife was busy carrying our second grandchild, we asked him for a simple plate of raw vegetables.

Since we'd become a couple again, having everyone back in the house was a major event involving lots of preparation on our parts. But we were ready. It was time for the children to come home—and we were prepared for the invasion of our peaceful nest.

A harbinger of things to come was Robert's phone call. "Can we have Christmas dinner on Christmas Eve instead?"

"Are you kidding? Everyone has already made their plans."

"Then I'm not coming."

"Sorry, son, it's not even an option."

Next, Elizabeth rang. She couldn't make her famous salad because she didn't have enough money to buy the ingredients, she had to work, and — anyway — she'd been sick.

"That's all right, dear, we'll do fine without it."

Finally, a call from Jack. "Mom, are you going to buy the stuff for Papa's Mix?"

"What?" It was Christmas Eve and he wanted me to drive twenty miles to the store right next door to him and buy the stuff!

"Yeah, we ran out of time and money. I haven't been working you know."

"That's all right, dear, we'll do fine without it."

Christmas day arrived. "Come early," I had implored. "We'll open gifts in the morning."

Elizabeth called. "We'll be there as soon as we can. We're sleeping in."

"Not a problem, but you do have to drive three hours."

Robert whined, "I don't want to come."

"Too bad. The turkey is already stuffed."

Jack announced, "We'll be there."

"Don't forget, dinner is at 2 P.M. On the dot."

Nuts and candies, chips and dips adorned the table. All was set. We were poised with cameras and videos to capture our grandbaby's delight. But, early came and went with no one in sight. Dinner, I determined, would be served on time no matter what.

1:55 P.M. In swooped the late-sleepers with salad in tow. Just as we bowed heads for prayer, the second family screeched into the drive. Hot food cooled, cold foods melted while baby was unbundled and greetings exchanged.

2:47 P.M. Dinner over, only leftovers graced the table — and still no sign of family number three.

Hours later, he and spouse arrived in a mood. You know the one. That five-year-old "I may be sitting on the outside, but I'm standing on the inside" attitude. It was clear he didn't want to be here and was going to make everyone pay. When hadn't he grown up?

Presents were opened and passed around; the grandbaby was cute and charming. But, in the midst of it all, I looked around the noisy room (while conversation tiptoed around Mr. Pouty) and observed my grown children. One having a temper tantrum (however silent) and the rest of them (after all these years) still trying to out-do the others. Before long, an old-fashioned, all-out, brother-sister verbal brawl broke loose.

I sighed. Indeed, the children had come home again. Only, not as the adults they were… but as the kids they used to be.

~Susan Stewart

45

Tracking Time

*The real voyage of discovery consists not of seeking new landscapes
but in having new eyes.*
~Marcel Proust

I woke to the sound of water rushing in the shower. For no discernible reason, my teenage daughter was up before dawn again. I squinted to see the clock's glowing red numbers—4:40 A.M.! I sank back into the pillow.

"One more week," I whispered. "Then Emily will be off to college."

For the first time in my life, I was going to be alone. My son had married in June, and then my husband was temporarily transferred out of state. Now my daughter planned to attend a local university and live in the dormitory. This fall, I would not only have an empty nest, but an empty house.

The cat tiptoed over the bedspread, stuck her whiskers in my face and purred. I turned over and tried to go back to sleep. Until a hair dryer buzzed. It was no use.

When I walked into the hallway, I almost tripped over a pile of Emily's Care Bears. "You don't want these anymore?" I asked outside the bathroom door.

"No," Emily said. "You can give them away."

I picked up the stuffed animals and threw them into a box in my closet. It was already full of her old books, purses, and jewelry. Emily didn't talk much about leaving home, but I got the feeling that I wasn't the only one counting down the days.

After breakfast, I tried to work at my computer while music blasted. "Can you turn down the radio?" I yelled.

Emily lowered the volume slightly. I shook my head and muttered, "One more week."

Move-in day at the college finally came. A woman behind a desk handed Emily a key, and she eagerly grabbed it and grinned. When I headed toward the elevator with her, she hesitated. "Mom, I don't want you to come up with me."

Another parent might have insisted, but I saw this as a step toward independence and allowed my daughter to move into the dorm by herself.

On my first morning alone, I woke to daylight and sighed. I looked forward to working in peace and quiet. But when I sat in front of my computer, I couldn't concentrate. Something was missing. I turned on some music — yes, that was it. I remembered when Emily went to pre-school I put cartoons on TV for background noise.

At 3:15 P.M., I heard a school bus rumble down the street and squeak to a stop next door. I suddenly felt old. The school years that had passed so slowly now seemed to have disappeared in a blink.

The next time I looked up from the computer screen, it was 6:30 already and dark outside. When my family had been home, I'd started dinner around 4:30 and we ate together at 6:00. Every night I'd served a balanced meal, something different, something they liked. Now I went to the kitchen and pulled out the frying pan. I scrambled two eggs and tossed in some leftover broccoli.

When I sat down at the kitchen table, the cat rubbed against my leg. "You miss her, too. Don't you, Midnight?" Emily's pampered cat jumped into my lap and I petted her soft ears. When the phone rang, she hopped down.

"So how do you like being alone?" my husband asked.

"I can see why people who live by themselves have pets," I said.

He laughed. "Are you going to end up one of those cat ladies?"

"I hope not!"

In the days that followed, I immersed myself in work, staying up late and sleeping in each morning. There was no child to keep me on a schedule.

When I didn't hear from Emily in two weeks, I phoned the dorm. Her roommate assured me that my daughter was still alive, but Em refused to return my calls. I was mortified. Had she discarded me like her Care Bears? Had she disowned me along with the cat? I'd been ready to let her go, but not like this. I walked aimlessly through the house, a hollow feeling growing inside me.

The days became colder and leaves fell from the trees. During the last week in October, my neighbors put up Halloween decorations, and I wondered if I should too. I'd never been alone on Halloween before, and I dreaded opening the door all night to strangers. Maybe I'd just turn out the lights and go to a movie.

With a heavy heart, I paged through our old photo albums and looked at pictures taken on other Halloweens—my son as a Smurf, my daughter as a princess. I thought of all the older people who gave treats to my kids over the years, even if they had no children at home.

On Halloween day, a key turning in the deadbolt startled me. Emily came in and set down her backpack. Without a hello, she asked, "Did you get candy?"

My breath caught in my throat. "Two big bags."

"Can I hand it out?"

"Sure."

She disappeared to her bedroom. When the doorbell rang, Emily swished down the stairs in her long pink prom dress from last spring. She clicked across the floor in high heels looking like an older version of the princess she'd been at six.

Emily grabbed the bowl of candy and opened the door. Two boys dressed like vampires yelled, "Trick or treat!" and she dropped chocolate bars into their bags. Midnight sat on the windowsill and hissed at them. It was as if the clock had been turned back a few years.

Before Emily went to bed, she told me she wanted to move back home and take the light rail to her classes. She didn't offer an excuse.

Undoubtedly dorm life wasn't what she thought it would be, just as an empty nest wasn't what I expected.

Early the next morning, I heard the sound of rushing water in the shower and smiled. It was a good sound. No. It was a wonderful sound.

~Mary E. Laufer

46

Ka-ding! Ka-ding!

If my doctor told me I had only six minutes to live,
I wouldn't brood. I'd type a little faster.
~Isaac Asimov

I put my last baby in college two weeks ago. The quiet is quieter than I imagined. But after a moment of self pity, I look at my computer and realize that this is a good thing. As a freelance writer, the wealth of creative solitude I now possess makes me feel like a kid out of school for summer vacation. All this time to write like a mad woman.

Ka-ding! Instant Messenger rings. IM for short.

"Momma, you busy?"

"I'm writing. How's school?" And it starts.

Blow-by-blow, choppy phrases about the roommate. My muse's spark starts blinking like a battery charger giving me warning that a few more seconds of playing second fiddle and it's leaving. So I minimize the IM block and continue my writing, knowing my son will type for a while without needed response from me. A couple of seconds and I'm back in the groove, composing some creative prose for an editor.

Ka-ding! Roomie is eating all his food and using his computer. "Mom, what do I do?"

"Go talk to the Resident Assistant on your hall. Be firm." Minimize — maximize article and continue typing after rereading the last paragraph.

Ka-ding! "I did that and she says if she doesn't see him, she can't do anything about it."

Minimize article — maximize IM. "Tell him in no uncertain terms to leave your stuff alone. Say you'll leave his stuff alone." Minimize IM — maximize article. Reread last paragraph again. Doesn't sound right. Delete.

Ka-ding! "Hey, how's it going?" Elder son's out of class for the day.

Minimize article — maximize second IM. "Fine. I'm writing and talking to your brother. Roommate problems." Minimize IM — max article. Why did I delete that last paragraph? Let's see, maybe I can reword it again...

Ka-ding! Ka-ding! Minimize article — max IM — max IM.

"But he's not going to listen to me. He's bigger. I hate this place!"

"Mom, this is the worst semester yet. These classes are already killing me."

"No you don't hate the place. Part of it is learning how to leave high school and adapt to being on your own at college." Minimize.

"You always say the semester is going to be your hardest yet and you continue to make the dean's list. We know you'll do your best and that's all we ask of you." Minimize.

Maximize article. Reread, delete, reread, delete. Is it me or is this story just not flowing? Maybe I picked the wrong angle entirely. I read from the beginning out loud to see how the words sound.

Ka-ding! Ka-ding!

"Not what I thought it would be."

"Should have gone to Clemson."

"Some weird people on my hall."

He's typing in staccato messages now, raising his voice via the number of dings. He needs an eyeball-to-eyeball discussion and a conclusive hug. He knows it; I know it; but the miles prevent it. The IMs ding on. A little guilty, I minimize the IM box , knowing I can't get a word in edgewise till he vents.

Ka-ding! Ka-ding!

Ka-ding! Elder son. "My apartment's too small. I can't store my trunk anywhere."

"Throw it in your truck until you visit your grandparents. They can store it." Minimize. The other son is still ka-dinging angrily. The second one is consoled for the moment and computer-chatting with several other friends simultaneously. How he does it is beyond my comprehension; I can't talk to the two of them and write a simple 700-word article.

Maximize article.

Ring! If this is a telemarketer I'll...

"Hey, Sweetie. How's your day going?" Husband decides to check up on his poor wife, lonely without her boys.

"What do you need?" I ask, then wish I hadn't.

"I don't need a thing, thank you very much. I was calling to check on you."

"Sorry."

"Getting lots done?"

I breathe slowly, trying to select words that won't express the impatience that had long ago kicked my writing muse out the door. "No, not yet." I try not to gnaw the phone.

Ka-ding! "Mom? You there? What do I do about this stupid roommate?"

Ka-ding! "Would Grandma mind if I came down this weekend?"

"Honey," husband says, "you've got all the time you need now. You've got no reason not to write like you've always wanted. Just ignore everything else!" Arrrrrghhhh!

Delete article. Count to ten.

"Son, talk to your brother about your roommate. He's a junior and can tell you better than I can. Gotta go. Love you." Close IM window.

"Call your grandmother and ask. Talk to your brother, too. He needs your help. Gotta go. On the phone." Close IM.

"Sweetie, I think I'll follow your advice right now. I'll see you when you get home tonight. Bye."

Turn off phone.

Shut down computer.

I pick up a pen from my desk and a notebook from my son's

empty bedroom and step to the back porch. One way or another, I'm writing this stupid story.

An hour later, I'm still sitting… and looking at blank paper.

He doesn't know anyone, so a bad roommate is not a good thing. And I didn't even ask which classes were giving the other son trouble.

Start up and login. "Hey there," I type. "I'm back."

Seconds tick by. Are they mad? Guilt eats at me.

Ka-ding! "Hey."

Ka-ding! "Yea."

"Get everything straight?" I open the door I closed a little hard before.

Ka-ding! "Mom, I'm seeing Grandma in two weeks. Busy with friends. Gotta go. Love you."

Ka-ding! "Mom, gotta get to class, and I'm talking to my room-mate right now."

"I just wanted to see if your problems were straightened out. I've been worrying about you," I typed and copied to both.

Ka-ding! Ka-ding!

"You worry too much. Bye."

"Geez, Mom, I'm not ten. Bye."

I smile to know the natural order is back in place. Peace settles over my monitor. And as I block my name on Instant Messenger, my muse creeps back and asks if it's safe to come out again.

~C. Hope Clark

For Better or For Worst

Blessed are the flexible, for they shall not be bent out of shape.
~Anonymous

"Listen."

"Listen to what?" asked my mildly interested husband, Doug. We sat side-by-side reading in front of the oscillating fan.

"That strange sound."

"What sound?"

"That sound."

"What is it that you hear, BJ?"

"Nothing." I could tell he seriously doubted my sanity.

"What do you mean nothing? What are you talking about?"

"The sound of silence."

Doug let out a sigh of relief that it wasn't some burglar I'd heard outside the window. "Better bottle it while you can. It seems like most things in life change."

Enjoying the peace and quiet once our two beloved and rowdy sons, Jeff and Jay, headed towards their own adventures in higher education, we just went about appreciating this new season of marriage. The silence wasn't something I dwelled on since I had, from the beginning, embraced the fact that children are on loan to us from God. We were only meant to do the best we could to raise them and then release them to fly independently. Up until now, our busy lives hadn't afforded us the opportunity to leisurely kick back and take advantage of any soothing sounds of silence.

But that wasn't the worst part.

Through life's transitions, we suddenly inherited our younger son Jay's two rather large and demanding housedogs. The older was a detached and continually whining Siberian husky named Cabo. The younger was a rambunctious and rascally chocolate Lab, Kirby. They double-dog-dared our jealous 115-pound white German Shepherd, Angel, to share her modest postage stamp-sized backyard domain. Yard clean-up was a constant challenge.

But that wasn't the worst part.

After a reasonable amount of time, we adjusted to our bulging house of continual fur-shedding creatures. And then, a few years after he was graduated and settled into the work force, our elder son, Jeff, contemplated the idea of studying for a master's degree. He inquired about the possibility of moving back home. In order to accomplish his career goal in a year and a half, Jeff reasoned, "I'll need to quit my job to return to school full time."

But that wasn't the worst part.

Jeff owned two robust indoor Labrador Retrievers. "Of course Kayla and Racer would accompany me," he added a bit apologetically. "And would you find it in your heart to welcome Monica, too?"

His steady girlfriend from out of town selflessly decided to get a job to support Jeff through school. And, oh, did I mention they were also expecting?

In a daydreaming moment, I tried to imagine the creative chaos this proposed living arrangement would produce. Our treasured sounds of silence would become only a memory because of a menagerie including four adults, one miniature human being with needy expectations (making her will known at all hours), and five energetic dogs we endearingly labeled, The Bumpus Hounds. All ten of us would be vying for personal space in a modest living area.

But that wasn't the worst part.

My amiable husband offered a workable solution: "We'd love to help you out. In order for us to do that, your sleeping arrangements would need to be different under our roof, and rules would need to be established that we all agree to, before you could move in. And we'll all have to take turns feeding, walking and cleaning up after the Bumpus Hounds."

I chimed in with my usual optimistic Pollyanna point of view, "It could actually be a wonderful experience for all of us."

And that it was.

Co-habiting turned into many blessings in disguise. The new living arrangement afforded all of us a chance to get to know each other on a deeper level. Jeff was no longer the innocent, wet-behind-the-ears kid we sent off to the University of California San Diego. Somewhere along life's time-line, he had transformed into an intelligent, multi-layered adult with thoughts, clever ideas, and a wisdom and expertise beyond his years. What a privilege to re-acquaint ourselves and bond with our adult son.

We were also grateful for the chance to embrace our shy future daughter-in-love in an up-close and personal way. Without this unexpected serendipity, it might have taken us many more years to form such a comfortable relationship with her.

Jeff's boomerang return also afforded us the unforgettable time of helping to care for our precious first grandchild. I can still see in my mind's eye, sweet innocent little Nicole lying in her tiny white lace-draped bassinette in the middle of our living room. As this helpless gift from God slept peacefully, snuggled sweetly in her pink blankie, a constant struggle ensued between the five Bumpus Hounds aggressively contending for the honor of standing watch over her crib.

But that wasn't the worst part.

Eventually, Cabo and Kirby found other homes. The newly-graduated Jeff with his bride Monica, daughter Nicole, and mellowed Kayla and Racer moved into their own nest. Things in ours once again returned to a long-forgotten normal.

"Listen." I whispered one cool, crisp fall evening as we sat side by side reading by the hearth in front of a dancing fire.

"Listen to what?" Doug abstractly answered.

"That's a strange sound."

"What sound?"

"That sound."

"What is it that you're hearing?"

"Nothing."

"Ah yes," Doug validated, "Once again it's that sound of silence."
And that was the worst part.

~BJ Jensen

48

They're Coming B-a-a-ck

*I*t's June, time for the annual natural phenomenon that ranks with the return of the swallows, the swimming of the salmon upstream, and the migration of the lemmings to the sea: The college kids are coming home.

Just when you've adjusted. Just when you've grown to cherish a house that stays clean and orderly. Just when you've learned to appreciate a refrigerator that doesn't empty in six minutes flat.

They're coming with their dirty laundry, term projects, a mountain of books, CDs, boom boxes, computers, printers, maybe even drums! And did they really have all that bedding when they left? Where did it come from and—where will it go?

Goodbye to quiet little dinners of chef salads or vegetable plates. Bring on the roasts, the chops. They'll want to forget the four days they survived on Bisquick pancakes last quarter when they were too broke to enter the supermarket.

Gird yourself for the glasses with petrified dregs that lurk behind the couch and under the coffee table. Make way for beach towels flung over railings and newspapers spread out on the floor.

Get set for fielding interminable phone calls. ("Couldn't get him on his cell. So, when did they leave? Which beach were they heading for?")

Rev up the washer, the dryer, the water heater. And resign yourself to a bath always running cold when you're in it.

Be prepared for your feet sticking to the kitchen floor. ("I thought I did wipe up the juice I spilled.") And last night's turkey loaf gone AWOL ("There was really a 'save' sign on it?")

Know that your shampoo won't be there when you're wet from head to toe, and that the hammer in the garage will be gone when you reach for it. And, of course, the orange juice container will be empty when you start breakfast.

Realize that even though they've cooked for themselves from September to June, you'll worry about what they'll eat when you leave them and dine out. You may even succumb to preparing something ahead for them.

But look forward, too, to seeing and hearing about their day-by-day experiences, their triumphs on summer jobs, if they're lucky enough to find them. ("Remember the kid who screamed bloody murder at the first swim lesson I taught? Well, he swam today.")

Prepare yourself for zany remarks and free-wheeling humor as the wild-and-crazy bunch gathers around the kitchen table. Maybe it's after body surfing or skateboarding or on their way out for the evening, or maybe just because.

Decide that the kid who can bench press twice his weight can surely rearrange the living room for you or move that potted tree you'd like to relocate from the front to the backyard.

Anticipate their light touch in moments of stress. ("Hey, you broke the faucet right off the sink? Mom, you animal!")

Expect observant comments. ("Tint your hair? Why would you want to cover up all those silver sparkles?")

Prepare to sit back as they challenge your spouse with profundities gleaned from this class or that. And as they dazzle you both with their insights.

It's June—and the kids are coming home. Yes!

~Beverly Bush Smith

Reprinted by permission of Randell Kruback.
©2007.

49

You Can't Go Home Again

ey, Mom, this is Stephen. If you're there, pick up. Mom? I'll keep talking to give you time to reach the phone.

I'm actually out front. I know I should be in class right now but I think I'm going to take some time off. Maybe try night school next fall.

So, I was sort of surprised when my house key didn't work. You must have changed the locks. What's with that? You didn't have some kind of home invasion, did you?

I was hoping I could crash here until I find my own place. Well, find a job first since I'll need to save up for the security deposit.

I know you moved all your quilting stuff into my room after I left because you started before I was out the front door. Assuming you're still using that space, maybe I can sleep on the living room couch.

Say, did you ever get the dryer fixed?

You thought I brought a ton of dirty laundry home on break? Well, you should see my back seat.

I hope you're—

Click.

Hi, Mom. Me again. The machine cut me off.

While I was redialing, I peeked in the garage. Your car's here. Don't tell me you're pretending not to be home.

Hey! I saw that curtain move.

Mom, I said I was sorry about the stain on the Oriental rug. And I apologized for the broken vase. And didn't I stop throwing parties when you were out of the house?

I know what you're thinking. When Bob Ross moved back in with his folks, he didn't leave until they put the house on the market and moved into a retirement community.

But didn't he keep their cars running well until then? Sure, he made a mess of their garage and started that fire but never once did they have to sit in line for an oil change.

Really, Mom. You don't have to worry about that happening with me. I'm not mechanical at all.

Mom?

Click.

~Stephen Rogers

Say "Cheese"

In the truest sense, freedom cannot be bestowed;
it must be achieved.
~Franklin D. Roosevelt

The Lautens have performed a special family ritual for what may be the last time: the annual first-day-of-school photo.

We started when Stephen headed to kindergarten to face the awesome challenge of crayoning, pasting and playing the sticks in the class band.

Two years later, Jane joined the photo. She wore a flowered dress made by her mother with one petal cut out, her "tickle spot." She remembers the dress to this day—and still hates it.

Another three years went by, and Richard went off to school for the first time. We recorded the three of them standing on our deck. Unfortunately, the picture is a little fuzzy. It was difficult for Mrs. Lautens to take the picture and click her heels in the air at the same time. The prospect of having half a day to herself was almost too much for the resident Love Goddess.

Each year we continued the practice. But by next spring we expect Stephen (who is twenty-five) and Jane (who is twenty-three) to be out of university, leaving only Richard (who is twenty) still in the halls of academe. Believe me, we can't wait.

To Mrs. Lautens, the empty nest syndrome is only a rumor. The one thing she wants desperately in life is to be lonely.

Not lonely, lonely, of course. Two still live at home, all three were at home during the summer, and the missus is getting a little eager to try all that emptiness she's read about.

After nearly twenty-six years, she's tired of holding her foot against the bathroom door and of reminding people it isn't against the law to make your own bed.

My wife, I suspect, suffers from mother-burnout. When she carries a huge bundle of laundry down the stairs, for example, she no longer wears a winsome smile on her lips nor does she trade light-hearted quips about the state of Richard's socks. She's more apt to say, "This being mother is for the birds."

Harder to believe, she even gets testy if she has to carry more than eight bags of groceries from the supermarket, especially if the phone rings and somebody (Jane) yells "Can you get it, Mom? I'm washing my hair" while she's staggering to the kitchen.

Yes, my wife is ready for some of that empty nest syndrome.

Me? I've written about the offspring for a quarter of a century. When they walk out the door, so may my career.

Anyway, we did get one final first-day-of-school picture of the three of them, even if we did have to take it a few days early because of Stephen's schedule.

Next year it's a photo of Mrs. Lautens. What setting do you use on the Canon for cartwheels?

~Gary Lautens

51

College Daze

*J*hesitate to commit these events to paper because I probably don't know what I'm doing and my son isn't here to stop me.

When we checked our entering freshman into his new dormitory at Arizona State University, he took the occasion to point out to my husband and me — vociferously — that we just didn't know anything. On the other hand, he did… which makes the next four years seem superfluous, not to mention a drain on our savings. Were it not for the nocturnal extracurricular activities in which he hoped to engage, the scheduled courses would only gild the lily.

"No, Dad, my textbooks don't go on that shelf. That's where I want my stereo."

"Mom, don't put my pens in that desk drawer. I'll never find them."

"Extra towels? Why do I need extra towels? I have a perfectly good one in the bathroom."

He orchestrated our every action from the comfort of his bed.

From now on, my husband and I will try to muddle through the days to come without the benefit of our son's counsel on every topic. And hopefully, with the passage of time, my facial tic will hardly be noticeable.

Our son has a male roommate and male suitemates, but from that point on the dynamics change. Coeds — each more eye-catching than the one before — live directly across the hall. Females are housed everywhere on his floor. It's a totally mixed-gender dorm. Our son, a recent graduate of an all-boys' high school, was trying hard to appear cool—with his hooded eyelids, a bored expression, and his I-can't-be-bothered attitude. But from long experience I'm familiar with every nuance of his act, and he was definitely drinking in the scenery and checking out the ladies.

That afternoon we old folks were bid a hasty goodbye. Our young man, far from needing to cling to the comfort and security of his family, was anxious to settle into his new and wonderful parent-free zone.

My husband and I treated ourselves to a dinner of steak and lobster, drowning our sorrows in melted butter. And all this delicious revenge was on a weeknight, no less. As we rattled around in the booth that was too vast for just the two of us, we discussed the events of that auspicious day. How could one textbook cost $75.00? Where had the years gone? How could our child suddenly be in college? When would we ever get the hang of being parents?

Today, I'm wallowing in painful luxury. Our son's bed is neatly made and his room is tidy. The rafters no longer shudder with the steady thud of the bass turned up to full volume. The refrigerator is stocked with healthful food and the door remains closed.

And, unbelievably, my familiar tic is gone.

~Lana Robertson Hayes

52

Sea Scape

*One doesn't discover new lands without consenting
to lose sight of the shore for a very long time.*
~André Gide

"Why aren't you coming home next month?" I asked my oldest son, but I didn't really want to hear the answer.

I was counting the weeks until Spring Break. Scott had slept and done homework through most of his Thanksgiving break. Christmas promised more days together, but the holiday rush of activities and visiting family left little time for uninterrupted talks.

I thought Spring Break would be our time to reconnect as a family. A time for Scott to hang out with his dad and younger brother. A time for us to talk.

Now my private hopes evaporated as Scott shared his own plans. A new friend from the dorm lived in the San Francisco area and had invited a group of guys to spend Spring Break at his home. Scott had never visited northern California.

"Would you and Dad be willing to chip in? Maybe half the amount you would have paid to fly me home?"

I tried to be excited as he enthused about the low cost of the trip. His friend's family would host the gang at night while they toured San Francisco by day. That meant free lodging. The cost of gas would be divided several ways. They'd be left with nominal expenses for lunches and activities. Who could pass up this opportunity?

At college, Scott had made new friends and found his wings. Now those wings would carry him away just when we expected him to return. This is how it goes, I realized. Once I let go, I'll never again control when he flies back to the nest.

"I'm sure we can chip in," I responded with forced cheerfulness. "We'll miss you, but I know you'll have a wonderful time."

Over the next few weeks, the group's plans morphed several times. Finally, they settled on a stop at our house during the trip home. We would get to share a few days of Spring Break with our son after all—along with all his buddies.

A few days into Spring Break the phone's ring interrupted my afternoon. I looked at the Caller ID. "Hey, Scott! How are you doing? Are you guys having fun?" I waited to hear the latest update on their itinerary.

"We're having a great time! Guess where I am right now?" I could hear an excited grin in my kid's voice.

"I have no idea." The Golden Gate Bridge, maybe? Alcatraz or Chinatown? He could be anywhere. "Just tell me."

"You've got to listen, Mom," he said mysteriously. "I want you to guess where I am."

I don't want to play this game, I thought with exasperation. How am I supposed to know where he is?

"Listen, Mom." Scott pleaded. "I'm holding out the phone for you to hear."

Then I heard it. The faint, unmistakable roar of wind and waves.

"Can you hear the ocean, Mom?" Scott yelled into the phone. "I'm at the beach!"

Scott has heard me talk about the beach all his life. I grew up an hour from the Gulf of Mexico where, summer after summer, my family vacationed along the Texas coastline. The beach is my refuge, my oasis. Whenever I feel stressed, I close my eyes and picture the sun glistening on foam-capped water or grass dancing on dunes and let my mind rest in peaceful oneness with the rhythmic lap of surf on sand. Memories of salt and sun soothe my mind.

Through the years, I've tried to share this passion for the beach with my sons. Whenever possible, we made a trip to the Gulf coast. We collected seashells and sunburns and filled our photo albums with memories.

Scott remembered. He remembered the picture of me dangling his toddler toes in the water. He thought back through all the family adventures that followed his first plunge into the surf. Scott knew how much his mom loved the beach, and he couldn't look at the ocean without thinking of her.

So he called. He broke away from the laughter and antics of his friends to dial my number. As the wind whipped his jacket, Scott brought the waves and sand to me through an outstretched cell phone.

At that moment, my hopes for quality time with my son were fulfilled. We went to the beach together during Spring Break.

~Donna Savage

Chapter 5

Empty Nesters

Wings and Wisdom

*Of all nature's gifts to the human race,
what is sweeter to a man than his children?
~Marcus Tullius Cicero*

Taking Flight

Worry often gives a small thing a big shadow.
~Swedish Proverb

My twenty-six-year-old daughter phoned, obviously excited. "Mom, I think I'll move to San Diego."

Did she say San Diego? Carolee was already somewhat on her own, but hadn't gone far; her rented townhouse was nearby in the Washington, D.C. area.

"San Diego?" I repeated, stunned. "You mean, as in California?"

"Yeah. California."

I sat down. She'd never been to San Diego. I'd never been to San Diego. I didn't know anyone who'd ever been to San Diego. I wasn't even sure where in California San Diego was.

"I checked my office's website and they have a branch there." Carolee's voice was dreamy. "It looks so pretty in pictures."

I glanced through the kitchen window at the muddy snow that had recently immobilized our area for the third time that winter, shivered, and pulled my sweater tighter.

I'd always wanted my children to be independent, to feel free to follow their dreams. But she planned to move as far away as she could without falling into the Pacific Ocean. Why, aside from two family trips, she'd never been farther west than West Virginia. I wanted to lift her back into the nest or, at the very least, tie a very long string onto her so I could tug her back when I needed to.

It wasn't long before my husband and I loaded her suitcases and her cat into the back seat of our car. Carolee sat with her arm around Maggie's travel cage. She wore a coat and knit hat. She'd caught a cold. She looked so small.

The check-in line at the airport was long. The clerk, who reminded me of a sloth blinking in the sunlight, was deliberate and wouldn't be hurried. Carolee missed her flight; her bags made the trip without her. I looked over at my daughter, expecting her to be upset. She was, but not like I thought she'd be. Instead, she was angry, pacing like a fluffed-up chick.

"Here. Watch Maggie. I'll be right back." Carolee handed me the cat carrier and marched over to the ticketing supervisor. After a long, animated discussion, my little girl returned triumphant. She would be on the next flight. Upgraded.

While we waited, I studied Carolee so that I would remember everything about her. Like Alice in Wonderland, she morphed before my eyes. She got younger, and younger and the cat carrier on the table next to her grew bigger and bigger. She was a little kid… not old enough to go off on her own… especially to a place where she didn't know anyone.

Too soon, airline personnel took the cat and called Carolee's flight. Maggie meowed pitifully, echoing the way I felt.

We walked Carolee to the gate.

"Be careful. Don't talk to strangers." I attempted a feeble smile.

"Mom, you worry too much. I'll be fine." She grinned and gave her father and me a hug.

Was she being brave? Was it all bravado? We hugged her back and waved as she disappeared through the door and down the ramp.

I reached for a Kleenex and headed for the ladies' room where I threw cold water on my eyes.

As we drove away from the airport, I pictured her sitting in the plane, feet dangling shy of the floor, swallowed by the seat. And — even though I knew the cat was in the hold — I imagined Maggie huddled under my daughter's seat, mewing sadly as they flew away.

Carolee called when she arrived in San Diego.

"How was your flight?" I asked, recalling the sad picture I carried in my head.

My daughter laughed. "It was great," she enthused. "Did you know they have real silverware and dishes in first class? And they give you magazines to read? I had hot towels and I ate smoked salmon. It was very elegant—the best flight I've ever had!"

I had to smile, partly at her excitement and partly at my racing, motherly imagination. I guess when a child leaves home, your point of view depends a great deal on which side of the tarmac you're standing.

~Michele Ivy Davis

54

My Mother's Daughter

That which seems the height of absurdity in one generation
often becomes the height of wisdom in another.
~Adlai Stevenson

Mom used to be carefree, a happy-go-lucky woman. She dealt with the endless mishaps of raising five kids with take-it-in-stride abandon. No sooner was one hurdle cleared than a new one surfaced. She was the ball in a game of pinball—constantly bounced to and fro with bells ringing.

Decades ago, one by one, we left her nest to begin nests of our own. I don't recall Mom worrying much as we packed up and moved out. Instead, we heard an audible sigh of relief, quickly followed by a frenzy of re-decorating the rooms we had just vacated.

Now in her late sixties, she's still a lot of fun to be with, she's still hard-working, and she's still a beautiful woman inside and out. But she's acquired a new habit that's beginning to make me uncomfortable. She worries. And since she retired, her life has slowed down and she has even more time to worry.

Throughout the years of raising my own kids, I sometimes called Mom when a mishap occurred. But lately I'd been fighting the urge, hesitating to burden her even more.

"Mom, how did you do it?" I finally asked one day while we lunched.

My husband Chuck and I had deposited our son Chase for his freshman year at college. The pain of cutting the cord from our first-born was so raw I couldn't even say his name without a lump clogging my throat. I thought I had been prepared, and I was; he had everything he needed for his dorm room, and then some. But what I never expected were the grief-like symptoms of not having one of my children at home anymore.

I was just getting a handle on raising him, and then he's gone?

Daughter Chelsea was next in line. It wouldn't be long before I'd have to do this once again. My mother, however, let go five times.

"How did you ever get through this?" I asked, dabbing at my eyes.

"Ahhh, yes," Mom nodded her head slightly and smiled reflectively.

She's smiling? I couldn't believe it.

"There was such constant commotion for so many years that I guess I reached a point where I became anxious to get my own life back."

"But you made it look so easy."

"Oh no, it was never easy. It's just that there was always so much to do. I worried while I worked. As a mother yourself, you know you start worrying from the moment you find out you are pregnant. And it never stops."

It never stops? I shook my head in dismay. Why did I think this job had an end to it?

For years, I had daydreamed about what I would do after the kids moved out. I assumed I would go back to being my carefree self again. And that's when it dawned on me.

It wasn't my mother who had been the lighthearted one—it was me. Mom had always worried about us; I just hadn't noticed. I had been so busy spreading my wings and then making my own nest that I never stopped to think about the adjustments Mom made at each leave-taking.

That is, not until now.

As I glance into my son's empty room, I once again resist the urge to call him, just to "check in."

"He'll let us know if he needs something," my husband constantly reassures me.

Still, he could be sick, or out of money, or…

I flip the page in my daily calendar and realize it's been three days since I've heard from Mom. I pick up the phone to call her, suddenly needing the comfort of her reassuring voice.

"Mom, it's me. I'm just checking in," I hear myself say.

And suddenly it becomes clear. As I watch my children spread their wings in anticipation of leaving our nest, I, like my mom, want them to know my wings are bigger and will always be able to wrap around theirs.

From the generations of women preceding me, the worry torch has been passed. I am my mother's daughter, after all.

~Connie Sturm Cameron

55

An October Garden

*I*t's a landscape of brown and bent things, the October Garden. Some may find it easy to consider such a plot—blasted by a killing frost and marked by desiccated plants whose shapes conjure up a nearly human gesture of surrender—and imagine that this is the end of things. But if we are honest with ourselves, we acknowledge that the October garden signifies but one notch on a wheel always rolling forward, toward another flowering and fruiting, another harvest, and another dormancy. We can only take our place in the cycle, flower and fruit in our turn, and celebrate the forward motion through all of its phases.

When my daughter Kelsey was a toddler, she loved to join me in the garden, especially during the planting phase. She trundled around with a small hand-spade I gave her, digging holes in the soil and dropping in small pebbles or bits of twig or, sometimes, imaginary seeds. Then with great care she would cover these deposits with a little soil and pat it all down nicely.

I realized early on that to avoid chaos in my own planned garden beds, I needed to provide her a space of her own, and so was born Kelsey's Corner. There she was free to dig and plant as she wished without any interference from me. I gave her any seeds she wanted, let her experiment and learn as I had about what grows where and why.

Over time, that little patch grew into a favorite place in the garden. Kelsey learned she had to plan ahead and select plants that would thrive in the microclimate of that particular space. She also learned to weed and water and do all that a garden plot requires. Her tastes ran to flowers—marigolds, poppies, forget-me-nots, daisies, and a wild rosebush we transplanted from another spot in the yard. This corner reached its peak when she was in her adolescent years, still tied to the family unit, to the house and yard.

As she approached high school, Kelsey's focus strayed from the garden. I didn't resist this change, nor did I resent it. It seemed inevitable that something as simple and mundane as working in the dirt gave way to the flash and charm of a budding social life. Her plot fell victim to neglect and I gradually assumed stewardship of the space. Even so, I knew it always would be Kelsey's Corner.

Now my daughter is eighteen, in the last weeks of her high school career. Our mailbox is laden with college catalogs, reminding me that the world has come for this young woman and she will soon answer its call. Her leaving is both a transformative event for her and similarly, a major change for me and her mother.

We are, in fact, already in the transition.

But it is mid-April in Colorado, with the usual fits and starts of spring. Two inches of snow cover the ground one morning but melt by mid-afternoon under a brilliant sun. The next day, a brisk wind tears small branches off the elms and scatters them in the front yard. The following day, the weather is so warm and the sun so hot, I have to take frequent breaks in the shade as I putter about the garden, clearing refuse from the previous season and turning the soil to inspect its condition. The next day, a cold rain falls and turns to slushy snow at dusk.

In Kelsey's Corner, a few Echinacea plants stand, their stiff brown stems fully arced so the seed heads drop their bounty to the soil. And sure enough, there at the feet of the dead stalks, the plants are sending up the first green shoots.

So it is I can't look at this transition in my life as the end of anything. It is merely one point on a cycle that will repeat, always the same in its larger revolution but colored and shaped uniquely with each turn. Now the wheel will roll with Kelsey as she moves into her adult life.

Let her live as she will, let her return when she can, and whether she comes alone or in company, she'll be welcomed home. I'll keep the garden until then, and will tend Kelsey's Corner faithfully. It will cycle annually, as it should, as it must. So will my wife and I, rolling on toward a different phase of our lives together, one that promises a rich harvest we can only now guess at.

~Chris Ransick

56

The Stress of a Mess

Brittany came home in May for her summer break and I braced myself. I remembered my own first night home from freshman year. Mom told me not to stay up too late because I had to work the next day. Oh, great, I thought, summer is going to be all rules and restrictions after a year of freedom!

I don't recall what I actually said to my mom, but Brittany told me she "stays up until all hours at school, and why should it be more important to be well rested for a summer job than for classes?"

I was warned that college kids invariably think their parents aren't quite as intelligent as they once believed. Sure enough, within her first twenty-four hours back, Brittany said something along the lines of "I know better because I'm in college." Her dad squelched that pretty fast by telling her he has an MBA, her mom has a BS, and Brittany has only one year under her belt.

On her first night back, I helped Brittany unpack. Otherwise, I knew she would live out of a suitcase all summer. I was in her closet folding tee shirts into stacks: whites, pinks, blacks. From the corner of my eye, I saw Brittany carry a suitcase to her dresser, dump the contents, and close the underwear drawer with her knee.

She caught me watching. "You can do what you want in my closet, but I want the drawer like this." She squared her shoulders in defiance. "At school, I decided it's less stressful this way."

How could a mess not be stressful? I shrugged and let it go.

Until a few days later.

I carried a load of meticulously folded laundry into her room and put everything away—except the underwear. I opened the dresser drawer and looked from my neat stack to her sprawling heap.

Should I fold and organize the drawer and risk "stressing" her?

Should I toss my neat stack into her jumble?

My eyes wandered to a picture on the dresser top, a photograph of me holding Brittany when she was a baby. I thought about how fast the years go; I thought about the shortness of summer break.

With a secret grin, I set my neat pile in the middle of her heap—and serenely closed the drawer.

~Nancy Geiger

Dance, Daughter, Dance

Parents give their children roots and wings.
Roots to know where home is,
wings to fly away and exercise what's been taught them.
~Jonas Salk

y daughter Christin is exuberant, full of life and love, quizzical and intelligent, and at times incredibly challenging. As a child, she could be exasperating. As a teenager, there were days I simply wanted to strangle her. Now that she's a young adult, frustration still creeps in from time to time, especially if I don't give her the answers she wants to hear.

I remember a day when she was seven years old. I had my plate full of busy-ness as I cooked lunch while four preschoolers bounced around the kitchen in anticipation of grilled cheese sandwiches. Christin bounded into the kitchen with two shirts clenched in her tiny fists. She wanted me to tell her which shirt matched best with pink and green pinstriped shorts.

"It doesn't matter which one you wear," I told her, "They both look nice."

Annoyed, she demanded, "Tell me Mom!"

"Well, which one do you like?"

Her voice got louder as she insisted that I tell her which one to wear—right now.

I glared and growled, "You decide!" With a firm finger pointed in the direction of her room, I commanded, "I don't care which one you wear. Go put one on—right now."

With pursed lips, she stomped her way back to her bedroom. A few minutes later, she plodded down the hallway with her Care Bear suitcase overstuffed with clothes and toys. She stopped at the front door and with a defiant stare announced, "I'm leaving, and I'm never coming back!"

"See ya!" I said.

She marched out the door, slamming it behind her.

I turned the stove burner off and went to the living room window to monitor my audacious, redheaded runaway. There she stood in the front yard, clutching her bag, looking up the street, then toward the front door before making her way down the sidewalk, constantly looking back. Before she reached the fifth house, I caved.

I've certainly learned a lot since those days, and no matter if she's seven or twenty, letting go is never easy.

Tomorrow morning, Christin will move to Florida to test her newly sprouted adulthood; tonight she came to my place for dinner. She's excited about her adventure, yet full of questions about leaping into the unknown.

"No matter what life dishes out," I simply advised, "don't let anything harden your heart. Keep your passion alive for life's journeys."

Before she left, we listened to Lee Ann Womack's song, "I Hope You Dance." I wrapped my arms around her and told her much I love her, that I'm glad she's in my life, that I'm honored to be her mom. I hugged her goodbye and watched her leave.

She walked to her car, constantly looking back at me. This time, with a smile and a wave, Christin said, "I love you, Mom."

I never gave her any answers, but I think I said the right things.

~Karen Landrum

58

Five O'Clock Shadow

Don't let yesterday use up too much of today.
~Cherokee Proverb

Five o'clock at the mall.

I once fantasized about shopping at that hour. I imagined having the mall to myself. I visualized shopping—while other moms negotiated rush hour traffic to chauffeur their kids to (take your pick, I've done every one) soccer-baseball-basketball-swim-cheerleading practice. All, of course, situated on opposite ends of town from each other. I dreamed of sauntering through mostly deserted stores while other moms supervised homework, raced to the grocery, and started dinner.

As a nurse practitioner/midwife, I'd dealt with my share of patients who wore long faces when their kids left home. And I didn't get it. Why was everyone so sad? I would be elated to see my five heading out the door. After mothering a blended family—with seven years between the youngest and oldest, I looked forward to knowing my children as adults. No glumness for me.

When our first son left for college, we adopted a Golden Retriever puppy. He required more time and attention than a newborn baby, and, of course, it all landed on my chore list. Upon the second son's departure, we acquired the cat; I preferred our boys with their bottomless stomachs and mountains of laundry. They soared at college, becoming the independent young men we had raised them to be.

With three teenagers still at home, I was drawn more than ever to my vision of the mall at that magical hour. And, almost overnight, it happened.

After getting my hair done at the salon one afternoon, I sat on a bench overlooking the mall's rushing waterfall. I pulled out my cell phone to arrange a dinner date with my husband when I noticed the time: Five o'clock. Straight up. On the dot!

And there I was, smack in the middle of the sparsely populated mall. Without special planning, without real forethought, I'd done it. I had achieved my dream.

So why wasn't I jumping up and down in glee? Why wasn't I shouting "Free at last! Free at last! I'm free, free at last!" Now was my Big Opportunity. I could have the full attention of any sales clerk, in any store. I could have my pick of umpteen empty dressing rooms. I could be the first in line at the checkout counter. Why, I could be the only customer at the checkout counter.

Instead, tears slithered down my face, my chest felt heavy, and loneliness threatened to suffocate me.

Could it be that I missed the conversations in the car as the kids told me about their day? Did I long to yell, "Dinner's ready!" and try to avoid the stampede of hungry teenagers? Did I mourn the fights over who would ride shotgun? Walk the dog? Feed the cat?

But wasn't this what I desired and worked for all those years? Just as my kids had craved and worked for their independence?

For the first time, I really got it. I understood the melancholy ache, the emptiness my patients had confided to me. The heavy-heartedness so many felt and feared. Suddenly, I felt less calloused and more understanding.

And — like I'd advised so many of my patients — I knew I needed to take a lesson from my fledglings and rejoice in my own newfound freedom. It was time for me to welcome this next season of life and move on.

My heart still ached, but, hey, I had the mall to myself. I breathed a deep sigh, wiped my eyes, and left a message for my husband that

I couldn't do dinner. Then, I headed into the nearest store—and shopped until the mall closed four hours later.

~Patricia Cena Evans

59

Nest-less and Restless

t has been over a week since I vacuumed and several months since I washed the windows. Yet, I see no crumbs under the table or fingerprints streaking the mirrors. Bedroom floors are clutter-free; dresser drawers are neatly closed. No muddy footprints spot the clean kitchen floor. No messy piles crowd the floor of the coat closet. No melted crayons stain seats in the family van.

More than two decades of family laughter, lively arguments, practical jokes, noisy meals, late-night parties, dorky games, boring chores, pillow fights, and tugs of war ring in my ears. Two decades of school work, library books, Saturday night movies, sharing clothes, sneaking food, decorating birthday cakes, hanging streamers and balloons crowd my mind.

Empty Nest Syndrome snickers at me all day long. I see sneaky eyes behind the never-shrinking stack of clean towels as I soak in the tub for the second time in one weekend. A mischievous finger pokes among the items in the sparsely-filled dishwasher and taunting laughter peals from the washer and dryer. I feel a kick against the back of my seat and catch a glimpse of a child's head in my rearview mirror.

Strangely, I do not know why I am haunted by these sights and sounds. I cannot make sense of this peculiar Syndrome. Or why I should be experiencing it.

I did not just send my last child off to college, wipe lingering tears as my youngest walked down the aisle, watch with arms akimbo as my kids cleaned the last of their belongings from the attic and basement, sell my children's unbelievably small bicycles in a sale on the front lawn, or take the final load of toddler clothes to Goodwill.

In fact, well, I am not even a mother.

So what has left me with an empty nest?

Was it the twenty-two noisy years I lived with my five siblings under our parents' roof? Could it be that the constant activity of my childhood left me anxious for the unlimited time, peace, and quiet I have now? Was it the chaos I grew up with that makes me desperate for voices to echo in the house, for stacks of bowls and dishes to fill the sink, for muddy footprints to tip-toe across the kitchen floor?

I've flown the coop.

I left the mess.

Yet I'm the one suffering from Empty Nest Syndrome!

~Sarah Stringfield

60

Chicken Soup for the Soul

Seventeen

*When you re-read a classic
you do not see in the book more than you did before.
You see more in you than there was before.*
~Clifton Fadiman

"*I* can't wait to get out of here!"

My mother didn't answer; she just turned and left the room. Left me standing in the middle of the floor with the echoes of my angry words to keep me company.

Looking back on it now, I suppose she was either too hurt to respond to my teenage tantrum, or couldn't understand it. The oldest of eleven, my mother had never harbored such a fervent wish as mine. She had never wanted to leave home, and only did so because "it was time." I knew she didn't remember being a teenager. She was too old.

Our differences were irreconcilable. She was trying to hold me back, to keep me the baby. I would be graduating in a few weeks, and in two months more, I would be eighteen. No one would be able to tell me what to do then.

Was it so hard for her to understand my desire to be on my own?

Due to my father's job transfer, I was uprooted my senior year in high school. We moved from Oklahoma to West Virginia, and I was anxious to get back to my old friends, to the life we'd planned for our post-high school years.

Those plans included moving from the small rural Oklahoma

community we had grown up in to the hustle of the metropolis: Oklahoma City. The five of us planned to rent a large house, find jobs, and make it "out there" on our own.

Our plans didn't include going to college. After all, we reasoned, plenty of people made it in the world without a college degree. My own parents were examples of that. So what was the big deal? And how could I bear living at home one minute longer than absolutely necessary?

Mom and I never really talked about that day again. It had been a particularly heated argument. She said things she shouldn't have. She was unreasonable. Set in her ways. And spoiled. She wanted everything her way. Why couldn't she see my side of things?

I flopped down on the bed, and let the tears come. I would remember this, I vowed. And I'd never treat my own children like that.

For all my wisdom and forethought, life didn't work out as we had planned. Two of our five-some got pregnant the last two months of high school; another decided to move in with her older sibling. That left just two, and it would prove to be nearly impossible to find a place we could afford. The reality of rent payments, utility fees, and spartan meals held little appeal. Our dream of being independent lost its luster.

I decided maybe I could live at home a while longer and go to college. But I didn't have to like it. After all, I had a mother who couldn't possibly understand me. She had called our plan foolhardy! Five girls, banded together, were indestructible. We could have taken Oklahoma City by storm. If what she had predicted hadn't happened quite so… predictably.

Besides, she was one of the oldest moms I knew. My friends all had younger moms; moms who weren't so set in their ways, moms who would at least try to understand.

Today, as a mother myself, I breathe a sigh of relief for the headstrong, willful teenage girl that I was. I live in Oklahoma City and there are places I will not venture, even now. As a young girl, I wouldn't have had the good sense to stay home. My mother knew that.

When my daughter, Jessica, turned seventeen, her birthday came with an attitude. Suddenly, her mom just didn't "get it" anymore.

Amidst her tears, eye-rolling, and fits of temper, I tried to remind myself what it was like to be seventeen. I remembered that long-ago time when I felt so misunderstood and insignificant, when I thought I knew it all, when I felt invincible.

And seeing it all replayed over thirty years later, I silently asked for forgiveness. Forgiveness for my own youthful inability to understand how great a parent's love, how boundless a mother's wisdom and understanding.

"I can't wait to get out of here!" Jessica yells, tears threatening.

I pull her to me and hug her. She tries to remain stiffly defiant, but finally, I feel her relax, her arms coming around my waist.

"I can't wait to get out of here!" I'm sure there were times when my aged, out-of-touch, controlling mother couldn't wait either.

I once promised myself to remember that argument. And I do. Only now I truly understand what those words meant to my mother: A loss and a longing, a promise and a prayer, an escape and an exile.

In another thirty years, perhaps Jessica will be standing on the other side of the fence and hearing those same words. I can only hope she, too, will always remember seventeen.

~Cheryl Pierson

Night Calls

Inch by inch, life's a cinch;
yard by hard, life is hard.
~Anonymous

I watched my baby sister carry the last load of dorm essentials to Mother's car and tried to contain my emotions. It was hard to believe the little girl with the crooked pony tail had transformed into this beautiful young woman. Kelsey was exuberant, nervous, and achingly sad all at the same time.

My husband and I had driven up for the weekend to see her off. Since Friday night she had meticulously organized her things. Each item of clothing had been folded and refolded. Dorm supply lists checked and rechecked. And now, on Sunday afternoon, Kelsey was leaving. I stuffed in her comforter and matching throw pillows and slammed the trunk.

"Well, you're all ready to go." I gave her one last lingering hug.

"I wish you could come with us tomorrow," she whispered into my ear.

"Me too." I wiped a tear from my cheek. "But Ryan has to be back at work, and besides there isn't any room in that car for me!"

My husband carried our luggage out the door. "Good luck," he said. "You're going to love college. You'll be fine, don't worry."

My parents joined us all in the driveway and Ryan and I got into our car.

"Call me tomorrow night," I told Kelsey. "I want to hear all about move-in day."

"I will." She choked back tears. My parents put their arms around Kelsey's shoulders as we pulled away.

"Hey Kelsey!" I shouted before we disappeared around the corner. "Remember to have fun!"

The next day I couldn't stop thinking about her. Was she all moved in? Had she met any new friends? Was she homesick? Kelsey had been the only child for a long time—ten years separated us—and I worried about her adjustment.

At midnight the phone woke me.

"It's me," Kelsey said. "I want to go home. Emily, I hate it here. It's so different from home."

"It's just new," I said reassuringly. "Anything new is scary at first. Just relax and take it one day at a time."

We chatted for a few minutes and she seemed to relax a little.

"Why don't you just go to sleep?" I suggested. "You've had a long day and things will look much better in the morning."

"You always know the right thing to say, Em. Thanks."

"I was homesick when I went to college, too. Mom gave me the same advice I'm giving you. And Kelsey," I added, "I'm just a phone call away."

I half expected a desperate phone call the next day, but my fears were misplaced. I didn't hear from her that day, or the next, or the next. When she finally got around to calling, she was already so busy with new friends and exciting activities that we only managed a five minute conversation.

So, I was startled a week later when the phone rang again at midnight.

"Em…" A sob strangled my name. "I hate this."

For a moment I stared at the phone, half asleep and confused. "Kelsey?" I asked. "What's going on? I thought you were having a great time!"

But only quiet crying broke the silence at the other end. Then a long pause. "This isn't Kelsey, Emily. It's Mom."

"Mom? What's wrong? Did something happen to Dad?"

"No nothing's wrong with either of us. It's just—the house is so empty now."

For a moment I sat there, feeling foolish and ashamed. All this time I had been worrying about my sister and hadn't given a second thought to how my parents were adjusting.

"Oh, Mom," I soothed, "it's okay."

"We haven't had an empty house in twenty-seven years. It doesn't seem right."

"Yeah, I bet it's weird. But think how clean it will stay!"

She laughed a little, but the echo of sadness lingered.

"Hey," I said softly, "you're going to be fine. This is a whole new chapter for you and Dad."

"It's just so empty here. I hate it."

As a mother now myself, I could almost feel the visceral pain she was experiencing. I didn't know what to say to make her hurt go away, so I passed on the same kernel of wisdom she had given me years before. "It's just new. Anything new is scary at first. Take it one day at a time." I smiled into the phone. "And remember, I'm just a phone call away."

~Emily E. Weaver

62

Connections

Biology is the least of what makes someone a mother.
~Oprah Winfrey

I'm un-bonding.

For those of you young moms, perhaps even rocking your newborn as you read this, un-bonding is the opposite of what you're doing now: the nursing, the cooing, the cuddling. All those things, we're told as new mothers, are crucial to establish a unique, one-of-a-kind connection between mother and child.

The experts are right. It works.

I did everything they suggested in order to bond with my son, or to attach, as they now say. I talked to him from the first moment the stick turned blue, so he'd know my voice. I took him from the nurse immediately after delivery, so I would be the first to embrace him in his new world. For weeks it was all about us and getting to know and trust each other. And when he gazed at me for the first time, looking right into my eyes, recognizing me and smiling that toothless smile, I simply melted.

We had connected, just like they said we would. We were tight.

Now, I'm stuck. Having bonded so well—more like Super Glue than regular Elmer's, I'm finding it a bit difficult to undo it all. The little boy who melted my heart is now researching colleges. He will turn eighteen on his next birthday. It's time to let go. And, like childbirth, it's more difficult than I expected.

Truthfully, it's a negative process. Detach. Separation. These are difficult words. Even harder, these negatives are positive things when your baby is no longer a baby. In fact, they are necessary in order to form a new, healthy, adult relationship. Yet, no one prepared me for this part.

Where are the nurses now?

My mother offered hints. She cried when I went away to college. She still mails grocery coupons to me and we talk every day on the phone. But other than witnessing her reaction to my own departure, no experts are telling me what to do and how to do it. No un-bonding Lamaze coaches in sight. I'm on my own to do this part of mothering, to undo the connection we've forged.

It's like ripping a Band-Aid off your arm that miraculously stayed stuck to you after an entire week of showering. It stings. And it leaves a mark. Yet, I know instinctively that letting him go is as natural as giving birth.

I just didn't know it would hurt the same.

~Kimberly Porrazzo

63

Pedal Power

Life is like riding a bicycle.
To keep your balance, you must keep moving.
~Albert Einstein

The memory is as clear as the bright blue sky on that summer afternoon almost twenty years ago. I stood on the sidewalk in front of our house, gripping the seat of my son's red bicycle and praying I'd have enough strength for the task ahead.

Matthew, his fifth birthday barely behind him, had decided it was time to take off his training wheels. Time to ride a two-wheeler, like the big kids in the neighborhood. One foot on a pedal, one still on the ground, he turned and looked over his shoulder.

"Ready, Mom?"

No.

I took a deep breath. "Okay."

"Don't let me fall."

"I won't," I promised. "I'll hold on until you get the hang of it."

And we were off, Matthew making his tentative way down the sidewalk, me trotting along behind, trying to keep the bike balanced so it wouldn't tip over. Down to the end of the block and back again, over and over, me getting more and more winded, Matthew growing more and more confident.

"I think you're ready," I told him finally, trying to steady my voice as I had steadied the bike. "You'll stay balanced as long as you keep pedaling."

Matthew nodded, his face reflecting the eagerness and determination that were so much a part of his personality. He was my first-born, always eager to get going, always bumping against my instinct to hold tighter. The child destined to poke the first hole in our family cocoon.

We started off again. "Just keep pedaling," I said, and it became a refrain I repeated over and over as we picked up speed. "Keep pedaling… keep pedaling… keep pedaling."

When I let go he glided on, wobbly but upright, the momentum carrying him down the sidewalk alone. I had to stop chanting then. I couldn't get the words past the lump in my throat.

I knew it was a moment to celebrate. After all, this was the very essence of parenting: to nurture, to teach, to hold your child steady until it's time for him to go it alone. And I was proud of all that Matthew had accomplished so far.

But I couldn't help feeling sad that every step in that journey would take him farther and farther away from me. There would be no going back to training wheels, no going back to toddler-hood or infancy. I knew I would have to face forward, focusing my energy on the future and trusting that something wonderful was waiting for him there.

Over the next few years, I helped both of Matthew's younger brothers learn to ride that same red bike. "Keep pedaling!" I called, as they took their turns heading down the sidewalk.

The phrase found its way into our family language, becoming a kind of shorthand for forging ahead. We'd use it when anyone felt discouraged or uncertain about a direction he'd chosen. "It will be okay," I'd assure them. "Just keep pedaling." And they knew exactly what I meant.

The last time I remember saying it, my youngest son needed encouragement. His two brothers were away at college and David was feeling lonely.

"I miss having them here to talk to," he said. "I miss all the fun we used to have."

"So do I," I told him. "But you know things can't stay the same. It was time for them to go. And there are lots more great times waiting out there for you. I promise. Just keep pedaling." He sighed but managed a weak smile.

Now David is the one going off to college. In a few months, he'll graduate from high school and head down the sidewalk to whatever his future holds. I'll send him off, like his brother before him with love and prayers, hoping I've provided him with the skills he'll need.

Only this time it will be different. After twenty-four years, there will be no children in the house. No Legos or soccer balls underfoot, no scout troops to lead or dances to chaperone. Parenthood, with its all-consuming activities and responsibilities, has shaped my life for so long that it's hard to imagine any other shape.

And yet, there is so much to look forward to, so much to cherish about a life in which my husband and I are free to pursue new dreams and ambitions. It's time to explore new sidewalks of our own, to see where they take us.

After all, life doesn't run backward. There is only forward. There is only the never-ending challenge of keeping your balance. I know I'll be fine if I just keep pedaling.

~Carol Grund

Surprise Guest

One half of knowing what you want is
knowing what you must give up before you get it.
~Sidney Howard

My emotions hung in the cold morning air just like my breath as my son headed back to college. As I watched his taillights fade in the dark hour before dawn, I realized he left behind a mixture of sadness and relief. Sadness, of course, because he would be missed. When he leaves, his vibrancy, energy, enthusiasm, and youthfulness all follow him out the door. Sometimes it seems as though my son is bigger than life. When he is home, the whole family dynamic changes. The house feels more alive, fuller somehow. The relief I felt at his departure, though, blind-sided me. I deflated like a balloon.

As he disappeared from view, I returned to my coffee and the quiet. I was left with a house that felt a little too big, even though I still have two at home. Although my high school daughters fill our house with laughter and secrets and long talks, a part of me is missing now. The vibrancy of the girls is, dare I say, quieter; it's different from young male energy. The place seems a little too hushed, a little too settled.

Yet, I have to confess a part of me felt released when my son left. How awful is that? I have grown to like peacefulness. I like my steady routine, not the roller-coaster ride his energy brings. When he is home, life is up and down, exciting because you never know which way he is going to go next. His boisterous pounding on the piano, his booming voice that echoes against our high ceilings, and his staying up all hours add a level of vitality our home lacks without him.

This child I once tucked in at night, who hosted friends to play video games and watch movies. This child I watched grow from the gangly youth with braces into a young man sporting a goatee and independent ideas about life. This child who, somewhere along the road, college transformed into an adult guest, visiting for the holidays.

How can I miss him and want him gone all in the same heartbeat? How did this happen? Is the change something that occurred in me? When did I form a definition of home that didn't include him? Am I a bad mother for such traitorous thoughts?

I was so eager to see him, to have him back with us. Why did I breathe a sigh of relief when he left? Could it be that my heart now sees my child as independent of me? Instead of the grief I felt a year ago when he first left, I feel… satisfied. It feels right for his homecomings to be visits. His life is out there, and mine is right here.

And that's okay.

~Kerry Krycho

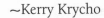

Swings and Things

Maturity knows no age. It is a concept that can only become a reality when one completely relinquishes their childhood tendencies and fully embraces the ideals valued by those already matured.

~Andy Masty

$\mathcal{I}$ knew it was going to happen; I'd seen pictures and plans. But I wasn't prepared for what met my eyes when I left college life behind for a weekend. I washed vegetables at the kitchen sink when my eyes lifted to the window. I scanned the backyard I'd seen a million times before and...

My childhood touchstone, my Mecca—my swing set—was gone.

As my parents closed the door on my childhood and packed up twenty-one years of life to move to their dream retirement home on a Maine lake, they'd pulled down the three swings that, for years, had been swung only by the wind.

When they bought the house, it was just that. A house. But with carpentry skills honed by friends and lots of hard labor from my grandfather and uncles, my dad transformed the house into a home within five years of his big purchase. With the addition of a beamed family room and a finished, carpeted basement, it became the perfect place to raise a growing family.

On the side of the wood barn he erected for a private get-away, Dad built a miniature house, just for us girls. With a shingled roof and deep purple shutters, it provided hours of playtime.

And right in front of our little house was the swing set.

Dad mounted the swings on an arch of telephone poles he "borrowed" from his job. With its little clubhouse that culminated in a plastic wavy slide, the custom-made set was envied by neighbors and friends.

When I left for college, I never envisioned someone else waking up on Christmas morning in my home. New owners wouldn't know how to live there.

They wouldn't know the playhouse windows are the perfect height to perch behind and play ice cream shop. They wouldn't remember how long it took my dad to set the basketball hoop at the exact height to ensure a perfect shot by a little girl. They wouldn't know how to step on the right side of the seventh stair to avoid the squeak that betrayed a curfew-breaker.

"It feels like we kids are on our own now," I accused Mom one day when she asked me to sort through boxes brimming with old school papers.

"Didn't it ever occur to you that your dad and I are starting a life on our own because our work is done?" She looked me in the eye. "And that in Maine we'll wake up every day to remember you guys as kids, playing there in the water?"

For my parents, those two annual weeks in Maine encapsulated my childhood. Memories of my first wobbly bicycle ride down the driveway at home and waiting for the bus on my first day of school have faded; they prefer to reminisce about a sunfish dangling from my pole and the look on my face when I felt the slimy scales.

I guess I should have seen it coming. After all, they'd been talking about retiring to Maine for as long as I could remember. Still, it had seemed an eternity away.

Apparently, eternity arrived this year. They're simply biding time until the last of their ducklings graduates from high school. My mother can no longer look out her bedroom windows without envisioning the view of the lake she'll have in six months.

When Dad showed me his plans for the new house, I was forced to swallow every selfish, petty thought I had. His eyes grew a little misty as he pointed out the sandy plot around the cove where my mom could finally have the garden she'd dreamed about—and the beach where grandchildren would play some day. I followed his finger as it traced the lines of the first floor and a big, square room with three windows to overlook the lake. There it was, scrawled in my dad's handwriting: Caitlin's Room.

And, on the tidy rectangle representing the porch, another little square: The Porch Swing. I could almost hear its tired groan as it held the weight of his children. His hoped-for grandchildren.

Time has a way of turning the pages, I decided.

My parents would start fresh with a new home, a new life. Yet, drawn right into the plans for their future were their ties to the past—their memories.

And my own.

~Caitlin Bailey

Empty Nesters

Left Behind

A pleasure isn't full grown until it is remembered.
~C.S. Lewis

66

Empty? Says Who?

There is nothing in which the birds differ more from man than the way
in which they can build and yet leave a landscape as it was before.
~Robert Lynd

When we moved to Colorado, we did not buy a rustic, multi-level lodge on several wooded, mountainous acres somewhere in the Rockies; we ended up with a brick, split-entry tract home, on a quarter-acre lot in the middle of town.

But it was home, and it was a great place to raise a family. We had enough bedrooms, bathrooms, and living space for our five children and all of their friends. For nearly twenty years, we entertained crowds of young people (and their parents) and enjoyed every bit of it. Each Christmas Open House was literally an open house — where scores of guests generated so much body heat we opened all the windows to cool the place down.

Then, one by one, the kids moved out, and as the saying goes, they only came home to visit. Now all that's left is to walk through the quiet house and savor the memories.

Downstairs, our oldest son's bedroom still has posters and pictures of airplanes all over the walls. In one corner are stacks of boxes containing flight manuals, college texts, and gear collected from years in Boy Scouts, Junior ROTC, and the Air Force Academy. In the other corner are boxes of miscellaneous belongings left behind by other children we took in and "adopted" for a while.

In his closet — well, in his closet are toy guns and swords, radio-controlled airplanes, all his old USAFA uniforms, several formals and prom dresses that aren't his, school projects, piles of books in Russian and English, and envelopes and shoe boxes containing official correspondence and old love letters. His dresser drawers hold the clothing he didn't take to the Air Force.

We heave a sigh and visit the bedroom our youngest daughter commandeered when the oldest moved out. (She transported all her sister's belongings to the attic.) Shelves on three walls display her extensive doll and tea set collections. On her dresser are the untidy remains of a triumphant high school senior year: drum sticks, band music, a drum major's baton, cards from well-wishers, discarded gift wrap, and a wad of dirty clothes.

The still-unmade bed holds a pair of pajamas and whatever else didn't fit into her suitcase when she packed for college. The hamper harbors dirty clothes, waiting for her to come home and wash them. We wade through a floor piled with college brochures and old class notes to peek into the closet—full of dresses, shoes, and several boxes of childhood mementos. We have to duck under the pet net full of stuffed animals to get out of her room.

We walk through the bar area, past several boxes of stuff we're storing for three "adopted" daughters. After they graduated from high school, they lived with us (not all at once, thankfully) to escape difficult family situations, and their parents dumped most of their belongings on them. One went into the Navy, one into the Air Force, and one married our oldest son. They left the boxes here with the promise they'd retrieve them when they got more room.

We enter the middle daughter's bedroom with caution. The walls are a collage of Broadway posters, inspirational placards, pictures of Paris and Vienna, brightly colored ceramic masks, bulletin boards, and photographs. Behind the door are bins of sheet music. At the foot of the bed sits a box of her favorite hats. Strewn everywhere are class notes, applications, old reports, and assignments. There's her scrapbooking stuff in that corner. Here are her cape, bow, and magic wand. Along one wall, an industrial-strength music stand balances three flutes and a piccolo. Beneath squat two suitcases that didn't accompany her to Chile.

We go upstairs and tiptoe quietly past the room of our twelve-year-old son, the only child still living here. It looks like a typical middle schooler's room, but for some reason, today it doesn't look all that bad—not after what we've seen downstairs.

The next bedroom was our home office... until our son's fiancée moved into it for a year before they got married. Mixed with family records are boxes of her childhood keepsakes and a stack of leftovers from the wedding preparations. And in the closet? A wedding dress, more clothes, more memorabilia.

We risk a peek into the attic. This is where we keep our Christmas decorations and suitcases—and about ten boxes of memories belonging to our oldest daughter. That explains why our roof didn't blow away in last winter's gales.

Now we go down to the garage. It's a two-car, but there's only room for one. Why? Because here are my oldest son's skiing and camping gear, his snowshoes, all our children's bicycles and sleds, my youngest son's Power Wheel dump truck, a six foot long wooden aircraft carrier, and all of the toys they outgrew but couldn't bear to throw away.

We miss our children terribly, but one question keeps nagging at my brain: What is this empty nest we keep hearing about? The kids may have flown, but we're stuck with their droppings.

~Robert Depew

67

Hats Off!

You see much more of your children once they leave home.
~Lucille Ball

I thought I did a good job preparing my children to leave the nest. They knew how to do their laundry, sew on missing buttons, balance a checkbook, and keep themselves from starving.

As the time approached for them to test their wings, I was more than ready to trade in my old hats — Cook, Chauffeur, Maid, Nurse — for some new and more self-indulgent ones. I actually looked forward to the empty nest. No tears for me. But I wasn't insensitive. No, I would wait until their cars were fully out of the driveway before I did my Snoopy dance.

Then it happened. They were gone — off to make their place in the world. Our daughter was the first to leave, followed four years later by our son. Free at last! We could eat whatever we wanted for dinner at whatever time we wanted. I could put the scissors in the drawer and find them still there a week later. I could take a shower and not run out of hot water just as I finished lathering.

It wasn't that I didn't miss them, but our newfound freedom was exhilarating. Slowly, however, a subtle fear welled inside me. What if I did such a good job of preparing my children to be on their own that they no longer needed me, or worse still, wanted me?

My husband tried to assure me that my fears were unwarranted. "They'll still need you, just in a different way."

During their college years they did seem to occasionally want my advice, although more as an emergency resource than anything.

"Mom, we're going to make pizza. What is your sauce recipe?" Or, "Mom, how do I get a grease stain out of my new blouse?" And there was always the proverbial, "Mom, can you cover my phone bill this month? I'm a little short on funds."

After they married, I expected their phone calls to become less frequent. After all, they now had children and spouses to occupy their time. But to my amazement the phone calls actually increased. Suddenly I was wearing my old hats again: Dr. Mom, Chef Mom, and Resource Mom.

"Mom, the baby has a strange rash. What do you think it could be?"

"I can't diagnose it over the phone. I think you should call your doctor."

"Mom, I have a pound of hamburger that's been in the refrigerator for a week. Do you think it's still good?"

"I don't know. If it still smells okay then it's probably fine to cook. If everyone gets sick then it probably wasn't."

"Mom, where can I get parts for my mixer?"

"Try a Google search. I'm sure you'll find something online."

Almost every day one or both children called for trivial reasons. Finally, after returning the telephone to its cradle, I looked at my husband in despair. "I don't think I prepared our children as well as I thought. I don't know what they would do if I suddenly died. They call me for every little thing."

A slight smile crossed his face. "They could probably answer all those questions on their own, but did it ever dawn on you that maybe they just like talking with you?"

My blank expression revealed I had never considered that possibility.

"You taught them to be self-sufficient, but you also taught them to care. You'll always be an important person in their lives and this is just their way of showing you that."

As I considered what he said, my head suddenly felt a little bare.

No matter how many new hats I wore, none would be quite as comfortable as those old familiar ones. And, thankfully, some hats never go out of style.

~Caroleah Johnson

68

Cheers!

Right there, between the pickles and the olives, I fell apart. I was trying to get a head start on shopping for three sons who would walk out the door to three different colleges in a month. My hands seemed glued to the grocery cart, my eyes welled with tears, and in a matter of moments, my heart skipped beats like a Broadway dancer ignoring a choreographer's instructions.

I just can't do this, at least not today, I thought. I still have time to get it all together.

More correctly, time had me—right in its grip.

"Hey, Ma, I don't see any sheets or socks. Remember the list Notre Dame sent?" inquired my soon-to-be freshman Dan. "And it's all got to have my name tags sewn on everything. Have we got a problem here?"

"Don't worry about me, Mama," Bill said, "I'll be living with five other guys in a house down at Eastern. Forget sheets or towels, think food, Mama, think food."

Mike, our returning junior, was headed to Northern Illinois. "Mom, take care of them," he nodded in Bill and Dan's direction. "Remember, I'm living with four girls this year. They're doing the cooking and laundry. I take care of their cars, odd jobs around the apartment, the grocery shopping and tutor them in calculus. Truly, I don't need anything."

Mike had stepped into the shoes of being the big brother, the year our oldest son, Jack, married his college sweetheart. The shoes fit him just fine.

Somehow, it all came together. Boxes, trunks, bags, and sports equipment filled our family van each weekend as we drove one or the other off to college: the land of no curfews, no parents, no matching socks. As hard as it was on John and me, in retrospect, it was harder still on our youngest child, Amy, who would begin high school after Labor Day. She detested being the only child at home, and slept each night in one of her brother's beds, crying herself to sleep.

We three became The Family. The Family ate dinner out. The Family went to church and volleyball games together. The Family took road trips to visit each of the boys. Truth be told, all the attention was suffocating her. Putting her parents up for adoption seemed like a great idea.

Seasons changed, the boys came home for holidays and visits, dirty laundry dragging behind them. We still missed them, but it wasn't long before we were asking, "So, when does school start again?"

Caps and gowns were donned, diplomas received and home they came. Now independent young men, they looked at home as a Class-A boarding house. They had new careers and no curfews. The stereo rocked, the phone jangled, and our drive resembled discards from Jake's Used Car Lot.

Another August rolled around and Amy left for college. Same routine, same row of pickles and olives. I should have been stronger, but this was Amy, our only daughter. She was breaking up The Family.

After college, Amy and her flaky roommate moved in. The day they chose to move, our home was a hundred pounds lighter as they borrowed supplies.

A year later, John and I celebrated our wedding anniversary. Over dinner and candlelight John said, "Do you realize we've been married thirty-four years and have never been alone?"

"We must have been alone, somewhere along the way." I winked. "We have five children to show for it!"

That summer, Dan entered Law School in Wisconsin. Counting

the boys who'd already married and moved, and Amy in her apartment, that left us... let's see... alone. A-l-o-n-e. Alone! It hit us right between the eyes, like a little boy's squirt gun on a hot July day.

I wandered their bedrooms, listening to the silence. This was it, I realized. This was real.

Returning to the kitchen, I was flabbergasted to see John beaming like a hundred-watt bulb. In his hands were two Waterford wine glasses, used only for the most special of occasions.

As he handed one to me, his tired eyes teared. Our glasses clinked in a weary toast.

"Here's to us, kid. Alone at last. Now it's our turn."

~Alice Collins

69

The Treasure Chest

There are chapters in every life which are seldom read
and certainly not aloud.
~Carol Shields

"Your ma's in the hospital." Daddy's worried voice came over the phone.

I'd been dreading that call since my parents moved from Colorado to Phoenix. Dizzy spells which had plagued Mama for years occurred more frequently in recent months. She blamed her health problems on Arizona's weather and wanted to move back to Colorado. It fell to me to go to Phoenix and help them pack up.

"I'll get there as soon as I can," I told Daddy.

I braced myself for the physical effort it would take to actually move all their stuff. You see, they saved things. Married in the summer of 1929, before the Great Depression, they learned to make do with what they had. If they needed something, they fashioned it from odds and ends, bits and pieces, of whatever clutter had amassed in the basement. If it couldn't be created from their salvage, Daddy had a ready response: "We don't need it."

Mama was home from the hospital when I arrived, but clearly not well. As soon as I stepped into their tiny home, I could see that housekeeping had deteriorated badly. Mail strewn haphazardly on a table, a hodge-podge of outdated prescriptions stashed in the bathroom medicine cabinet.

But the sight that stopped me cold was the old cedar chest. It was, I knew, crammed to overflowing with relics collected throughout their marriage. That was the starting place—space made there would allow real necessities to be packed for the move.

The chest had been Daddy's engagement gift to his bride. When we moved to Colorado from Missouri, he strapped it atop the car where it baked and bleached under the Kansas sun. We must have presented a curious sight to all who passed us on old Highway 40.

The chest held a quilt made by the grandmother I'd never known. It cradled Mama's wedding dress, a purple fringed concoction quite stylish in its day. And photographs. Boxes and boxes of old photos. Unsmiling, stiffly posed relatives from bygone times, peering with hollow eyes at the camera. A black and white of Mama and Daddy on their wedding day.

Mercy, I knew Mama would never give up those heirlooms. The "keeper" pile was growing. I would simply have to question all other items in the chest, deny their usefulness, and convince Mama to toss each outdated article.

As intent as an archaeologist, I continued burrowing. Honestly! The chest housed outgrown baby clothes. A beaded handbag my sister and I used for dress-up. Report cards from our elementary school days all the way through high school.

Then the most ridiculous piece appeared. I picked it up, in wonder that Mama had kept it all these years. When I entered junior high, I had decided that my long pigtails would never survive higher education. Those pulled-tight braids looked stupid, and I was tired of boys yanking them. For the first time in my life, the tresses, so long that I could sit on them, were cut.

But Mama had salvaged the long locks from the beauty parlor floor, lovingly plaited them one last time into a thick braid, tied it off with a blue ribbon, and tucked it away in the chest. I sighed in exasperation and tossed the hank of hair onto the discard pile.

Then, I noticed a shiny object hiding in a corner of the chest. I pulled it out and drew in a sharp breath. A clay plaque, bearing two tiny handprints, covered in gilt paint. The impressions were my daughter's. Sherry had made that little gift for me one long-ago Mother's Day. Her name was scrawled into the clay.

Tears stung the back of my eyes. I'd discarded that plaque years ago in one of our many moves. Apparently Mama salvaged it. The next thought that occurred to me was hard to bear. Three months hence, my husband would be presenting those hands, now all grown up, to Sherry's groom.

Suddenly I understood. After her kids left home, Mama had softened their departures with relics... memories to recall our childhoods.

After only a slight hesitation, I returned the plaque to its niche. Then I cast a fond look at the discard pile, picked up my shiny golden braid, and replaced it gently in Mama's treasure chest.

~Mary K. McClanahan

70

Discarded Memories

The past is not a package we can lay away.
~Emily Dickinson

*J*en had hauled her bed, dresser, clothes, and whatever else she felt a nineteen-year-old Colorado girl would need for her move to the city where Tony Bennett left his heart.

Oh, yes, my baby girl — forsaking me, the local college, me, her friends, and me, to move west seeking something that I could not provide. I watched her drive away with a U-Haul, a fake smile plastered to my face, my arms waving as if they had a mind of their own.

A week later, it was time to brave her room. I trembled at the door. Taking a deep breath, I stepped in.

Along with the dust bunnies in the corners were things she'd left behind. Two boxes, one marked "Stuff to Save" and the other "Stuff to Toss." With a deep sigh, I sat down amid the dust bunnies and began a journey through my daughter's childhood.

My fingers riffled the discard box and discovered friendship notes, folded in intricate puzzles, from her sixth and seventh grades. Designated as refuse, I deduced they were open to viewing, and unfolded the origami shapes.

The notes were typical of prepubescent girls. Peppered with words such as rad and gross, they rambled about boys and crushes. The language was simple and crude in places, preteens experimenting in a world of hormones, competition, role-playing, and puppy love.

Looking further, I uncovered grade school notebooks and tattered artwork. I found clothes and shoes, stuffed animals, a library book (at least three years overdue), an empty cologne bottle, and her cheerleader megaphone. I lifted out a box of old costume jewelry I gave her when she was little.

As I sorted through the "bling," I recalled Jen playing dress-up in my long dresses.

"Mommy, look at me, I'm a princess!" She twirled and danced.

My heart ached with the memory—until something caught my eye. I pulled out a pair of 14 karat earrings I thought I had lost years ago. Jen loved those gold dangles and begged to play with them.

"Why, that little booger!" I gasped. She must have "borrowed" them and added them to her collection. I set them aside and moved to the other box, the things Jen obviously felt were keepers.

It held yearbooks, favorite photographs, and special occasion cards. Her varsity letter, her diving trophy, and the stuffed dog that was her constant companion as a youngster. Interspersed throughout were her diaries. My fingers itched to open them. After all, there was a lot I still wanted to know about her sixteenth year. I shrugged. Perhaps ignorance really was bliss. I chose not to violate her privacy and placed them aside, unread.

It was, I noticed, cathartic to sit in her bedroom. I accepted that it was Jen's time to go. And I knew it was my time to let her go.

Jen blossomed in San Francisco. She faced fears, accepted challenges, and wrote most of it down in journals. Journals I've never read. I didn't need to.

Our relationship matured. We had great phone chats those first few months and she shared her adjustment to the big city, a new job, new friends, and self-discovery.

After a time, I decided to paint the walls of her old bedroom and convert it into a guest room for her to use. Each time she visits, we sit and rub each other's feet—and tell stories from the Save Box of our memories.

~Linda Leary

71

Under Construction

Ambition is putting a ladder against the sky.
~American Proverb

"It really is an eyesore." My husband eyed the tree house.

Eighteen-year-old Michael, the youngest of our three sons, readily agreed.

Uncertain of its stability, I didn't want to worry about the young neighborhood children playing in the structure that hovered over our neighbor's yard, too. I also knew if it didn't come down now, it might stay there forever.

I envisioned the original "construction crew" gathering for the demolition and suggested to Michael that he gather those friends to help.

"Mom, it's no big deal. They won't want to help take it down." Knowingly, he asked, "Do you want to take pictures?"

Of course, I wanted to take pictures.

Eight years ago, slender dark-haired Michael approached me. "Mom, can we build a tree house in our yard?" Several friends stood behind him with pleading, hopeful looks on their preteen faces.

"Sure." I assumed it was a fantasy that would occupy them for the day. "Where do you want to build it?"

The boys had already scoped out the yard and chosen a towering pine at the northwest corner of our house. Sturdy branches made it a favorite for climbing.

Scrap lumber, saws, nails, hammers, and a sawhorse emerged

from the garage and basement as the boys started the project. The tree house became a focal point when children congregated at our house. Other kids came to watch and offer suggestions. I loved having them at our home. Not only did I know where my sons were, I enjoyed the noise and vibrancy of their friends.

Michael and a core group continued to modify the structure over several years. With no written plans or adult intervention, the construction site evolved from a plea and a plan to three levels of platforms meandering through branches high in the tree.

My rules evolved along with it. From "No one can be in the tree house unless I am home," to "No power tools unless I'm home," to "Be sure to call someone's mom if you fall out of the tree when I'm not home."

The boys tied a rope swing to one of the branches. The top level had a hinged roof, opened by pulling a rope that dangled to the ground. Rungs nailed to the trunk provided access to their dream house. Being permitted to climb the ladder became a rite of passage for younger cousins and friends' siblings.

Michael and his pals graduated from high school this spring, and our family hosted several parties during the summer. The construction crew and their friends didn't climb up the tree house. Not once.

Now, as my youngest readies for college, I find myself de-cluttering. I do not have plans to move, but I do have an urgent desire to purge my house. I've always discarded items we no longer need. Years ago, we offered our idle swing set to a neighboring family who dismantled it and moved it to their home. We gave away tricycles, rollerblades, and bikes as soon as our kids outgrew them.

And, besides, an uninhabited tree house sends an aura of loneliness, of longing for a past life. It's a tangible symbol of little kids. And my kids are moving on. There is no place in our family for it now.

The original construction crew is scattering. One boy left for college last week. By the end of the month, the rest will have spread to different states. I once took pictures of those boys building the tree house and its additions. Last weekend, I took pictures of Michael taking it down. He enjoyed demolishing it. I know his friends would have enjoyed helping him. I would have enjoyed watching them and taking pictures.

Seven large trees—elm, ash, cypress, and pine—grace our front yard, now devoid of basketballs, bicycles, and boys. To the objective eye, there is no evidence of children having lived here. But I know where to look: on the big pine with barely discernible imperfections left from a dismantled childhood. Enthusiastic adolescent boys plotted strategy, lashed ropes, and pounded nails to create their masterpiece. A contented young man on the brink of independence took it down by himself. He's moving on, building a new life.

So must I.

~Karen R. Gray-Keeler

Treasure

I have a little treasure box made of battered tin.
It's always where I need it, to place my treasure in.
I haven't any diamonds or sapphires of deep blue,
But the tin is overflowing with gifts I got from you.
I have the first sweet golden lock from your baby head,
Folded sheets with woven lace I used upon your bed.
I have all of your birthday cards and favorite reading book,
And when you're gone and it is cold, I'll sit and have a look.
Deep inside my memory box, a peacock feather bright;
We marveled at its colors shining in the light.
And then, of course, my necklace of little beads so red,
We sat and laughed for hours as we slipped them on a thread.
My favorite and most precious: your brilliant butterfly;
I held you sobbing in my arms when you knew
    that it would die.
Faded flowers and broken shells you found down by the sea,
All the cherished, simple gifts—with love from you to me.
Yet, despite the keepsakes in my tin, the treasure that I miss
Is your warm cheek, your eyes of blue, your silky head to kiss.

~Linda Bispham

Over Stuffed

Every increased possession loads us with a new weariness.
~John Ruskin

It's finally quiet.

For the first time in almost thirty years, my husband and I are alone in our house. Six children, a daughter-in-law, a son-in-law, and two grandchildren have lived under this roof. Now that they've all moved into their own homes, we have the house to ourselves. It's a pretty big house for just the two of us, but we have plans for all that empty space.

We want to turn one of the upstairs bedrooms into a library. We'll replace the carpet, install a fireplace, and build bookshelves. I already store a lot of books in that room and need to move them out while we remodel. The upstairs hall closet is, I decide, the perfect place to stack them. But it's full of winter coats, high school letter jackets, and the kids' sleeping bags.

With enthusiasm, I organize it all into plastic bins and ask my husband to store them in the shed.

"There's no room in the shed," Randy announces.

"Why? What's filling up the shed?"

"Legos."

Oh, yes, the boys' favorite toy. In fact, several large containers of Legos crowd the shed. Literally thousands of Lego parts and pieces. But one of our sons recently moved into a house.

"You have a garage now," I point out with logic. "Could you store the Legos in there, son?"

"I'd be happy to, Mom, but the lock doesn't work and I don't want to risk them being stolen. I don't want to put my scooter or golf clubs in there, either. Could you keep them for me?"

"Oh, sure." I decide they'll fit in the closet of the basement bedroom, where I can also put the coats and sleeping bags.

"There's no room in the closet," Randy comments.

"Why? What's filling up the closet?"

"Toys. A pirate ship. A train set. A chess board. You name it."

After considering the stack of bins, I remember the downstairs storage room.

"There's no space in the storage room," Randy says when I ask him to carry them for me.

"Why? What's filling up the storage room?"

Randy sighs. "You'd better have a look."

As it turns out, the storage room is filled with boxes that belong to my daughter and son-in-law, who recently moved into a townhouse.

"Could you come and get the rest of your things?" I implore them.

"That's stuff we're saving for a garage sale, Mom. We don't have room here. Can you just keep it until spring?"

No wonder the house doesn't feel empty, I think as I sit on a plastic bin, holding my head in my hands. Will these kids ever get their things moved out?

Just then the phone rings.

"Hi," my mom chirps. "Dad and I were just cleaning out the garage. And we're wondering—when can you take all the stuff you've stored here for years?"

~Donna Milligan Meadows

Table Talk

Blessed are the joy makers.
~Nathaniel Parker Willis

"One day, my table will be clear. Just a vase of flowers on it!" I muttered to myself.

Toys, textbooks, make-up, and sports gear littered the table top. My eyes darted to the tubes and bottles. Why couldn't the girls go to their rooms to paint their fingernails, argue about music, and discuss boyfriends? And, why didn't Ben take his friends upstairs to his room? Instead, they hung around the kitchen all weekend, giving blow-by-blow accounts of the soccer game they just lost... or won.

My kitchen was a place where arguments were born, acted out, and resolved. It was a place of tears and consolation. It was a place of laughter and swapping secrets. But it was not a room where I had peace and space to get on with my chores.

Each evening, I tripped over tennis rackets and sporting bags. I set the table around photographs and magazines, scolding the kids to clear their mess away. And in the midst of it all, I served home-made muffins, savory pies, or whatever else was on offer. Over time, I replaced kitchen chairs with broken backs or worn out from use.

Naturally, I often got involved in what the teens were saying, offering counsel, giving support, while all the things I had promised myself I would get done were left untouched. By the time the lot of them left, I shook my head at the piles of dirty dishes.

"One day," I vowed, "my table will be clear."

Carol got married, but my table remained cluttered. That still left Lesley with her friends and Ben with his friends to inhabit my kitchen. When Lesley moved into a flat, the house was emptier for a few weeks. Then Ben invited Archie to stay in Lesley's room… and my kitchen was full again.

Finally, the day came when Ben and Archie decided to take a year off from university, and tour and work in Europe. As Ben and I stood alone in my kitchen, bags piled everywhere, I said, "Well, soon I won't have to nag you night and day about the state of this place!"

Ben nodded agreement.

"I'll never understand. You all had rooms of your own. Why did you kids spend your lives in here?"

Ben shrugged "Because of you."

"Because of me?" I frowned.

"Oh, all the homemade cookies, bowls of soup and everything helped, but mainly it was you." Ben paused. "You were great company, mum. That's why all our friends came round."

He grinned at me. "This kitchen is the place of our happiest childhood memories. And, like Carol's pal once said, 'Your mum is the kitchen, really!'"

I bit back my tears as Ben swung me into his arms, "Don't get weepy. It's how we all feel about you and your kitchen." Ben hugged me. "The girls have promised to look in on you while Archie and I are away."

"Nonsense. They don't need to do that," I said. "At long last I will have the place to myself!" And I actually meant it at the time.

Two lonely weeks later, I glanced round my clean and tidy kitchen. Tears ran unchecked down my cheeks and dropped off my chin as I gave a small sob.

"I miss you all so much!" I admitted brokenly to the empty room.

If the kids and their friends had spent some of the best days of their life in here, so most definitely had I. I just wished that I had appreciated it more at the time and not nagged them so much.

I stared at my clean table with its lace napkins and vase of flowers, and I could see them all sitting there, the chatter, the clutter, the laughing. I closed my eyes, and it was almost as if I could hear them giggling, arguing, and just enjoying themselves.

The happy side of life, I realized, is often about clutter and chaos. Too often, the neat and tidy side has a touch of loneliness about it.

It won't be long, I know, before grandchildren appear and come round to my kitchen. Hopefully, their friends will come, too, with book bags and magazines, soccer balls and jerseys.

~Joyce Stark

75

Sold!

Change always comes bearing gifts.
~Price Pritchett

"Did you get what you asked for?" my friend had asked me earlier.

I pondered her question as I walked through the vacant rooms of our house one last time. Of course, she really meant, "Did the house bring the sale price you asked?"

The rooms echoed my footsteps as if they too were a bit sad at the emptiness so foreign to them. It was as if I were in a strange place. Had it really been seventeen years since I first came here with my husband and three children in tow?

It didn't seem so long ago that my thirteen-year-old daughter begged, "Can I have the room with the purple carpet?"

I peeked into her bedroom. The carpet remained—along with purple stenciling on the walls where she had created her work of art. Several times we'd considered redecorating the room, even to the point of buying paint. But we'd never followed through.

I meandered down the hall to Justin's room. I wondered how many times my husband repaired its walls after our wall-abuser child had joined the family a couple of years after we moved to this house.

In the living room, now so bare, I imagined I could hear the laughter and squeals of children sitting around the tree that stood in the bay window at Christmas time. I could almost see Rocky sprawled above everything as he arrogantly watched his kingdom of human peasants from his royal cat throne.

I turned toward the kitchen and cringed at the slight shadow on the floor next to the refrigerator where I once spilled an entire gallon of salad dressing. The carpet was new at the time and although I scrubbed with everything imaginable, the stain never completely came out.

I walked through the kitchen and down the steps to the family "wrecked room." The black cast-iron stove was an old friend that kept the basement warm in winter. I often sat a pot of ham and beans on the top of it to simmer all day. Against the east wall were carpet indentations from the old upright piano. It was there I taught Jeremy "Moonlight Sonata." And, just out the window, the kids played Fox and Geese in the snow.

The number of children around the house multiplied with play dates and sleepovers. Once, Jeanna asked to invite a few friends for her thirteenth birthday. A "few" turned into nineteen, and one decided to show the group how long he could hold his breath—until he passed out. I thought about writing the Surgeon General to request a sign on birthday supplies and candles—"WARNING: Children's parties can be hazardous to parental sanity."

I meandered into the yard and paused under towering maples that shaded the deck. I nodded approvingly at the garage standing where there was once nothing but lawn.

And, as I climbed into the van, I studied the house one last time.

"Did I get what I asked for?" I asked out loud.

Oh, yes, and so much more!

~Pamela Blaine

76

Catch and Release

An object in possession seldom retains the same charm
that it had in pursuit.
~Pliny the Younger

The long-awaited births of our two children created untold happiness for my husband and me. Caught up in our joy, I tried to save all our special moments. But not all icons of these memories fit neatly into scrapbooks. How on earth could I dispose of their things?

My answer was to save everything.

I kept the ribbons from my daughter's hair. Her interests blossomed into drama, gymnastics and dance, which resulted in costumes, uniforms, medals, and ribbons. I kept the cars and trucks my son drove in the sandbox. His drawings and inventions resided in every room. I couldn't toss a thing. I framed, displayed, stored, and cherished it all. Each item evoked a good feeling that I wanted to capture, so the saving continued.

But, as children do, mine grew up, moved out, and moved on.

One day, I awoke to a home full of too much love in the form of stuff. I knew some changes had to be made. I called my daughter. "I found fifteen dolls, each with a different smell and a different color."

"Mom," her exasperation was obvious, "those are Strawberry Shortcake dolls."

"Well, what should I…"

"I'm twenty-nine now. Release them, Mom!"

Another pile, another call. "I just found your love letters to..."

"Mom, that was in ninth grade."

"But I wondered if..."

"Shred them, Mom!"

This exchange went on for days. I suspect she used caller ID to avoid my inquiries. I needed a new tactic. Weekly, when I collected my grandson for his visits with us, I verbally listed items in the toss out pile for her approval.

She'd roll her lovely green eyes and say, "Mom, release them! I already have."

The process of sorting was tedious and heart-wrenching; I was thankful for her encouragement. How I'd loved those years when our home was full of activity and happy chaos. When we hosted the church group each week for dinner and singing. When we welcomed our children's friends—so well, in fact, one of them moved in for a year. Each item I touched snagged on a memory.

And a clear understanding dawned: Good memories didn't rely on the items in the closets, drawers, attic, and shed; they resided securely in my mind and heart.

Empty spaces emerged where once a train table whistled with activity and a car track zoomed with fun. Carpet appeared where elaborate Lego and Construx buildings once towered and Matchbox cars garaged at bedtime.

I donated shelves of stuffed animals; I adopted out boxes of Cabbage Patch babies.

But the books were the hardest. I relived hours of rocking chair readings with a baby in my lap and a storybook in my hands. It was hard to say goodbye... to both the books and the babies. As I gave them away, I felt my breath catch and I whispered a little blessing that the words and pictures would bring the same happiness to another mother and child.

While there was angst in parting with tangible memories, there were moments of laughter, too.

One holiday, I shared one of the more unusual "relics" I'd unearthed.

"Dears, look what I found."

"What on earth are those, Mom?"

"Oh," I grinned unabashedly, "pieces of your umbilical cords."

"Mom!"

"Well, what do you think I should...."

From the expressions on their faces, I knew there was only one thing to do — keep them.

~Marilyn Ross

Two's Company, Three's a Family

I watched him play patiently with his toddler for over seven hours on an airplane headed for Seattle. It was December 24th and we were finally visiting my newly married daughter after being separated for seven months. The family in the seats across the aisle vividly reminded me of numerous trips we had taken. I wished I could tap the young father on his shoulder and warn him to cherish this moment. Someday he might be saying goodbye and leaving his daughter on the other side of the country.

Since Shelly's fifth birthday, we traditionally enjoyed family vacations at least twice a year if not more. This cross country trip was our first alone since becoming empty nesters. Shelly begged us to join her and her new husband for their first holiday together. The last time I saw her, on Mother's Day weekend, she had hugged me goodbye in her wedding gown. I glanced at my watch when I felt the plane prepare for descent. In another hour or so we would be a family of three again—instead of only two.

We had reservations at a hotel near their home, not wanting to intrude on their newlywed privacy. Curt checked us in while I made the call. "We're here! I can't wait to see you both."

"I'll be there in five minutes or less. Scott had to work." Shelly's excitement bubbled through the air waves.

I turned to my husband feeling butterflies flutter in my stomach. "Do we look older?"

"It's only been seven months." He rolled his eyes and resumed playing with his Blackberry.

I watched him pace the worn carpet in front of the double doors in the lobby. Why was I so nervous? I was seeing my only child—the daughter I had shopped with, baked with, and tried on new make-up with for years. What was going on?

"I see her Jeep." Curt cleared his throat and stepped behind me.

The early dusk made it difficult to see more than an outline. Suddenly, the doors whooshed open. I blinked as a beautiful blond woman stepped into the warm entry area. My flesh and blood stood before me, but in that split second of recognition, as she spread her arms and wore a smile a mile wide—I panicked. Memories of twenty-two years of living with my Shelly struggled to connect with this person awaiting my hug. Our married daughter had a life separate from ours in a strange town with a man we hardly knew. I forced back my tears.

"Mom! You made it!" She flew into my arms, hugging me fiercely. Her father stepped forward and pulled her into one of the bear hugs she loved so much. We were together as a family again but something was missing... or changed.

Later that evening, I brought up my concerns to Curt. "I felt strange. Like we hardly knew her. Did you feel awkward?"

He reached for his pajamas. "I know what you mean. She really isn't our daughter like before. It's just you and me, babe." He winked.

I called my mother later to tell her we arrived safely and wish her a Merry Christmas. "Why didn't you warn me it would be different? Did you feel like that when I got married and moved away?"

"Children grow up. Shelly's a young wife now with her own home." My mother chuckled softly. "I remember seeing you for the first time after you moved away and I felt the same."

I grumbled that I should have been warned.

We spent Christmas with the in-laws and toured the city for a week. On Thursday, the three of us spent hours shopping at a local outlet. Shelly laughed and teased me about my taste in clothing while I countered with comments about her taste in shoes. Her father fell back into his routine of carrying our purchases to the car. Time passed too quickly.

On the night before we left, I quizzed my husband again about his feelings.

"She's a grown woman now. Another man takes care of her." He hugged me but not before I noticed the tears in his eyes.

Shelly joined us for breakfast and then walked us to our rental car. I told her I wouldn't cry but I lied. As one, we hugged in the rainy parking lot and promised not to let so much time pass between us again. My last view was her scarf blowing in the Seattle wind as she ran to her car.

"Aren't you glad we got here early?" We were first in the post-holiday line at Southwest to claim our seats for the long flight home. I unzipped our carry-on bag I'd packed with an assortment of snacks. My heart jumped when I spied two cards.

"Mom" and "Dad" were printed on separate envelopes in our daughter's bold handwriting. I caught my husband's eye. He reached for his note and tucked it into the book he was reading. I couldn't wait.

When I tore back the flap, a flowered card fell out. "Dear Mommy…"

I didn't need to read anymore.

~Terri E. Tiffany

Heart Strings

"**G**ood night, Austin," I tell my son as he closes his former bedroom door. College has snatched him; this is his first time home in months.

My heart sighs as I hear him upstairs shuffling around. I ache to hum a lullaby and cuddle him close, as I did two decades ago. I remember how fulfilled I felt, how being a mother of such a little bundle was all I needed in life. How my chest fizzed with bubbles of excitement as I felt the cadence of his breaths.

Now I have a twenty-year-old. Over the years of gradually pulling away, the bubbles all burst. It's the way it's supposed to be. It's the healthy way.

I walk down the hall to my room, sit on the loveseat, and pick up my book. I pine to gain fulfillment in another venue.

Softly, slowly, the pinging sound of his guitar wafts into my room. One note, followed by another, then another, flowing into a tune. It is the soft melody of one of my favorite songs. My heart coos. My home is no longer empty. I feel like a baby curled up in its mother's lap, being lulled.

My eyes close, embracing this moment, never wanting to let go of its grasp. I visualize Austin's young, manly fingers picking the strings with the speed of a hummingbird's wings, and then slowing down with the grace of a swan's ballet. I see his other hand hugging the guitar's neck, changing the chords effortlessly.

For several minutes, the music drifts down the hallway and

my soul fizzes. I dare not move. I dare not let him know my pleasure at this moment. A feeling like this must not be abated. It's too precious.

The novel waits. It, too, understands.

One song flows effortlessly into the next and I'm swept away to another time, another world.

Too soon, the last strains of music fade away. His feet shuffle. The echo of the frame resonates as Austin places the guitar tenderly into its case.

I sigh.

The floor jars, as he bounces his whole body onto his mattress, just as he did when he was eight. And nine. And ten. And now.

The spell is broken, but my soul remembers, it still remembers how to fizz. With each strum of the guitar, I once again embraced his cadenced breaths. He had cuddled my whole being, as I once cuddled his.

I can do only one thing. I put my hands together. Clap, clap, clap. The sound must reach through the floor above. Clap! Clap! Clap!

Silence. Then, a low giggle from his room.

There. There it is again. Those little bubbly fizzes tickling my soul.

~Rhonda Lane Phillips

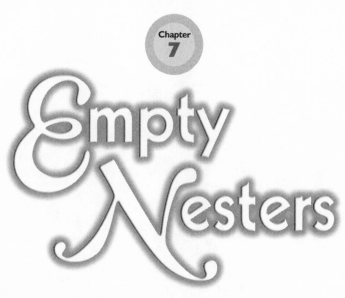

Branching Out

*You can clutch the past so tightly to your chest that it leaves your arms
too full to embrace the present.*
~Jan Glidewell

Silence

Your future depends on many things, but mostly on you.
~Frank Tyger

he house is suddenly cavernous and silent.

Beneath the decibels of arguing and excitement and frustration that once filled these rooms, the clock ticks and clicks in the living room. I can hear it from the bedroom at the back of the house. The refrigerator hums. A ghostly hand flips the light switches on and off. It is probably my imagination. I am not used to the silence.

I miss the sounds of the boys sleeping. The rustle of sheets and blankets kicked to the floor. Eddie's soft snores in the spring and fall when the air is full of pollen. David Scott mumbling in his sleep. I could count on the soft rise and fall of breathing from all three in the darkest hours of the night when sleep soothed away days full of homework and girlfriends and school. The sounds were a lullaby that eased me to sleep every night and without which there will be no sleep tonight.

There is still work to do, although not so much now. There is the house to clean, meals to cook, dishes to wash, groceries to buy, a yard to mow, and a large stack of books waiting to be read. The books waited patiently until there were no more demands on my time and I could sit and just read.

I read the same page over and over, waiting for something. I realize I am waiting to be interrupted by rips that need to be mended, shirts and jeans to iron, homework dilemmas to be solved, or arguments to referee. There is nothing but the ticking clock and the open book open on my lap, so I invite Connie for dinner.

"I've always wanted to have the time and the money to travel and just write."

Connie nods her head. "So, what's stopping you?"

"I can't afford it."

"Sure you can." My best friend's tone reminds me of a parent talking to a young child. She changes the subject. "How hard is it to set up your computer?"

"It's easy. The connections are color coded and…"

She interrupts. "Do you need anything special?"

"A phone line to connect to the Internet."

"Anything else?"

"Well, a high speed connection would be nice, but I don't have it here."

"Every motel has a phone and some of them have high speed connections."

"Yes, but…"

"But nothing." She interrupts again. "If you could afford to travel and write, you'd live in motels or hotels anyway."

"But I can't afford it. We went over this." Sometimes Connie was like a dog with a bone.

"So sell the house or rent it and hit the road. Take your job with you." Folding her arms across her chest, she waited for me to catch up.

The clocked ticked and clicked while excuses circled in my mind, but they were just excuses. "You're right. I could."

"What are you waiting for?"

"Winning the lottery."

"You don't need to win the lottery. You have a job you can take with you. You have direct deposit and you have your credit card. You pay your bills online or by phone. What are you waiting for?"

I hate it when Connie gets like this, the smug smile when she's right, but she's my best friend, my oldest friend, and even the devil should get her due once in a while.

Two weeks later, I fitted my computer neatly into the trunk of my car, organizing suitcases and books around the monitor and various parts. As I shut the trunk lid and went back into the house to make sure I hadn't forgotten anything, a wave of emotion took me by surprise. I expected fear, but not excitement. My heart pounded with a thrill of pending adventure I had not felt since the boys were young. The air was full of possibility.

After closing and locking the door, I got into the car and began the first leg of an adventure that took me to visit friends in Tennessee and then back to New Orleans to research an unsolved murder and disappearance from forty years earlier.

That was nearly a decade ago. In that time, I traveled to Florida in the winter, soaking up cold winds and chilling rains while running around town looking for a space heater. The murderous heat and mud rains of Dallas in the summer left me breathless. Torrential rains and spectacular frozen waterfalls of the Tennessee highlands dazzled me. The picture postcard haven of a bedroom community on the edge of the emerald necklace of parks and secret wildernesses surrounding Cleveland provided seclusion and peace. I visited and sampled the sights and sounds everywhere I traveled and finally came to rest in Colorado.

I fell in love with Colorado when my ex-husband and I were stationed at Lowry Air Force base over thirty years ago. This is where my oldest son was born and where I have always wanted to live.

Since coming back, I stayed for a while in the Denver suburbs, moving up into the mountains between Vail and Steamboat Springs to a cabin for a spell. Then I settled at the foot of Pikes Peak near the Garden of the Gods. My traveling days are far from over and I continue to work and write, but I do it from a converted Victorian, the mountains around Pikes Peak right outside my windows. Most mornings, it is quiet before the city and my neighbors wake. I look forward to the silence before beginning another busy day.

My boys all live on the shores of the Atlantic with their wives and their children. We keep in touch by e-mail and phone. Occasionally, I miss the arguments and constant demands that come with raising children. When I talk to my sons, my grandchildren clamor in the background, demanding attention.

I smile and wonder if one day my sons will pick up the threads of their own dreams when their children move out into the world. If not, I hope a good friend reminds them that no dream, not even old ones packed in mothballs, is out of reach when the silence deafens them.

~Jackie M. Cornwell

Learning to Fly

That which the fountain sends forth, returns to the fountain.
~Longfellow

A tinge of fear and a shiver runs through me as I stare at the date circled in red on the kitchen calendar. Inside the circle are two words emblazoned in capital letters: MOVING DAY.

My life will change drastically in exactly two weeks, because my husband and I have sold the home we've dwelled in for almost twenty years and we are moving to a condo. It's just the two of us.

My husband has an exciting job and feels fulfilled. But I retired a month ago, due to a large conglomerate gobbling my employer of twenty years. What am I going to do with my life?

It's not easy to sort old keepsakes and decide what we'll keep and what we'll donate to a charitable organization. Time is slipping by too quickly, and I feel overwhelmed by all that's left to do.

The garage is my husband's domain, but I remember I have a few things stored there, too. I scan the rafters above and spot a big black blob tucked away in plastic. I climb the ladder and toss the bag to the garage floor. I remove the plastic and ease myself down to sit in the old chair one last time. It's been years since the beanbag chair was in Nick's bedroom. My chest tightens, I feel a slight tug, and my heart aches a little. As I hold my head in my hands and try to choke back the tears, my mind swirls with memories.

My first inkling of my only son's wild imagination was when

he was three-and-a-half and enthralled with *The Wizard of Oz*. After watching his first television broadcast of the show, he ran into the kitchen straddling my new broom. He gulped for air between sobs and whined, "The broom won't fly. The broom won't fly."

I could barely contain my laughter, but I did. It took a while to console him, but he accepted my explanation that flying on a broom was only make-believe.

However, Nick's imagination soared. After watching a production of *Peter Pan*, he obsessed over the elfin-like boy who loved to fly and refused to grow up.

"Mommy, I'm not sleepy," Nick said, as I tucked him in that night. "When I close my eyes, I can see myself flying across the sky." I kissed his forehead and assured him he'd fall asleep soon.

The next morning, I was awakened by a loud thud. Immediately, I raced to Nick's bedroom.

"I learned to fly!" he announced.

He'd leaped from his top bunk bed into the black beanbag chair, splitting the seam I'd recently repaired. There he sat, covered with hundreds of tiny, white foam beans, grinning sheepishly, his cheeks flushed, the thrill of success making his blue eyes brighter than usual.

That incident ended Nick's interest in physically learning to fly, but it didn't deter his passion for musical theater—a passion that continued to evolve from kindergarten through high school. During his first year of college, Nick was offered a role in a national touring company of *A Chorus Line*. He asked us if he could choose performing over college.

"Pursue your dream. Go for it." We gave our blessings and proudly watched his career flourish.

Our house was empty much sooner than we'd planned. To ease our anguish, we focused on our jobs during the week, and as often as possible took weekend getaways and watched him perform.

Suddenly, the garage door opens, thrusting me back to reality.

"Surprise!" Nick shouts. "I have a couple of days off from the show. Thought you could use my help—I can help you pack."

"Oh, I am glad you came! It's going to be difficult for me to part with this old beanbag chair. Would you like to sit in it one more time?"

He plops his lanky frame into the beanbag chair and we laugh as the patched seam gives way. Foam beans escape, some flying about, others spilling onto the garage floor.

"Just like old times," Nick says. "Don't worry, I'm cleaning up this mess and tossing the chair in the dumpster."

Relieved, I give him a quick hug, and confide that I'm engulfed with memories I want to share and how I long to write fulltime now that I am retired. "But I'm afraid to give it a try."

"Mom, you always gave me free rein to indulge my imagination and reach my goals. Now it's my turn to support you. Go for it!"

That was thirteen years ago. Since then I have learned that an empty nest is a time to spread one's wings. I have learned to fly.

~Georgia A. Hubley

Reprinted by permission of Randell Kruback
© 2007.

81

A Different Drummer

Life is good, life is big.
Life beats a rhythm in every heart that beckons each of us
to join the dance.
~Annie Danielson

For years, I volunteered for school and civic projects. I chauffeured our daughters and their friends to meetings, endured their noisy sleepovers, survived their driving lessons without losing my sanity, and lost sleep lying awake nights until they arrived home safely from dates.

And I thrived on the frantic routine of raising them.

Yet after they left home and married, I didn't suffer the oh-so-common melancholy as did many of my friends. No, not me.

Oh, I'll admit at first I missed the drumming commotion of televisions and stereos blaring, phones ringing, and girls giggling as they raided pantry and refrigerator. But I didn't miss hours spent on laundry, ironing, and housecleaning. Now I was free to travel with my husband and resume our newlywed lifestyle.

I relished the luxury of uninterrupted time to pursue some of my favorite interests: music, sewing, and reading. One day, while researching Mideast cultures, I discovered belly dancing was a *danse du ventre* that dated to Biblical times. Envisioning its rousing movements, I was startled to learn it was considered a folk dance in some countries.

Hmmm. This could be interesting, I thought.

Its stimulating arm and body motions could firm my sagging muscles and redistribute middle-age weight. After more research, I decided its erotic moves might even be a good way to trim unwanted cellulite. Where could I learn how?

When I contacted our local Parks and Recreation Department, the woman on the other end of the phone actually snickered at my request before she finally took me seriously.

"In order to justify the expense of a teacher you'll need to sign up at least fifteen women." Her voice left me with the impression that she didn't think my idea was worth pursuing.

Fortunately, my neighbors did. By day's end, I had the required signatures. I took my petition to the recreation department and within a week, not one, but three classes were filled.

Mysterious Arabian music saturated the room at each lesson. We undulated to the passionate rhythms of zithers, tambourines, drums, flutes, and mandolins. We practiced serpentine arm and torso movements. We perfected the art of head slides, camel walks, and scooting shimmies.

Our instructor emphasized belly dancing as sensual and filled with emotion and stressed the importance of traditional attire.

Hmmm. Since I enjoy sewing maybe I should make a costume, I thought.

Referencing a costume book, I bought a blue two-piece bikini and shopped for sheer, matching material. I also bought a tape of stirring belly-dancing music and played it over and over, memorizing the two-two and two-four beat while I sewed pearls and rhinestones on my bodice, veil, and skirt band.

Without telling my husband, I juggled a secret schedule: attending classes, practicing, and sewing while he was at work. By the time lessons ended, I had mastered a fairly respectable dance routine. I plotted my debut several months later when my unsuspecting husband returned from a business trip.

As soon as I heard the grinding sound of the garage door opening, I clicked on the stereo and positioned myself strategically at the top of the stairs. Arrayed in a costume complete with dangling ear-rings and clinking bracelets and necklaces, I struck a sultry pose. I fluttered my eyelashes and performed abdominal flutters to the thrumming of exotic music.

My husband paused at the entry level — dropped both his jaw and his luggage — and leaned on the banister for the full effect. Grinning ear-to-ear, he watched my sinuous hip rolls, circles, and thrusts — a provocative display of everything I'd learned and rehearsed.

When the music and the movements ended, he dashed up the stairs, swept me into his arms... and whisked me off to our bedroom.

No, mourning the kids was never much of a problem for me. I simply danced to a different drummer.

~Sally Kelly-Engeman

82

Paris When It Sizzles

"Pinch me," says Susan as we cross the Seine from the Left Bank to face the sun-drenched Gothic towers of Notre Dame. "I can't believe we're back here."

We peel off jackets and join the throngs of tourists outside the cathedral. Despite Cole Porter's claim to love Paris in the summer, when it sizzles, it's only April and the temperature this afternoon hovers near eighty.

We'd visited Paris at earlier stages of our lives, but this trip is different, and our lives have changed. Back home, we left behind an empty nest. Our kids are no longer teenagers and have their own lives. Oddly, our only agenda now is to enjoy a relaxing week together in the City of Light — and to find each other again on our first trip alone in many years.

We sit on the wall facing Notre Dame and embrace like a pair of young lovers in a Cartier-Bresson photograph. "Thank you for bringing me here," Susan whispers as she nuzzles my neck.

We wander through the warm streets of the Left Bank and rest in the shade of the Luxembourg Gardens, where we recall renting little boats for our kids to sail on the pond. Having them grown and gone has been particularly difficult for me; being Dad was always my favorite job. On this trip, I'm certain, we'll revisit some of the places we once took them: Chartres, the Musee d'Orsay, the Louvre, Giverny, the Rodin Museum.

The timing of our trip is a bit odd. Two months before, I

celebrated my fifty-tenth birthday, but my freelance career is sputtering at low ebb, and work and cash are hard to come by. On the other hand, two of our closest friends have recently been diagnosed with cancer and started chemotherapy. Life and good health feel precious. Seize the time, I tell myself. Besides, we have lots of credit, more than we should ever use.

We've been lucky. On a business trip to Paris several months before, I reconnected with a cousin who offered me the small studio apartment he and his French wife keep for guests. So we cashed in 100,000 frequent flier miles for our roundtrip tickets and made plans to farm out the dog.

On the hottest day of our visit, we stroll into the Tuileries Gardens. A young couple occupies a wall near the Place de la Concorde, limbs entwined. We head for an empty bench, but it seems all of Paris is out today in the fine weather, and a young family sprints ahead to beat us to the seating. After several similar failures, we secure a bench in the shade and pass the time watching the parade of humanity and reading our books, both set in Paris. Soon I get drowsy, recline on the bench, and snooze with my head in her lap as she strokes my hair.

We visit Montmartre, shocked by the densely packed tourists patronizing the portrait artists in the square, even mid-week in the spring. We walk for hours across the city on another steamy day, down the Boulevard de Magenta, through the bridal and formal clothing districts, and eventually meet Cousin David for falafels in the Marais.

One day, I get a call from Eric, a Parisian colleague of mine who invites us on an outing. They graciously take us into their home for champagne and then out for lunch to a guinguette, a traditional cabaret/restaurant on the banks of the Marne. As we watch Eric and his wife Paule, both in their forties with young children, we see ourselves years before. We were older parents, too, working professionals thoroughly immersed in the job of raising kids. Paule tells us she often gets home late from work and uses familiar shortcuts to prepare meals.

Would parenting have been easier if we'd done it when we were younger? Certainly we might have had more stamina for the sleep-torture inflicted by our infants. Were we ready? Absolutely not. Do I want to go through it again? No way, but I wouldn't trade the experience for anything.

In the end, we revisit few of the places we took our kids. We linger in bed each morning, getting a late start on our touring, but relishing each other's company. Years before, the summer after I graduated from high school, my parents went to Europe for the first time. Their first trip ignited a mutual passion for travel that took my parents to many countries in the ensuing years.

I was the younger child in my family, about to flee the nest, but I had no clue that my folks were grieving, in their own way, for the tight family we had been… until the same thing happened to Susan and me. Now I understand their desire to travel. I think about them frequently as we swelter on our way to the Picasso Museum, near the end of our stay in Paris.

We walk to the Seine late in the day and hop a ride on the Bateaux Mouches. The cool air on the river is refreshing as the sun sets behind the city.

"You're my life," says Susan as she squeezes my hand. Porter's haunting lyrics sneak back into my consciousness and I concur: I love Paris every moment, every moment of the year. We sit very close, embrace in this most romantic setting, and face the future together.

~Bill Zarchy

83

A Slice of Paradise

It is a far, far better thing that I do, than I have ever done;
it is a far, far better rest that I go to, than I have ever known.
~Charles Dickens

I t's said that if you spread your bundles of joy with a few years in-between, they won't abandon you all at once. I'm not sure how Ken and I managed it, but the good Lord must have lent a hand as the kids left in tolerable stages.

Our son was born six years ahead of our daughters. My men had close times with all their guy stuff, while the girls and I were involved in perpetual tea parties, dance lessons, and Girl Scouts. After a little arm-twisting and greasing his palm, our son became a fine built-in babysitter. No more packing a half-asleep sitter into the car and driving her across town after midnight.

The day came when our son, his mini fridge, and his truck went off to college—followed by a stint in the military. But for two smart and spirited teenyboppers keeping us on our toes, we'd have been as homesick for him as he was for us.

A mere two grades apart, the girls savored their own special friends. Sports and cheerleading became their lives as they, too, sailed right past us, but always saving Sunday for family fun.

Then suddenly, no more relaxing on Saturdays with pancakes in the shape of bunnies and bears, or giggly campouts in the backyard playhouse. No more carpools with half a dozen dusty ball players, their bags, and overflowing Slurpies. No more freaky music that fairly rocked the house off its moorings. No more endless hours of clandestine phone calls.

When the older daughter hit the college dorms, I looked forward to less laundry. But her big laundry bag appeared in our hallway more often than not. The grocery bill looked like the national debt after numerous weekends of roommates and college chums rolling out sleeping bags upstairs and down.

The second daughter finished college, got married, and cast off to new horizons as we waved and threw weepy kisses. They had grown up, giving pleasure to replace any pain of their teen years. That made it all so worthwhile.

Ken and I looked at each other like strangers, barely knowing how to act in the sobering silence of our big deserted house. It was soon apparent that nobody left was handy with yard chores and window washing. We rattled about, living with empty rooms that cried out for fun, tempestuous moments, and raging hormones.

Finally, I took the bull by the horns, called our realtor, and viewed a glorious piece of wooded and streamed acreage teeming with wildlife. We had dreamed about a log home in the mountains only twenty minutes from town. So we did it. We kicked our traces. The old house in town sold with grand memories and no regrets. Now we were land owners with our own paradise.

I drew plans and ordered logs. Suddenly, along came our brood with their campers on more weekends than we could count. They helped us with the logs, the windows, the doors, and the roof, until three months later our son and his dad drove in the last spikes atop the loft. What was supposed to be a log cabin turned into a family lodge for any-and-all who cared to stay and saddle a bronc. We forged a homestead in God's wilderness that has kept our children returning and loving every minute of their parents' grit.

So the question arises... were we ever really empty nesters? Yes, but we unwittingly and happily waylaid its onset. We've sat and rocked in front of the fire on two-dog nights, swapping old times and old photos back and forth with adult children. What a grand celebration of a new lifestyle as I flipped a bunny pancake for our first grandbaby.

We sometimes yearn for the sleepless nights when the children were out; now it's our backs and knees that are out. Occasionally, the nest feels emptier than we like. We miss those magnificent beings we so lovingly shaped and molded into success stories. But we take some pleasure and pride in knowing we were adequate role models.

Not long ago I heard our youngest daughter remark, "I have every intention of raising my kids just like I was raised."

For us, that says it all.

~Kathe Campbell

84

Oh What A Trip

When our twin sons threw their caps in the air at their convocation ceremonies, my husband did the same with his empty wallet. It was more than a Kodak moment. It was a snapshot of the past, the present, and the future — in vivid color.

I wish I could say I was in the pictures, standing proudly between my tassel-capped twins, Mark and Matthew, but I wasn't. I was back home, one thousand miles away, recovering from surgery. I'll get over it… some day. Rick, bless his heart, taped both ceremonies for me.

About a month after they left home, Rick and I visited them on campus. (How else is a mother to know what her kids are up to?) The boys gave us guided tours of their dorm rooms (which took about three seconds), the campus, and the town. What I saw curbed my anxieties; what I didn't see, I tried not to think about.

I'd had nearly a quarter of a century to prepare myself for this bittersweet event when Mark and Matthew would leave home. It's not fair. Just when crow's feet and saggy skin were starting to take over my body, nature dealt me another blow: My first- and second-born left the nest.

Our children, all four of them, were a pain in utero (once they arrived, they were pure joy, naturally). I have suppressed the memories of months of nausea, high blood pressure, and blood-curdling screams (mine, not theirs) during their births. Held dearer in my memory are their smiling cherub faces, breastfeeding, preschool, soccer games, award ceremonies, and the ups and downs of parenting teenagers. Myriad remembrances still flood back. (Proof that my memory, at least, still works.)

When our twins left home to attend university, I cried copiously, starting months before their departure. Had I known they'd come back every summer and every Christmas holiday until their graduation, I would have used fewer tissues and saved a tree or two.

Mark and Matthew returned home three consecutive summers. On their last trip back, they brought two Golden Retriever puppies. I dog-sat while the boys were at work. (In addition to caring for the gecko, bird, and fish they left with me earlier.) At the end of the summer, I kissed the boys and the pups goodbye. For one silly little moment, it was a toss-up as to whom I would miss most—the kids or the dogs. The gecko, bird, and fish remain in my tender care until their passing, or until the boys reclaim them, whichever comes first.

Now, with our youngest child a year away from university, Rick and I are making plans for the next stage of our lives. He recently bought a pickup, and now he's eyeing fifth-wheel travel trailers. Occasionally, I catch him salivating over travel brochures on Alaska and the Yukon. I'm salivating over my own—on Hawaii and Tahiti, or anyplace involving bare feet on sandy beaches. Aahh… those warm, exotic beaches. I can see them; I can feel them; my feet are digging in the warm, seductive sand.

Wait a minute…

What's with the dreamy, far-away look in Rick's eyes? Are those lights dancing in his eyes a reflection of the Northern Lights—or some place involving snowshoes?

Oh well, the point is, with an empty nest behind us we'll be able to go whenever we want… wherever we want.

Gee. I hope the kids keep their porch lights on. We wouldn't want our RV to run over anything when we pull up in their driveways.

~Chantal Meijer

85

On Edge

"Well, that's the last of it," said Mom as she slammed the door of the U-Haul.

I put my arms around her and hugged tight. I was thrilled to have landed a new job, but hesitant because the company was two hours southeast of home—and my mother—in Oklahoma City. With my sister away at college, how would Mom manage all alone? Without us living here?

Our parents divorced when my sister Shelby was in preschool and I was a first grader. For the last twenty years, it had been just the three of us. Mom always put us girls first. When we ate out on payday every other Friday, Shelby and I took turns choosing the restaurants. Vacations were spent at amusement parks or other kid-friendly destinations. When we moved into a new house, Mom insisted she preferred the smallest bedroom for herself. She wasn't interested in activities outside of work and the idea of dating never entered her mind.

Or so I thought.

"I gassed up your tank so you should be able to drive straight through," Mom said with a smile.

"Are you worried about me being on the highway in this weather?" I asked. "The forecasters are predicting a snowstorm."

"Aw, it never snows that heavily in Oklahoma," she answered, practically pushing me into the driver's seat. "Leave now and you'll be cozy in your new apartment by the time the flurries start. Love you. Bye."

She hurried into the house. She didn't even look back. It was almost as if she were eager for me to leave.

For the next few weeks, I was busy. I settled into my new apartment. I worked extra hours at my job. It didn't occur to me that I hadn't talked to Mom in a few days. Then I realized she must be lonely and wondering why I hadn't made time for her.

After work that evening I called, but the answering machine picked up. I looked at my watch. Funny, she's usually home by six. When thirty minutes went by and she didn't return my call, I dialed again. No answer. Oh no, something's happened! I called four more times. Where could she be?

At 8:45 P.M., my phone rang.

"Stephanie, what's wrong?" asked Mom, her voice thick with concern.

"Nothing's wrong with me. Why haven't you been answering the phone?"

Mom sighed. "For heavens sake, I thought something was the matter."

"No, you just didn't answer. What were you doing?"

She hesitated. "I went out to eat with a friend." Her voice held an odd lilt. "I joined a singles group a few weeks ago. I'm meeting the nicest people. And tonight, I had a date with…"

Mom kept chattering, but I'd stopped listening.

My forty-five-year-old mother on a date? I collapsed on the sofa like a rag doll.

When she finally took a breath, I interjected, "Glad you're okay. Gotta get up early tomorrow. Love you. Bye."

I couldn't sleep that night. A singles group? Dating? Next she'd have a boyfriend!

A few weeks later, Mom drove down and met me for dinner. Her ulterior motive was to introduce me to her Special Someone. He seemed okay, but I didn't understand why Mom wanted to date. After all, she had Shelby and me. Why would she need someone else in her life? And the two of them gazed into each other's eyes like love-struck high schoolers.

Then the holidays arrived. Mom brought him to the family Thanksgiving dinner. After the dishes were washed, I cornered Grandma in the bedroom.

"They seem to be getting serious," I complained. "You don't think they'll get married, do you?"

Grandma grinned like she was pleased with the notion. "Stephanie, your mom is a young woman. She deserves some happiness now."

"But she was perfectly happy before!" I flailed my arms in the air to make my point.

Grandma put her hands on my shoulders. "Honey, it's okay. Just because your mother has a boyfriend doesn't mean she loves you any less."

I sat on the bed. Grandma took my hands in hers. "You and Shelby are young women now with lives of your own. Pretty soon you will marry and have children. Your mom is making a new life for herself, too." Grandma's explanation was as soft as her smile. "Trust me. She has enough love for all of us."

I nodded my head. "It's just so hard. Everything's going to change."

"Just because life changes doesn't mean it will be for the worse." Grandma put her arm around me and we walked into the living room. Mom and her beau sat surrounded by aunts, uncles, and cousins. Her eyes sparkled as she laughed and talked.

For the first time, I saw her not only as my mother, but as a woman. A woman who, much like me, was on the verge of starting an exciting new phase of her life, ready to fly.

And I understood.

~Stephanie Welcher Thompson

Headed to Hollywood

In 1980, with a two-year-old on my hip, I decided to take the biggest risk we had ever taken.

"Let's sell our house and move to Hollywood," I said to my husband. "It's time to take our dreams seriously."

His eyes lit up. "Are you serious?"

"Yes! All you've ever wanted to do is make movies, and all I want to do is sing. Let's go for it."

Rich had to drive through snow most days to repair telephones, while I sang radio commercials at a local recording studio. We were aching for something more in our lives.

"You're on, get the For Sale sign!" He said.

Six months later, we pulled into Los Angeles with a truck full of furniture and an apartment next to the YMCA.

"I'll be a star in six months. There are record companies on every corner," I crooned.

But first, Rich had to register for film classes at night school.

"My teacher is a Hollywood director," Rich announced after the first class. "He's going to let us film a fake TV commercial for our assignment. You can't believe the cameras and mics we get to use!"

I waited for him after school in the six-story parking garage. And I found work singing commercials, recorded a demo, and waited for a record company to call me.

"I'm twenty-three years old," I complained one day. "I'm almost past my prime. What's taking so long?"

Sirens blared in front of our apartment nightly, and every morning, a homeless woman picked through the dumpster. That first summer, temperatures soared to one hundred degrees. Rich battled heat and traffic on his job repairing telephones and hurried to school each evening. We were in deep debt and dreamed of a backyard with a swing set for little Chris. There was a toddler play yard in our complex: One swing on a square of grass with a fence around it. Pathetic.

"Let's drive up the coast," Rich said one Saturday. "We gotta get out of this heat."

Forty minutes north of Hollywood we came upon something amazing.

"What is this place?" Rich asked.

He exited into a little village with tree-lined streets, fountains and flowers; lovely homes with palm trees, stone walkways and a lake—an actual body of water, cool and clear, with kids fishing from the shore. Flowers lined the shops and a little bakery with tables sat out front. We stepped out of the car and gasped.

"It's not as hot here. It's like we're on vacation somewhere gorgeous," I said.

We went in and eyed the amazing pastries under glass.

"Two of everything you got." Rich laughed as he approached the counter.

"Cookie!" Chris yelled with glee.

We sat outside and ate chocolate-dipped croissants as the scent of honeysuckle filled the air.

"Umm. Let's just live here," I suggested with a sigh.

"This place is awesome," Rich agreed. "I want to drive around and explore."

We made a ritual of it. Most Saturdays, we headed north until the city disappeared and the hills turned green. We ate pastries and fantasized about living there. One weekend we even went to a realtor's open house. The model was modest but cost three times more than our starter home back in the cold Midwest.

"I wish I could buy this stucco house for you." Rich stared at the palm tree standing sentinel.

"Why don't we pray for a miracle?" I suggested. "God could give us that house. I could get a recording contract or you could work on a movie, or who knows? Let's just pray."

As we sat in the car, we asked God to let us buy that house and live in beautiful Westlake Village.

Eighteen months later, we moved. Not to the house in Westlake, but back to the cold. In debt up to our ears and completely discouraged, we'd been eaten up by a city that spits out dreamers on a regular basis.

A little brother for Chris came the following year, and we raised our sons in a small town in Colorado where houses were cheap and there were backyards with swing sets. We went through sixteen winters, three sets of skis, and fourteen windshields that cracked every time we drove to the mountains behind a gravel-spitting snowplow.

In 2001, our younger son graduated from Rocky Mountain High. A college dorm and life out of state called to him, and he answered. By August, like his older brother, he was gone.

One evening the phone rang.

"I'm not coming home this summer," he said. "I got this college internship. Isn't it exciting? I don't have to come home!"

"Oh, that's wonderful." I choked back tears.

I hung up the phone. "He's not coming home," I said. "What are we doing here? Why are we rattling around this big house? Even the boys don't want to live here."

Rich put his arms around me. "Now don't cry. This whole thing began with just you and me, remember? Now where were we? Weren't you and I following some kind of dream at one time?"

"You know what I'm thinking?" I said.

"What?"

"I'm thinking we go back to Los Angeles and do what we love. All you've ever wanted to do is make movies, and I can write or teach theater. What the heck are we waiting around here for?"

Rich sighed deeply. "I may be fifty, but I ain't done yet!"

It's now been five years since we packed our children's bedrooms into boxes and moved to the West Coast. Last year, Rich won his third Telly Award for his work on a TV commercial, while I've been publishing stories and teaching drama.

Less than two miles from the model home where we prayed thirty years ago, we bought a stucco ranch with a palm tree. On Saturdays, we walk down to the corner bakery and enjoy a scone, sitting under the exact California oak where we sat before. Little did we know God was unfolding a joyous plan he had reserved for us in a magical little town called Westlake. All because a man in his fifties wasn't afraid to say, "I ain't done yet!"

~Carla Riehl

Taking Note

Birds sing after a storm;
why shouldn't people feel as free to delight in
whatever sunlight remains in them?
~Rose Kennedy

The dark thoughts lingered, like storm clouds that splattered rain against the windows of my hollow house. I missed caring for my three children, now grown with children of their own. I no longer felt needed or productive.

Free time—so elusive during days of PTA meetings, endless laundry, and sibling squabbles—was now a challenge during these golden days of freedom. I was reluctant to be the senior citizen who says, "I'm very busy! I have a doctor's appointment in three weeks." Even though I exercised, attended social events, and worked in my rose garden, the truth was, I wasn't as active as I used to be... and I missed it.

To fill my days, I cleaned cupboards that didn't need it, organized closets I'd straightened recently, and polished silver I never used. This rainy day, I cleaned the drawers in my desk, hoping the task would somehow organize my thoughts. I sharpened pencils, threw out old calendars, and updated my address book. When I worked my way to the bottom drawer, I discovered a stash of forgotten notes and cards I had collected over the years. In case I decided to save them, I located a scrapbook with a red rose on the cover and brought it to the desk.

I recognized Steven's familiar scrawl on a Mother's Day card. "I am so proud of you and your accomplishments. Thanks for raising a great brood of children."

A note from Betsy said, "Thanks for making such an effort to come see us. You're so thoughtful and we appreciate you so much."

Lori, a mother of five children under the age of eight, wrote, "We can't thank you enough for all your help these past ten days. What a relief to know the kids were in good hands while we were away. You plugged into so many areas."

I spied my husband's handwriting on a card that once accompanied a floral arrangement. "I missed you and I love you. Jim."

"I enjoy having you in our ladies' Bible study," said a note from the leader. "Thank you for sharing yourself and your wisdom with us!"

And there were more.

Time slipped away, the rain stopped, and the sun began to peek through fluffy clouds. As I continued to read the warm thoughts from family and friends, I was touched by their appreciation for holiday dinners, birthday celebrations, and the needs I had met. I added these precious memories to my scrapbook and smiled as I remembered those happy times when I touched the lives of others. Now, their loving thoughts were comforting me when I needed a tender touch. I finished, then put the scrapbook away, knowing I would open it again on days when gray clouds filled my soul.

I decided it was time to get out of the house and focus on new ways to serve others.

I volunteered to deliver Meals on Wheels to shut-ins, raise funds for charities, and become secretary of our neighborhood association. I mentored aspiring authors in my writing group and sent notes of encouragement and appreciation to family and friends. I abandoned my routine for several months to nurture my daughter, Betsy, through a difficult pregnancy. I helped my daughter-in-law care for her premature baby. Over time, my cupboards looked messy, my rose garden sprouted weeds, and my silver tarnished.

As I attacked the weeds early one morning, I marveled at a dew-sprinkled rosebud. Soon, it would reach its prime and fade; its petals

would wrinkle and fall. But the rose would continue to bring pleasure—when I gathered the petals to arrange in a crystal bowl and
enjoy their dried fragrance.

And I suddenly understood the symbolism: I may no longer be
a rosebud, but I can be potpourri!

~Miriam Hill

The Exodus

Vision is not enough; it must be combined with venture.
It is not enough to stare up the steps; we must step up the stairs.
~Vaclav

great victory had been won.

Convincing my father to pull up his California roots and move to Oklahoma hadn't been easy for my mother, but somehow she managed. She could hardly believe it herself. She was finally going home to the Heartland of her youth.

And why shouldn't she embark on this new journey? With my older sister living on her own and me off at college, she saw no reason to sit and pine for her children. Not that she didn't miss us. Already she had found countless reasons to visit, lugging bags of food and household supplies to our doorsteps.

Mom refused to surrender to the Empty Nest Syndrome (ENS) — at least in the traditional sense — as so many of her friends had done. No, she decided to fill her maternal void by forging a new chapter of her life. This time would be for her and my father, a chance to start over.

A strong, determined woman, she turned her dreams into reality almost at once. The Pioneer Spirit also proved catchy among other family members. Smitten by the prospect of adventure and road dust, these aunts, uncles, and cousins happily packed their bags, sold their homes, and joined the southbound caravan. Yessirree, the Great

Exodus was shaping into epic proportions. Sort of like *The Grapes of Wrath*, only in reverse. And with U-Hauls and AAA insurance.

Back again in the Sooner State, Mom wasted no time securing property and a new house built to her own specifications. In his letters, Dad described her as "a woman possessed" and "a firecracker."

He was right. The first time I saw the new homestead a year later, I was in awe. The sprawling house offered much more room than our cramped A-frame on a tennis court-sized lot back in Los Angeles. Plus, Mom was now surrounded by a lush landscape of winding lawn, woods, and a huge vegetable garden. She built a fence with an attached pen in case she decided to add livestock in the future!

I was so thrilled for my mother. She could enjoy a higher standard of life, with some serious room to stretch and play. I also saw other dimensions to her, talents she kept hidden during my childhood. I couldn't remember seeing her happier than she was in the country, back in her own element. In fact, over the next ten years, my mother doted on her new home like a fussing parent; I even joked that she had replaced her children with a different offspring—her personal Tara.

A decade later, when a doctor delivered his grim prognosis—she was dying of brain cancer and only had weeks to live—she decided to stay at home and forego useless treatments. This was where she wanted to die, she told us, on her own land, in her own home. So a hospice nurse was secured and Mom, surrounded by her devoted family at the lovely, dream home she had designed, passed away peacefully one chilly December afternoon.

Before her death, my mother said something I will never forget. "Be lucky like me. Have people around you and a place you love to call your own. Then you will never be lonely or sad."

Her message was a lesson, a living illustration of strength in the midst of despair. My mother taught by example: Her decision to transform her ENS into a dynamic journey of self-growth and determination was the greatest gift she could have given us.

~Al Serradell

Stepping Out

There is a bit of insanity in dancing
that does everybody a great deal of good.
~Edwin Denby

When our youngest son left for college, I was suddenly conscious of the differences. When I hung towels, they stayed hung. No textbooks cascaded from the end table. No one barged in the door yelling, "Mom, I need the car!" while I was on a long distance call.

I could take a box of crackers from the cupboard and find more than a handful of crumbs. I could pour a glass of milk from the carton without wondering if I should strain it. Food stayed in the refrigerator for unconscionable periods of time. In fact, I discovered cheese could dry to a rubberized state.

I reveled in the change.

But gradually, I realized there was something I missed. Gangly bodies draped over the furniture. Lively chatter. Wry comments on current events. Witty names for everyday objects—a whole different language. I missed the laughter, the fun, being part of a happening world.

I realized my husband and I were in danger. Our life was so comfortable and predictable that we would soon be fossils: Mr. and Mrs. Curmudgeon, grumping from morning to night that the newspaper wasn't thrown on the porch. That fresh fruit doesn't taste like it used to. That neighborhood kids won't stay off the grass. It was an awful picture.

What we needed, I decided, was to get a life!

So I signed us up for dance classes. And, since a friend signed up with me and each husband was told the other had already agreed, we found ourselves in the mirrored basement of a couple who expected to teach us the Texas Two-Step. Theirs was a Texas-sized challenge. But they looked kind of cute in their boots and denim, and they also looked like they were having fun.

First came basic instructions:

"Face each other. Stagger your feet. You both cannot stand on the same piece of floor at the same time. You have to take turns," she said.

"Your feet should never leave your legs," he said.

Comedian, I thought.

"Men step forward on your left foot. Ladies step back on your right. Keep your knees bent," she said.

"No wooden legs," he said.

That's what you think, I thought.

Following instructions, we clasped each other in a death grip and muttered under our breaths. "Sloooow, sloooow, quick quick. Slooow, slooow, quick quick."

No one watched; the others were busy conducting their own personal scrimmage.

Slow-Slow-Quick-Quick was followed by Ladies Underarm Turn. When we managed that without strangulation, the teacher introduced us to Horseshoe.

"Arms firm but not stiff," she said.

"No spaghetti arms! Stop that loosey goosey," he said

Easy for you to say, I thought.

What's more we were expected to make eye contact… with each other… and smile.

Sometimes our expressions were anything but friendly. There were whispered comments.

"Not that foot!"

"I'm supposed to be here!"

"How can I do this when you're doing that?"

As the evening wore on, we wore out. The teachers divided the couples to teach a line dance. Each of us was on his own. We learned to Vine Right: right, behind, right. And Vine Left: left, behind, left. Hop, we could handle. Stomp came quite naturally. We could even hop and clap at the same time! We could feel the rhythm. We laughed. We were having fun—together!

There was no talk about skipping the next lesson. We finished the session. We took another class and learned the Triple Step. With Lariats. We learned the Cotton-Eyed Joe, with Cross Kicks. We learned the County Line Cha Cha, with Military Turns. We learned the Tush Push, with… well, Tush Pushes.

When our kids called, we had something to talk about. We kept them in stitches. Sometimes they couldn't understand. They raised their brows when my husband bought cowboy boots for the first time in his life.

Then, pressured by friends, we found ourselves in square dance lessons. Learning the calls exercised our brains; executing them exercised our brains and our bodies. We added to our own special language. Now it included Do Passo, Half Sashay, See Saw, and Tea Cup Chain.

I bought a couple of full skirts and dance shoes. They looked like the Mary Janes I wore in grade school. I started to wear prairie skirts. My husband got into bolo ties. I felt like I was in disguise, but we were having fun.

Our circle of friends widened and deepened. Our schedule is so full the kids ask, "When is a good time for us to visit?"

It's a whole new, happening world—and we are part of it. The therapy took. We got a life!

~Nancy M. Peterson

All Is Calm

I turned to search my husband's face as, together, we choked out the words to "Silent Night" on the drive home. Countless memories of singing this carol to Shelly at bedtime raced through my mind. Why hadn't we chosen "I Saw Mommy Kissing Santa Claus" instead?

"Please let's go to the Christmas cantata this month. It's *The Nativity*. I bought tickets." I waited for my husband to open my car door. "We haven't been to one in years. It will put us in the holiday mood."

Curt smiled and went around to his side of the car. "If I can get a nap in first."

This was our first holiday season alone as a couple. Our only child had moved away on Mother's Day weekend after marrying her college sweetheart. We lived in Florida; she lived in Seattle. We couldn't be farther apart. If it weren't for cell phones and unlimited minutes, I wasn't sure either of us could have survived this long.

We arrived for the eight o'clock showing, the last performance of twelve. Thankfully, we noticed some friends as we made our way to our seats. Their daughter had recently married but her husband was stationed in the military so she lived nearby. Tonight she played an angel in the show.

I couldn't help but remember the many cantatas Shelly and Curt had performed over the years. In the weeks leading up to Christmas, they spent long evenings rehearsing their lines while I applauded their efforts.

Someone tapped my shoulder. "Terri, I want you to meet our daughters and their families."

I turned around in my seat. A church friend sat with her two beautiful daughters and a son-in-law toting a sleepy toddler. "This is our grandson." She stroked his blond curls. They were a good-looking family, out for a special evening together.

"It's great to meet you all. How nice you can spend the holidays together." I glanced over their heads and was struck by how many family units were seated together or milling the aisles. Why on earth did we ever move away from our families back north? We'd lived in Florida for five years but always had our daughter with us. Our nest was as empty as the manger on the stage.

"It's starting… shhh." My husband nudged my arm. I refocused on the set and watched as the players gracefully took their places. The choir resonated from both sides while the angels bent forward from above.

And then they sang our song.

"Silent night…" More like silent days.

"All is calm…" Too calm and quiet.

"Mother and child…" Just the mother. No child. No one to shop with or ask for another wardrobe opinion.

I struggled with my heightened senses throughout the whole first stanza. Where had time gone? Shelly was supposed to be part of our lives—making us a whole family—not leaving two people alone. Especially at Christmas.

Curt reached for my hand. His grip was strong, as strong as the day we married. I turned to watch him swipe the dampness from his eyes and suddenly understood what a blessing I had beside me.

I didn't have to get lost in my own recollections. My husband of thirty years shared more than my memories; he shared my loneliness. We could reminisce together. And, together, we would share new experiences. We would create new memories.

Together. Just the two of us.

~Terri E. Tiffany

 **Home Sweet Nest**

*You can never go home again,
but the truth is you can never leave home,
so it's all right.*
~Maya Angelou

Hoops

I see them.
They command my attention
as I drive through the neighborhoods,
on my way to work, church, groceries.
The silent sentinels missing their youth.
Backboards faded.
Nets torn.
Rims bent.
Waiting to be used, restored or taken down.
Oh! To hear those sneakers slap the tarmac.
The bounce of the ball.
What a crowd used to gather!
Another sign of an empty nest.

~Peggy Vommaro

92

The Big Picture

We're watching a show on our new big screen TV. My husband and I are enjoying something or other, feet up on the new ottoman, the smell of paint still fresh.

We love the room. It's our romantic hideaway. No laundry, dressers, messy beds. Just our couch and chairs, a table for tea in the morning, and our new television.

"It's the first room we've ever had with all new furniture," I remind him, still amazed. We've been married for over thirty years and each of our rooms contains furniture from many, many years, some dating as far back as our individual apartments before we married.

But not this room. Everything is new, including the floor, the windows, the sliding door. We are in heaven. I just bought the last thing for the room, a furry rug for the old dog—one of the last remnants of our long life with children. And the old cat purring beside me, of course.

Ted's leg is up because of arthritis. I recently broke my foot, tripping on an old boot. No problem, we have our new ottoman.

"We've been around the block, the four of us," he says, looking at four content, well-worn elders.

The show is over and we're off to other activities. E-mail, likely. We've not quite decided what to call this new room. The Porch? The TV Room? We tried The Family Room, but that didn't quite fit since there are only the two of us left now that the kids are on their own.

The room is still new; it will find its name.

We swore, "No kids coming here with friends to watch football on this big screen."

The kids—young and working to make their way—don't have big screen TV yet. They have small children with early bedtimes. Not us, we smirk. Free at last!

When our favorite football team missed the Super Bowl by one game, we sighed in relief. "Whew! Now the kids won't want to watch our television." Super Bowl day came and went. We both peered out the window from time to time to see if their cars pulled up. "Just to check on the game anyway." They didn't.

We lost interest and watched something else.

Tonight we expect no children. We enjoy ourselves immensely in our new room. Getting ready for bed, I call downstairs to my husband, "Don't forget to turn out the lights in Tommy's old room."

I know that's a name that will stick—at least for awhile. The baby is gone and his room is ours. It took years for Jody's old room to be renamed Ted's Office and even when Sarah got married and moved away, her old room took a long time to be called The Guest Room.

Our romantic new room will take a long time to outgrow our last child and his legacy in our home. Maybe it doesn't matter, because our son will be back. They all will. After all, we own the best TV.

~Dorothy Firman

93

Moving On

Be patient with yourself.
Self-growth is tender; it's holy ground.
There's no greater investment.
~Stephen R. Covey

I recoiled at Dad's words and drew a deep breath, as if someone had socked me in the gut. I thought I must have misunderstood what he said.

Staring into his coffee cup, my father repeated his announcement that he wanted to sell, maybe move closer to town. "Since your mom's death," he confessed, "I just don't have the heart to live here any more."

He admitted the four-acre spread was too big for him to properly manage. He was ready to move on.

"But I'm not," I silently countered, still at a loss for words.

Even after putting my life on hold, a grown man such as me was content to live in his parents' home, to act as caregiver whenever the need arose. It had been a year since I'd received that chilling phone call ("Al, this is Dad. Your mother has... cancer.") and hopped the first Oklahoma-bound plane out of LAX. I had to see my mother, to support her as she battled a terrible disease.

After she died, I stayed to help Dad become independent, teaching him to cook, shop, do laundry—to live alone after thirty-odd years of marriage. Of course, I hadn't planned on staying for twelve months; I simply felt I was needed. Unfortunately, in the process, I had lost my independence and desire to leave.

Selling the house, I felt, was like disposing of the past, turning his back on his family—especially his wife. How could he want to leave this place, the culmination of their dreams? I recalled when, more than ten years ago, they had left the hustle and bustle of California city life for this quiet, rural town. With my sister and me grown, they started over. They purchased this property, built a house to Mom's specifications, and put their thumbprint all over it.

Their letters and phone calls were full of enthusiasm, like two middle-aged kids in the midst of a giant candy store. I was probably envious. I was in the city, my nose buried in a pile of college books, stressing over tuition and exams, and trying to prove myself every step of the way. And there they were, playing and having fun.

Now, everything had changed.

With my father's shocking announcement still ringing in my ears, I went for a walk around the grounds, hiking across the garden paths, to the edge of the woods. But I failed to experience the serenity, the peaceful beauty of my surroundings.

Something's missing, I realized. But what? I looked around at the familiar landscaping, confused.

The property wore the look of neglect. From the un-mown grass and shapeless hedges to the broken posts in the fence, my parents' yard was in shambles. An abandoned wheelbarrow and rake resting beneath the shade of a cottonwood tree told the story—Dad wasn't neglecting his work; he simply couldn't bring himself to do it anymore.

The yard work was something he'd shared with Mom. They enjoyed working outdoors. Together. Clearly those joyous tasks were now tedious chores.

I felt a second gut-punch as I realized Dad was right—he didn't have the heart to continue living and working here. Selling this property would not take away his memories. But the time had come for him—and me—to take those beautiful reminiscences and move forward. How selfish and unfair of me to expect him to stay here, a prisoner to his grief. He needed a fresh start, perhaps even a life with someone new.

I also understood how unhealthy it was for me to remain here, sheltered from my life and the world outside these gates.

I laughed to myself. At thirty, I suddenly felt as I had so long ago when I moved out and started life at a college dorm. I recalled my fears and doubts for the new chapter awaiting me, the strength I needed to take that first step.

I couldn't believe it: Years after I first left home, my parents were still teaching me to move on. To be a man.

~Al Serradell

94

Chicken Soup for the Soul

Home Improvements

Mistakes are the portals of discovery.
~James Joyce

Our only son moved into his own apartment and the company I worked for shut down. With no one to parent and no job to report to, I suddenly found myself at loose ends. Reluctant to face the rounds of interviews for a new job, I used my severance pay to tide me over.

After cleaning and reorganizing every cupboard in the house, I settled into a routine of housework and daytime TV programs, a lot of which were home décor and handyman shows. These people were magicians who could transform a tired, boring house into a showpiece in just a short time. It looked easy and effortless, something even I could manage.

Light, airy open space seemed popular on the shows. They knocked down and replaced walls in half an hour. What if I removed the wall between my dark entrance hall and the living room? It would be a nice surprise for my husband, Jim, who—although never handy about the house—possessed nearly every tool known to mankind.

I found the sledgehammer in the shed and stood in the hallway. After a few deep breaths, I summoned the courage to take a bash at the pristine wall. With that initial crack, I was committed.

The first few whacks came easily and the lathe and plaster fell smoothly away. But as a layer of fine dust settled over the room, it didn't seem so simple. I surveyed the hip-deep mess.

"This isn't the way it looks when they remodel on TV," I muttered.

I'd never seen the hosts sweat. Nor did they have dust and plaster clinging to their faces like I did. And I'd certainly never watched them clean up debris.

A big hole gaped in my wall; the stairs were obstructed by chunks of plaster. The damage was done. It wasn't as if Jim wouldn't notice.

"What can I do but go on?" My words echoed against the rubble.

Every hammer swing got harder and harder. It took about twenty more minutes before I truly regretted my decision and hated those smug people on television who obviously weren't showing the true details of what happens during a major remodel. No matter where I stepped, things dug into my feet. My shirt was torn. Every inch of my body ached.

By the time Jim got home, it looked like the house had taken a direct hit from a scud missile — and I had been the main target. Panic pinched his face, and he began to grumble. Something about supporting walls? Well, harrumph. The shows never mentioned those.

So, I dug into the rest of my severance money and spent it all… on a contractor we hired to finish the project.

Now our house is light, airy and open. Yet the living room doesn't seem as cozy and nothing stops a cold draught from sweeping through when someone comes to the front door in the dead of winter. I guess the shows don't focus on snug and practical, only on good looks.

In the end, I didn't learn much about renovating. But I learned a lot about moving beyond an empty nest. I learned there is a lot more to life than what appears on the surface. That when you try new things, you don't always get the results you want. That you should never stop trying. And that, sometimes, you have to start with the first hammer swing.

I am going to do so much better at my next project.

~Christine Kettle

95

Where's the Beef?

But when the time comes that a man has had his dinner,
then the true man comes to the surface.
~Mark Twain

Home. I hadn't been there for the past fifteen months. Everything had changed. The times, the streets, the weather. I traded Vietnam's hot and humid Mekong Delta for my wintry Colorado home. A home that had once been filled with three siblings, two dogs, a cat, three red-ear turtles, and my parents. All that remained were my parents and the dogs.

Politics and protests aside, I felt thankful but guilty to be home again. I felt thankful for a respite from the carnage that had taken a toll on my heart and mind; I felt guilty that my friends were still in harm's way.

My parents, although grateful to have me back, were a bit puzzled by some of my post-war behavior.

Loud, unexpected noises sent me to the floor looking for cover. Old, familiar things like refrigeration now seemed new. I often spent minutes at a time with my hands in the freezer compartment, just enjoying the wonderful, cold air.

The scents and sounds coming from the kitchen were one of the comforts of being back. My mother had gone all out to make sure this was a great homecoming. With my older brothers out of state at college and me in the Navy, the house had seemed empty to her. She knew I'd missed her cooking, so she had planned and shopped and baked. She prepared homemade delights, particularly yellow rice and chicken, my favorite.

What she didn't know was that I'd consumed too much chicken and rice in Vietnam; it was the last thing I wanted to eat at home. And my mother was startled when I drenched the entire plateful in Tabasco sauce. It was something I'd done overseas. We all did it, covering our C-RATs and proving the old GI culinary philosophy, "If it's hot enough, it'll kill the taste of most anything."

Later that night, I rose from my old familiar bed to raid the kitchen. After all, I figured my mother had filled it with things to tempt me.

I wasn't disappointed. Standing in the light of the refrigerator, I plucked two fresh eggs from the container and set them on the counter. I found bacon and a potato I peeled at lightning speed for homemade hash browns. There was bread for toast… but I hankered for something more. This was "real" food and I intended to make the most of it.

Scrounging further, I uncovered a Tupperware container that held the best treasure—some of my mother's homemade corned beef hash. Proof positive that she wanted to please her home-again son.

"All right, Mom!" I whispered and licked my lips in anticipation.

Emptying it into the frying pan, I let it simmer before I cracked a couple of eggs onto the mountain of hash. Like two large yellow eyes, they peered up at me. Perfection!

"The mess cooks in My Tho would be proud," I muttered.

I dished the gastronomical masterpiece onto a large dinner plate along with the hash browns, toast, and bacon. Then I reached for the half bottle of Tabasco sauce and emptied it over the top.

Pouring myself a large glass of milk, I sat down at the kitchen table and dug in.

Although it was delicious, it wasn't the taste I remembered. Maybe my taste buds had been influenced by all the Southeast Asian cuisine I'd consumed? Not that I cared. I was home, and Mom, delighted to have me back, had thoughtfully made the hash for me. I downed every last bite.

I dutifully hand-washed my plate, the frying pan, and the Tupperware. Then I retrieved the morning paper from the steps and wandered into the living room.

My mother's alarm clock jangled. When I heard her move around, I padded into the kitchen to visit with her.

That's when she noticed the Tupperware container on the drain board.

"Patrick," she said, "what did you do with the dog food?"

I looked at her quizzically, rolled my eyes, then shrugged. "You know," I winked, "with a little Tabasco sauce, it wasn't half bad!"

~Patrick Mendoza

96

Rewinding the Clock

Her voice on the phone was weary. I could tell instantly that Amy, our middle daughter, was on overload. But I dared not ask. At least not yet.

Amy resides in Manhattan, works in the entertainment industry, and lives a life that I could tolerate for about three days. She darts from crisis to crisis, juggles three phone lines, lives on the Internet, and seems to spend at least half her life in corporate meetings. But Amy—high-energy, hard-driving Amy—thrives on it.

On this night, however, the pace seemed to have caught up with her. And she clearly needed some down-time. As it turned out, Amy's company was doing some work in the Philadelphia-South Jersey area, her old stomping grounds. And if it was okay, could she spend a couple of nights with us, making our home her headquarters, instead of staying with her colleagues at a hotel?

Okay with us? We hadn't spent sustained time with this middle daughter since the week of her wedding four years and two babies ago. That was the last time she had actually stayed under our roof for four consecutive nights. So not only was it okay, it was absolutely, positively terrific.

Off-site parenting is the natural evolution of our kids leaving home. But it's always fascinating to reunite with an adult child for a length of time.

Amy arrived looking a bit bedraggled from a long day and a train ride into Philadelphia that had run into mechanical problems. Just what this overworked young woman didn't need.

It was even more gratifying than I'd expected to pamper her with home cooking and to see her delight. It was the plainest of plain food: meatloaf and the crispy, oven-baked potatoes Amy always loved. But our Manhattan daughter—who dines on sushi and exotic Cuban food, Thai delicacies and Mediterranean dishes I can't even pronounce—devoured my meatloaf like there was no tomorrow.

That night, she practically fell asleep in the middle of a sentence. Her father and I helped Amy climb the stairs and watched her crumble into an exhausted heap in the bed from her old room. Suddenly, we felt like parents again.

For the next three days, we devoured our time with this daughter whose life is still something of a mystery to us. Between her phone calls and meetings, we found opportunities to remember old times, family lore, and all the patchwork of memories that define this thing called "family."

Amy and I ate peanut butter and apricot jelly sandwiches on crackers like we had when she was in high school. We took a walk in our old neighborhood so we could both reminisce about life in that wonderful house where another family was now building memories. And one morning, Amy and I even attempted a yoga session from a tape on the family room VCR.

We laughed a lot, read, and got sentimental over crazy old family photos. For this blink of time, we were just parents and a daughter again, minus all the profound changes in our lives.

I think Amy enjoyed suspending time just as much as we did. I could swear that she looked younger than she had two days before.

But too soon, our daughter was standing beside a stuffed suitcase and a briefcase bulging with papers. Too soon, real life nipped at her heels.

We drove Amy to the train in Philadelphia, knowing this brief reunion might not be repeated for months. Maybe years. But we hugged our middle daughter goodbye, grateful that in the middle of all our hectic lives, we had had this lovely interlude, this chance to rewind the relentless clock.

And if we've learned one thing by this stage of our lives, it's this: In parenting, you seize the moment, whenever and however it comes. And you savor it for all it's worth.

~Sally Friedman

Reprinted by permission of Randall Kruback.
©2007.

97

Street Wise

$\mathcal{M}$y wife and I, now grandparents, recently bought a pair of ten-speed bicycles, taking our first ride together since our college days, when we lived on macaroni and cheese and our transportation was entirely leg-powered.

We practiced on the street in front of the house, shaky at first, like a couple of kids learning to ride. We finally managed to roll forward in a straight line, up on two wheels again, and our confidence increased as the skills and memories returned. Some things you never forget. Like riding a bike.

Later, I sat on the front porch and reflected that this is the same street where I taught our younger daughter Shelly to ride when she was only five or six. Girls' bicycles were usually pink or purple in those days, and flower decals were more crucial than air in the tires.

I heard almost-forgotten voices floating over from the street, carried on my imagination through the hot air of a summer afternoon long past.

"I can't do it, Daddy."

"You can, Shelly. I'll hold you until you get going."

Dozens of times I ran this street behind my young daughter, propping her up as she peddled. Finally, I'd hold my breath and let go, allowing her to fall, but never to fail.

One day, she wobbled away in something like a straight line and was up on her own two wheels. "That's it, that's it, you're riding! Way to go, Shelly! Look at you now!"

Shelly spent most of that summer riding the street with her friends, stopping long enough to make announcements: "I skinned my toe and it hurts."

"Told you not to ride in flip-flops. Let's take a look, I bet we can fix it."

"Daddy, the chain came off."

"No big deal, let's take a look, I bet we can fix it."

"Daddy, I need a bigger bike."

"Yes, Shelly, I know you do. Let's take a look."

And then one day, "Dad... I need a car."

The memory went slightly out of focus, but I discovered a proud daddy's grin on my face, all over again.

This wise old rascal of a street skinned tender knees and bruised young egos. But it also built confidence and fostered independence.

This wise old street allowed our kids to face the possibility of failure, but it also provided pathways to their success. It watched our kids grow and move from bikes to cars. Then it watched them grow up and move from our home to their own.

This street welcomed them back, eventually, with children of their own. A new generation of kids who now draw on it with chalk. Skate on it with roller blades. Ride on it with pink and purple bikes. And sometimes skin their knees.

My wife and I are too old to risk skinning our knees, and our egos are beyond bruising. We re-learned bicycle riding—carefully, without falling down—on this same street. Some things you never forget.

Other things you must remember to remember. As I did from my porch, while the old street out front carried kids past our house on bicycles, peddling their way to the future, and going much too fast.

Later, returning from an errand, I parked the car in the driveway. Across the street were two girls about eight years old. One was on roller skates, the other had her bicycle—with flower decals—turned upside down, wheels in the air.

"What's the problem?" I asked from the front yard.

"Chain came off. I can't get it back on."

"Let's take a look," I replied, crossing this street I have crossed so many times, on so many similar errands, "I bet we can fix it."

~Ted Thompson

Weekend Washerwoman

My work load has diminished,
The kids are college bound.
I made myself a sewing room
With free time I have found.

The chores don't eat up time,
It's all within my power.
The laundry that once took all day
Now barely takes an hour.

But, whoops, here comes the weekend,
And kids pop in the door
With seven bags of laundry that
They dump out on the floor.

Mom's work is never done,
And really, that's okay.
Just don't get any notions
Of coming home to stay!

~Beverly F. Walker

The Lyons' Tale

It is hard to pick up the pieces of an old life
when you know you can never go back.
~J.R.R. Tolkien

I love being home.

Home is where I can really let loose, be my whole self. I can talk more, smile bigger, and laugh harder, and the best part is that my joy is returned, gesture for gesture, from each member of my family. I miss them more each time I come back.

There are only five of us, and since we oldest two siblings left to pursue degrees, home life has been difficult for my sister, left to endure high school with just my parents and the dog.

I knew it was hard on her. Quiet and artistic, Kassie often spent weekends going on dates with my parents. Still, I never knew exactly how she felt until one summer just after my college graduation.

My whole family gathered around the dinner table. Pots of steaming food passed hands while the Lyons clan used this treasured time to retell old tales, talk about our lives, and share great laughs.

I sighed, wishing the hour would never end, but started slightly when Mom announced, "Did you know Kassie published in *The DaVega Bicycle?*"

I remembered that the high school literary journal printed articles, narratives, and poetry along with submitted artwork. "Congrats, Kass! What drawings did you submit?"

She studied her food while Mom handed me a copy of the

journal. Curious, I thumbed through the first few pages, glancing over titles and pictures, until I found a submission by Kassie Lyons. "You submitted an essay?"

She nodded, red-faced.

Amazed, I began to read aloud:

I am the collector of memories in my family. I am the only one who bothers with the dusty shoe boxes of yesteryear. The albums of photographs I put together immortalize every event in the life of my family. All those little details, all the fine print, all the pictures, all the memorabilia—I have in safe keeping.

Glancing through one of the scrapbooks that I put together, I find it—a silly, spontaneous photograph. I remember that moment like it was yesterday.

It was taken in the front yard of my house in the sunset of a Kansas summer day. Mom wanted a family photo. My sister thought we should do a pyramid. So Dad, Mom, and my brother got on their hands and knees while my sister and I climbed onto their backs. We smiled as we wobbled; there was a bright flash of light, then laugher.

That evening was just another copyrighted Lyons-family spontaneous moment of insanity, but there would not be many more like it. Though no great tragedy has ever hit the Lyons, one inevitable element did. Time.

That picture was taken just before my brother left on a two-year church mission to the Philippines and my sister left for BYU. It captures the true Lyons spirit—my dorky dad with his lopsided grin; my beautiful, exotic mother with her dark skin; my genius brother with a quiet, mischievous gleam in his eye; my entertaining sister with her contagious laughter; and last of all me, with my slightly awkward, braces-filled smile.

The Lyons clan does everything together. We quote the same movies, read the same books, and occasionally wear the same clothes. We will always be close, but it will never be the same. We're growing up and we're growing apart, and it breaks my heart.

~Kassie N. Lyons

Silence filled the kitchen as I finished reading. My heart pounded as I tried to process what I had just read. I skimmed over my sister's essay again, a hard knot in my throat. We all sat around the dinner table, despondent yet awed by the words of the youngest of us all.

"It's going to be okay, Kass. You'll see."

She looked at me through hopeful, teary eyes. "Maybe."

Since that dinner, my brother got engaged, Kassie started her first year at university, and I became a fulltime working wife. Now, I'm obligated to share my holidays with another family whose traditions and customs differ greatly from my own. I find myself fighting, like Kassie, to keep the memories alive, fighting to spend as much time with my family as possible. I'm in denial. I hate to think my family will never be the same. That Kassie was right.

Empty Nest Syndrome, they call it. Apparently it applies just to the parents.

I wonder: What do they call it for the children?

~Chelsea Lyons Pyle with Kassie N. Lyons

Giggles in the Dark

*W*ith my husband away fighting a large brush fire in Northern California, I'd had a lot on my plate that week. Only my daughter and I were home for the evening, and I yearned for just a few minutes of quiet conversation with her. In just a few short weeks she would graduate from high school and take a job in San Diego.

I was hoping for some together time while we prepared supper, but Terra had homework and laundry and wanted to write a few letters to friends. We gobbled dinner and retreated to our rooms to complete our long To Do lists.

I fell into bed, completely exhausted. After a few minutes, I heard snippets of conversation and bits of laughter coming from her room. Normally, we have a cut off time for late-night telephone conversations, but I found myself feeling more lenient than usual, knowing her time at home was fleeting.

Even so, I had my limits. "Keep it down, Terra!" I called from my bed.

She complied for a few minutes, then the talking and giggling started again.

"Terra, I'm trying to sleep!"

Silence. But it wasn't long before I was roused by more giggles. "Be quiet and go to bed!"

After my fifth request, I decided to make sure she understood how serious I was. Marching in, hands on hips, I stopped short.

There she was in the dark, sprawled across her bed on her back, legs crossed, twirling the phone cord between her toes and giggling. The giggle that made me smile no matter what. The giggle that reduced me to laughing out loud. The same giggle that today still moves me to laughter and tears. And, in that moment, I wanted nothing more than to capture the delightful scene in my mind and my heart. Soon, it would be gone forever.

That evening is now a long-ago memory. But every once in a while, when I walk into my office (her old bedroom), I don't see the desk or my bulging bookshelves or the pictures on the wall. Transported back in time, I see only my beautiful daughter—on the threshold of her future—sprawled across her bed and talking late into the night.

And I swear I hear her giggles in the dark.

~Sheri L. Torelli

The Heart
of the Matter

The emptiness isn't in the home; it's in the hands.

My home still has lots of beds. My home still has many chairs at the table. My cupboards still have stacks of dishes and countless spoons and forks.

Not too long ago, my hands were busy all day, laundering sheets and making beds. I spent hours scooting chairs so I could sweep under them. The dishwasher hummed constantly, and there was usually a pile of dirty dishes waiting for the next load. Now my hands aren't as busy with housekeeping duties. I keep them busy doing other things — like dialing the phone and writing letters and e-mails.

The emptiness isn't in the home; it's in the car.

I still have a vehicle with many seatbelts. Not too long ago I lived in the car. If I wasn't driving someone to school or church, I was madly driving a son to pick up school books he left somewhere. I carried reading material in my purse so I had something to do while waiting for play practice to end. We talked in the car. I knew what troubled our daughters because they opened up when we had one-on-one time in the car. Our car was the original chat room.

Now my car sits in the garage most of the time. When I drive, I have CDs and coupons all over the front passenger seat because I usually drive alone.

The emptiness isn't in the home; it's in the ears.

We still have lots of movies and CDs. We even have cassette tapes and long playing vinyl records. We also have a very nice stereo AM-FM radio. Not too long ago, the first place I headed when coming in from an errand was to turn down the stereo four notches. The music was always on—in the family room and in every bedroom.

We never needed an intercom because our kids had their own system. They yelled. "Mom, where's my yellow notebook?" or "Mom, did you remember to buy me a new calculator?" They didn't wait until I was in the room with them. They blurted out their demands from wherever they were to wherever I was as loud as necessary to get the job done. I learned the meaning of cacophony.

Now, the house is so quiet I hear the ice maker drop cubes into its bin. I hear the fan on the furnace start and stop. Sometimes, if I'm lucky, I hear the phone ring.

The emptiness isn't in the home; it's in the heart.

My home still has all the furniture we've ever had. Plus, we have closets, dressers, tubs, and boxes full of belongings… awaiting the day the children own homes big enough to hold it. We have sheet music, toys, books, and hairbrushes. What we don't have is people fighting over them.

What we don't have are daily emergencies. Once, I grumbled when I found out at bedtime we had to go to the store for a school item. Once, I groaned when I found out at bedtime (always bedtime) that a pair of pants needed to be shortened. Yet, even as I grumbled and groaned, I felt empowered because I could do those things for my kids. Now, the only time I grumble and groan is when they don't call.

It's the Xtreme sport called "raising a family" that gives a home its heart. Without the family, the house might still be full, but it's missing a piece of its heart.

~Wanda Lynne Quist

Meet Our Contributors

Chicken Soup for the Soul

Meet Our Contributors!

Caitlin Q. Bailey, journalist by trade and writer at heart, has been writing for various anthologies, magazines, and newspapers since age eight. Daughter of Kathy and Bob and sister of Erin and Kevin, Caitlin's now thrilled to call both Maine and Connecticut home. E-mail: caitlinqbailey@gmail.com.

Kathryn Ann Begnaud is a freelance writer with many essays published in religious publications, some serious, some humorous. A lay homilist for ten years, she has been married to Blake over thirty-five years. She is mother to five sons, grandmother to four. Contact her at bkbegnaud@msn.com.

Born in Kent, England, **Linda Bispham** now lives on the Sunshine Coast, Australia. Linda shares her happy and chaotic home with her husband and three children. Her spare time is spent camping, traveling, and writing. Linda's poetry, children's books, and excerpts from her novels can be viewed at www.loobispham.com.au.

Pamela Blaine writes "Pam's Corner" for her local newspaper. Her stories have been published in magazines, newspapers, and books. She is a church pianist and has a CD of songs she has written. Her goals are to write to encourage and to preserve family history for her children.

Jean Bobb and her husband Doug live in Phoenix, Arizona with their two labradoodles. They enjoy spending time with friends and family, and visiting their daughters in Southern California.

Beatrice E. Brown received her B.A. from Rutgers University and has enjoyed a career in biotechnology. Currently owner-operator of a restaurant, she enjoys cooking, traveling, and photography. Her writing projects include an adventure novel and short stories about her amazing dog. E-mail: beabrown@care2.com.

Nancy Burnett completed her Ph.D. from Texas Tech University in 1987. She is a Jungian psychotherapist in Denver. Her clientele includes individuals and families affected by TBI. She also creates and facilitates workshops and retreats for women. Nancy's writing projects include creative nonfiction. Please contact her through: www.healingexpression.com.

Sue Cameron is a Bible teacher, speaker, and author. She writes on assignment for *Focus on the Family Magazine*. Her work appears in numerous devotional books and secular newspapers. Sue enjoys worshiping through dance and drama, teaching at writer's conferences, mentoring younger women, and being called Grammy. E-mail: epcwf@yahoo.com.

Connie Sturm Cameron is a freelance writer and speaker who lives in her country empty nest with her husband Chuck. She has been published in dozens of periodicals and is the author of the book *God's Gentle Nudges*. Contact her at P.O. Box 30, Glenford, OH 43739; www.conniecameron.com; or conniec@netpluscom.com.

Kathe M. Campbell lives on a Montana mountain with her mammoth donkey, Keeshond, and a few kitties. She is a prolific writer on Alzheimer's, and her stories are found on many ezines. Kathe contributes to the *Chicken Soup for the Soul* series, numerous anthologies, *RX for Writers*, and medical journals. Contact bigskyadj@in-tch.com.

C. Hope Clark (hope@fundsforwriters.com) received her agricultural degree from Clemson University. She retired in her forties to freelance and is currently editor and founder of FundsforWriters.com, a *Writer's Digest* award-winning website. She writes on the banks of Lake Murray, South Carolina, composing nonfiction by day and agricultural mysteries at night.

Lisa Coalwell and her husband Gib are living happily ever after in the foothills of Colorado's Rocky Mountains. A collection of critters fills their empty nest now that their three children are independent young adults. Lisa is an elementary school teacher and freelance writer.

For twenty-six years, **Alice Collins** has written her weekly columns, "Cookies'n Chaos," and "Love'n Leftovers," in the Chicago area.

J. M. Cornwell is a nationally syndicated freelance journalist, award-winning writer, editor, and book reviewer who lives in the Colorado Rockies. Her work has appeared in *Columbus Monthly, The New York Times, Ohio Magazine, The Celebrity Cafe, Haunted Encounters, and Cup of Comfort*. Please e-mail her at fixnwrtr@gmail.com.

A mother and grandmother first, **Robin Crain** has worked as a secretary at a Kansas middle school for twenty years and does private-duty nursing. Writing stories about her adventures with her grandchildren, students, and senior friends has been a hobby for years. She enjoys reading, camping and traveling.

Jean Davidson resides in Pocatello, Idaho. She enjoys family, devises home remodeling projects, and does historical research. Her stories have been published in *The Rocking Chair Reader* series; *A Cup of Comfort* series; *Portneuf Valley Parents* magazine; and *Deseret Morning News*. She is writing a novel about women of the Old West.

Michele Ivy Davis is a freelance writer whose stories and articles have appeared in magazines, anthologies, newspapers, and law enforcement publications. Her young adult novel, *Evangeline Brown and the Cadillac Motel*, was published by Dutton (Penguin Group USA) and has won national and international awards. Learn more at www.MicheleIvyDavis.com.

Ray Depew is a writer, teacher, and engineer. He and his wife Valerie, also a teacher, have five children and one grandchild. He enjoys playing in the mountains of Colorado, making music, and creating bedtime stories for children. He can be reached at rdepew57@msn.com.

Ruth Douillette is a retired teacher, freelance writer, and photographer. Her essays have appeared in *The Christian Science Monitor*, *Chicken Soup for the Coffee Lover's Soul*, and a breast cancer anthology. She is associate editor for *The Internet Review of Books*, www.internetreviewofbooks.com.

Drema Drudge received her B.S. from Manchester College in 2007. She and her husband Barry live in North Manchester, Indiana. They have two children, Mia and Zack, and a son-in-law, Adam. Drema writes fiction and is attending Spalding University for her M.F.A. degree.

Nancy Erskine holds a B.A. degree from California State Polytechnic University, Pomona. She enjoys baseball, traveling, cooking, and photography. Please e-mail her at nancy@TheDogEaredPages.com.

Dorothy Firman (dfirman@comcast.net) is the co-author of three *Chicken Soup for the Soul* books including *Chicken Soup for the Mother & Daughter Soul* and *Chicken Soup for the Father and Son Soul*. She is the author of *Daughters and Mothers, Making it Work*. She is a psychotherapist, life coach, and speaker specializing in holistic and spiritual psychology.

Although her nest emptied some years ago, the experience never left **Sally Friedman**. Family life is her writing focus for national publications. A frequent contributor to the *Chicken Soup for the Soul* series, Sally lives in Moorestown, New Jersey with her husband, retired NJ Superior Court Judge Victor Friedman. E-mail: pinegander@aol.com.

Nancy Geiger graduated from Iowa State University, married a West Point graduate the next week and worked as a U.S. Customs inspector in Europe for the next three years covering a territory of Holland, Germany and Belgium. Back in the States she was a travel agent for American Express and is now a freelance writer and owns an online store called givitup. Nancy's interests are: her faith, business and marketing, travel, snow and water skiing, yardwork, learning and reading. Please email her at ng0425@embarqmail.com.

Beverly Ginsberg has been a published freelance writer for over sixty years, starting in high school as a city newspaper reporter. She also held writing positions in national advertising and in college public relations.

With a B.A. in education and an M.A. in applied behavioral sciences, **Gail Goeller** spent most of her career as a trainer and management consultant. In 2004 at age sixty-two, she fulfilled a lifelong dream by writing and publishing *Coming of Age with Aging Parents: The Bungles, Battles, and Blessings*.

After a twenty-year nursing career, **Pamela Goldstein** turned to her passion—writing. She has completed three full manuscripts and has several short stories accepted for publications. She produces/hosts the 'Boker Tov' radio show in Windsor/Detroit, and is heard worldwide via Internet. E-mail Pam at boker_tov2002@yahoo.ca.

Marian Gormley writes from Northern Virginia about parenting, family life, education, health, and the arts for regional, national, and international publications. She has stories in *Chicken Soup for Every Mom's Soul* and *Chicken Soup for the Soul: Recipes for Busy Moms*. She has a background in software engineering, public relations, and marketing.

Karen Gray-Keeler treasures the privilege of sharing in the lives of her three sons—Daniel, Brian, and Michael—and the new worlds they continue to open for her. She's a graduate of Washington University and of Indiana University School of Law, Indianapolis and lives with her husband Tom near Chicago.

Freelance writer **Carol A. Grund** lives in Williamston, MI, and works for her district library system. Since 2001, her work has appeared in many children's magazines, including *Cobblestone*, *Ladybug*, *Pockets* and *Plays*. She considers her three grown sons to be her greatest inspiration and finest achievement.

Bonnie Compton Hanson is author of several books for adults and children, including the popular *Ponytail Girls* series, plus hundreds of published articles and poems (including twenty-five for Chicken Soup for the Soul). She speaks to MOPS, seniors, schools, and women's groups and leads writing seminars. Contact bonnieh1@worldnet.att.net.

Lana Robertson Hayes has an M.A. in education. She has authored many humorous essays and articles. A former teacher, she wields her pen at life's absurdities, which amuse her, and her family's antics, which strike her as hilarious. Contact her at Britishtea@aol.com.

Karen Heywood is a poet, playwright, and award-winning essayist living her dreams in mid-Missouri. She and her husband began caring for children with moderate to severe special needs in 2005. Karen graduated magna cum laude from Stephens College in Columbia, Missouri with a B.F.A. in creative writing in May 2007.

Miriam Hill is co-author of *Fabulous Florida* and a frequent contributor to *Chicken Soup for the Soul* books. She's been published in *The Christian Science Monitor, Grit, St. Petersburg Times, Sacramento Bee* and *Poynter Online.* Miriam's manuscript received Honorable Mention for Inspirational Writing in a *Writer's Digest* competition.

Georgia A. Hubley retired after twenty years in financial management to write fulltime. Her work has appeared in the *Chicken Soup for the Soul* series, *Christian Science Monitor, Plus Magazine, Birds and Blooms Magazine, Story Circle Journal, Capper's* and other publications. She resides with her husband in Henderson, NV. Contact her at GEOHUB@aol.com

BJ Jensen is an international speaker, author, dramatist, and the Director of the LOVE IN MOTION Signing Choir (www.signingchoir. com). BJ and husband Dr. Doug, co-founders of CREATE LOVING RELATIONSHIPS Ministries (www.createlovingrelationships.org) live in San Diego near their son, daughter-in-love, and three wonderful granddaughters.

Caroleah Johnson lives in Northern California where she is a dental hygienist, writer, speaker, and artisan bread baker. She has been published in *Upper Room* and several *Chicken Soup for the Soul* books. She is currently working on her first novel.Visit her blog at http:// caroleah.com.

Sally Kelly-Engeman is a freelance writer with many publishing credits. In addition to reading, writing and researching, she enjoys ballroom dancing and traveling the world with her husband. She can be reached at sallyfk@juno.com.

Born in Glasgow Scotland, **Christine Kettle** is a longtime resident of small-town Ontario. Happily married for over thirty years, she enjoys reading, travel, and writing. Christine gave up a corporate career to try lots of new experiences—some really great, others not so great, but always grateful for the opportunities.

A speaker for Stonecroft Ministries, **Karen Kilby** resides in Kingwood, Texas with her husband, David. A Certified Personality Trainer with CLASServices, Inc., Karen helps people understand themselves and others through her seminar presentations. She has published in *Chicken Soup for the Soul* books as well as other publications. Please e-mail her at krkilby@kingwoodcable.net.

Karen Kosman is an inspirational speaker and author whose stories of joy and zest for life have appeared in several magazines and books. *Wounded by Words*, her book on verbal abuse, offers needed encouragement for victims. Karen enjoys her grandchildren, swimming, and gardening. Email her at ComKosman@aol.com.

Rand Kruback received his Bachelor of Fine Arts degree from Colorado State University. He has created illustrations and cartoons for Hewlett-Packard, Agilent Technologies, Group Publishing, Zondervan Publishing, CSU and others. He also paints and sculpts, exhibiting and selling works in Colorado, New Mexico, and Wyoming. Contact Rand at rand@randkruback.com.

Kerry Krycho received her B.S. from the School of Journalism at the University of Colorado in 1985. She is an editor for a nonprofit publisher. She enjoys reading, skiing, and learning to mountain bike. Kerry loves writing a variety of genres. Please e-mail her at Kerry@Krycho.net.

Jeannie Lancaster is a freelance writer in Loveland, Colorado. She graduated from the University of Northern Colorado with a B.A. in communications at a "mature" age. Jeannie has written for healthcare publications for a number of years and now returns to her love of storytelling through poetry and prose.

Karen Landrum has published stories in *Chicken Soup for the Kid's Soul 2* and *You Look Too Young to be a Mom*. She writes articles for local publication and enjoys sharing her reflections in her website journal at www.writeheart.com.

Mary Laufer is a freelance writer whose work has been published in over ten anthologies. Her recent credits include poems in *Bombshells: War Stories and Poems by Women on the Homefront* (OmniArts, 2007) and *Beautiful Women — Like You and Me* (BW Books, 2007). She lives in Forest Grove, Oregon.

Gary Lautens, a popular Canadian humorist and syndicated columnist, wrote for the *Toronto Star* newspapers. Collections of his columns have been published as books. Gary twice won the national Stephen Leacock Award for Humour. For more information log on to the website of his son Stephen Lautens, also a writer, at www.lautens.com.

Linda Leary wrote in earnest when her daughter left home and soon created a new career path, filling her time with stories, poetry, magazine articles, interviews, and women's leadership groups. For her, life has truly begun — again — at midlife.

Donna Lowich received her Master's degree in Library Science from Rutgers University in 1978 and works as an Information Specialist for the Christopher Reeve Foundation. She enjoys writing about her family. Donna lives in New Jersey with her husband, Walter. E-mail her at DonnaLowich@aol.com.

Chelsea A. Lyons Pyle received her B.A. in English from Brigham Young University, Provo. A senior writer for *Schooled Magazine,* she is soon to be published in the scholarly journal *Interdisciplinary Humanities*. **Kassie N. Lyons** is a sophomore at BYU, Idaho studying art. Together they love to watch movies, talk movies, plan movie projects, and obsess about anything British. They hope to one day host their own critics' program.

Ruth Magan is the author of *Laughing With Angels, Visions of Earth Beyond 2012*, and *My Angel, My Friend*, a children's book. Her humor and lighthearted spirit shine throughout her books. Ruth travels the globe giving seminars. She lives in California and in Tasmania. Please e-mail her at ruth-magan@ruthmagan.com.

Columnist **Derek Maul's** credits range from *The Tampa Tribune* to *Newsweek* to *Guideposts*. His books: *Get Real: A Spiritual Journey for Men*, and *In My Heart I Carry A Star* are available from Upper Room Books. Derek shares his empty nest with his wife, Rebekah. Contact him at Derekmaul@Gmail.com.

Mary K. McClanahan, a retired English teacher and author of an English textbook, holds a B.A. from the University of Colorado. "The Treasure Chest" is taken from one chapter in her nonfiction manuscript, *Miracles and Other Stuff*. She is a member of Mensa. E-mail her at maryd2mac@comcast.net.

Alice McGhee graduated from Cedarville University. She has articles published in several devotional books. Her passions are teaching Bible study classes, singing in the church choir, and participating in mission activities. Her six grandchildren keep her on her toes. She can be reached at a.m.mcghee@att.net.

Kathleen McNamara is a fourth generation Californian who lives in the San Francisco Bay Area. Her husband Michael is an award-winning photographer (www.mdmphotostudio.com) and they often combine their work for photojournalism projects. She holds an M.A. from the University of Wisconsin, Madison.

Donna Milligan Meadows is the mother of six adult children—including triplets. She worked for many years as an elementary school librarian and, someday, hopes to write a children's book. She loves reading, traveling, gardening, and especially reading to her grandchildren. Please e-mail her at meadowsdonna@hotmail.com.

Chantal Meijer is a freelance writer living in Terrace, British Columbia, Canada with her husband Rick. Now full-fledged empty nesters, they visit their far-flung kids as often as they can. Chantal's essays, articles and features have appeared in regional and national publications. She can be reached at Meijer@telus.net.

Follow the dirt road in your soul to **Carol Mell's** "Humbug Mountain" at www.NewWest.net and the *Albuquerque Journal North* where she takes a humorous gander at Taos and all places west. You're danged if you do and danged if you don't so you might just as well. E-mail: carolmell@msn.com.

Internationally acclaimed folk-singer/storyteller **Patrick Mendoza** produced numerous recordings and a documentary film. He authored *Song of Sorrow: Massacre at Sand Creek, Four Great Rivers to Cross, Extraordinary People in Extraordinary Times*, and *Between Midnight and Morning*. A Navy veteran, Pat also worked as a police officer. Contact www.patmendoza.com.

M. Carolyn Miller, M.A., is a personal growth columnist, author, and educator whose work is grounded in psychology, mythology, and writing. Forced to rewrite her own story at fifty, Carolyn now leads personal development workshops that show others how to unearth their unique gifts and stories. Visit www.mythiclives.com or carolyn@mythiclives.com.

Sebastian Moraga received his B.A. at Washington State University in 2002 and is a reporter in North Central Washington State. He enjoys swimming, reading, tennis, and coaching youth soccer. He wants to become a columnist after he finishes pursuing his M.A. degree in 2009.

Amy Newmark has four children living outside the nest—two in college and two grown stepchildren. She spent most of her fulltime parenting years working part-time in the world of telecommunications and finance, when she wasn't driving on field trips and buying emergency poster board late on a Sunday night.

Tiffany O'Neill was raised in California's Central Valley. She now makes her home in New Jersey where she enjoys life as a freelance writer, wife, and stay-at-home mom of two daughters. Please e-mail her at oneill_tiffany@yahoo.com.

Jean Padgett raised five children and has been a foster parent to many others. She now lives in an empty nest with her husband and best friend John. She loves to read and write and plans to travel. Please e-mail her at jpadgett13@cogeco.ca.

Carol Panerio lives with her husband in Spearfish, South Dakota. After raising two children while teaching piano, she had a third child, retired from teaching, and discovered the fun of writing personal essays and fiction, as well as learning to speak Italian. E-mail her at acarprushmore.com.

Mark Parisi's "off the mark" comics, syndicated since 1987, are distributed by United Media. His humor also graces greeting cards, T-shirts, calendars, magazines, newsletters, and books. Check out: offthemark.com. Lynn is his wife/business partner. Their daughter, Jen, contributes inspiration (as do three cats).

Nancy M. Peterson has been writing for publication for forty years. Her humor, essays, fiction, poetry, and articles appear in national and regional magazines and newspapers. A native of Western Nebraska and resident of Colorado, Nancy's greatest interest is writing history about the West. Visit www.nancympeterson.com.

Rhonda Lane Phillips is a reading specialist at an elementary school in Western Virginia, as well as an online instructor for Virginia Tech, her alma mater. She enjoys traveling and volunteering for her church and Gideons. Being Savannah's Nana wonderfully fills the empty nest that Austin and his sister created.

Cheryl Pierson is a freelance editor who lives in the Oklahoma City area. She teaches classes on novel and short story writing for adults and teens. Cheryl is currently working on her sixth novel, including a screenplay adaptation. E-mail her at cheryl@westwindsmedia.com.

Stephanie Piro lives with her family in New Hampshire. The Saturday Chick, she is one of King Features' team of women cartoonists, Six Chix. Stephanie designs gift items for her company, Strip T's. *My Cat Loves Me Naked*, her new book, is available at bookstores everywhere. Visit www.stephaniepiro.com. Contact stephaniepiro@verizon.net.

Kimberly A. Porrazzo is Chief Content Officer for Newport Beach-based Churm Media where she oversees five magazine titles and Web sites. She is an author and award-winning columnist who frequently writes on family issues. Porrazzo is author of *The Nanny Kit*, (Viking Penguin) and of *The Santa Secret: The Truth About Santa Claus*, (www.thesantasecret.com) She is also the founder of MyWomanOwnedBusiness.com, the "myspace" for female entrepreneurs. Contact her at kimberlyporrazzo@cox.net.

Wanda Lynne Quist holds a bachelor's degree in education and has spent her career years raising eight children with her husband Robert. They have seventeen grandchildren with more on the way. She enjoys writing poetry and light prose, sewing, quilting, and hiking. E-mail her at wanda@lpbroadband.net.

Chris Ransick, Denver's Poet Laureate, won a Colorado Book Award in 2003 for his first book, *Never Summer*. He is the author of a collection of short fiction, *A Return To Emptiness*, and published his most recent poetry collection, *Lost Songs & Last Chances*, in 2006.

Carla Riehl teaches theater in Los Angeles, where she lives with her entrepreneurial husband Rich. Carla is involved in music, writing, and speaking and inspiring others to get in touch with the personal plan God has for their lives. Both sons, college grads, are pursuing exciting careers.

Over five hundred of **Stephen D. Rogers's** stories and poems have been selected to appear in more than a hundred publications. His website, www.stephendrogers.com, includes a list of new and upcoming titles as well as other timely information.

Marilyn (Lynn) M. Ross, a graduate of Arkansas State University, teaches special education in Prince William Co., VA. She lives with her husband Bob and is the mother of John, Lori, and grandmother of Alex. Favorites include writing, photography and album making. Contact lynn.ross96@gmail.com.

Donna Savage is a pastor's wife, writer, and speaker who encourages others to experience God's joy. A previous Chicken Soup for the Soul contributor, her work has appeared in *Today's Christian Woman, Marriage Partnership*, and *Discipleship Journal*. Donna and Hoyt live in Las Vegas, and have two sons. Contact her at donnasavagelv@cox.net.

Al Serradell received his M.A. from the University of Central Oklahoma, Edmond, in 1991. Al co-owns an editing firm in Oklahoma City, where he teaches creative writing. Currently, he is working on an anthology for mid-lifers with a sense of humor.

Beverly Bush Smith has written over 500 articles and five books, including *Caught in the Middle, Wings of a Dove*, and *Evidence of Things Unseen*. She lives in Southern California and skis and hikes in the Sierras with her engineer husband, two sons, and three grandchildren. Contact b2smith@pacbell.net.

Vie Stallings Herlocker is a retired elementary assistant principal. She has published in *Guideposts, Angels on Earth*, and other magazines. She coauthored *Building Better Schools by Engaging Support Staff*. E-mail her at vieherlocker@violetwrites.com.

Joyce Stark retired from local government to write a travel book on her many journeys in the United States. She wrote a story book on teaching a second language to young children and is now working on a collection of her own stories. Contact her at joric.stark@virgin.net.

Susan K. Stewart is an inspirational writer, speaker, and teacher. She and her husband Bob have three children, five grandchildren, and three granddogs. Susan advocates on behalf of those dealing with serious mental illness and their family members. Contact Susan at susan@skstewart.com.

Sarah Stringfield is the author of *Marone Memoirs: An Immigrant Story* (Xlibris Corporation, 2003). She was published in *Christian Miracles: Amazing Stories of God's Helping Hand in Our Everyday Lives* (Adams Media, 2005) and has two works in progress. Sarah is a fulltime journalism student in North Carolina. Visit www.themovingpen.com.

Stephanie Welcher Thompson enjoys writing and scrapbooking when she's apart from husband Michael and their five-year-old daughter Micah. A contributing editor at *Guideposts* and *Angels on Earth* magazines, she feels blessed to be included in a dozen *Chicken Soup for the Soul* books. Contact her at P.O. Box 1502, Edmond, OK 73083 or stephanie@stateofchange.net.

Ted A. Thompson is a freelance writer living in Harrison, AR with his wife Roxanne. Ted is a former advertising copywriter with interests in boating and motorcycling. He writes a popular monthly perspective and humor column for *Houseboat Magazine* titled "Notes from the Stern." Contact tedthompson@alltel.net.

After careers as a counselor and bookstore owner, **Terri Tiffany** now encourages others through her inspirational writings to treasure the moments God gifts them. She lives in Florida with her best friend and husband of thirty years. E-mail her at terri.tiffany@yahoo.com.

Sheri Torelli teaches organization seminars all across the United States. She is the co-author of two books. Sheri is married to her high school sweetheart, Tim, and they live in Riverside, CA. They have been married for thirty years and have two grown children. Please email her at: sheri@emiliebarnes.com.

Margaret Ann Vommaro is the mother of two grown sons. While anxiously awaiting grandchildren, she works as a geriatric nurse. Peggy enjoys living on beautiful Lake Erie, serving as music minister at her church, and being creative.

Beverly Walker enjoys writing, photography, and scrapbooking pictures of her grandchildren. Her stories appear in *Angel Cats: Divine Messengers of Comfort* by Allen and Linda Anderson, and in *Chicken Soup for the Cat Lover's Soul*, *Chicken Soup for the Soul in Menopause*, and *Chicken Soup for the Soul: A Tribute to Moms*.

Emily Weaver lives in Springfield, Missouri with her husband and two children. Her work can also be found in *Chicken Soup for the New Mom's Soul*. She enjoys gardening, staying home with her kids, traveling, and writing. She can be reached at emily-weaver@sbcglobal.net.

Marjorie Woodall lives in Olympia, Washington, with her new husband and visits her two awesome grown children in California as often as she can. She makes her living as a freelance copyeditor and proofreader and is a frequent contributor to *Chicken Soup for the Soul* books. Contact her at marjoriewoodall@hotmail.com.

Leslie Yeaton Koepke, an author and speaker, uses life experiences to equip and connect with teens, parents, twenty-somethings, and women. She traveled for Focus on the Family as their international spokesperson for abstinence and youth issues. Leslie is a wife, mom, and mentor living in Colorado. Visit her at www.leslieyk.com.

Bill Zarchy (www.billzarchy.com) is a writer, teacher, and director of photography. His film credits include *West Wing Documentary, Conceiving Ada* and *Read You Like A Book*. He has published numerous essays, tales from the road, and technical articles, and he teaches at San Francisco State University.

Meet the Authors

Chicken Soup for the Soul

Who Is
Jack Canfield?

*J*ack Canfield is the co-creator and editor of the *Chicken Soup for the Soul* series, which *Time* magazine has called "the publishing phenomenon of the decade." Jack is also the co-author of eight other bestselling books including *The Success Principles™: How to Get from Where You Are to Where You Want to Be*, *Dare to Win*, *The Aladdin Factor*, *You've Got to Read This Book*, and *The Power of Focus: How to Hit Your Business and Personal and Financial Targets with Absolute Certainty*.

Jack has recently developed a telephone coaching program and an online coaching program based on his most recent book *The Success Principles*. He also offers a seven-day *Breakthrough to Success* seminar every summer, which attracts 400 people from fifteen countries around the world.

Jack is the CEO of the Canfield Training Group in Santa Barbara, California, and founder of the Foundation for Self-Esteem in Culver City, California. He has conducted intensive personal and professional development seminars on the principles of success for over a million people in twenty-three countries. Jack is a dynamic keynote speaker and he has spoken to hundreds of thousands of others at more than 1,000 corporations, universities, professional conferences and conventions, and has been seen by millions more on national television shows such as *The Today Show*, *Fox and Friends*, *Inside Edition*, *Hard Copy*, *CNN's Talk Back Live*, *20/20*, *Eye to Eye*, and the *NBC Nightly News* and the *CBS Evening News*.

Jack is the recipient of many awards and honors, including three honorary doctorates and a *Guinness World Records Certificate* for having seven books from the *Chicken Soup for the Soul* series appearing on the *New York Times* bestseller list on May 24, 1998.

To write to Jack or for inquiries about Jack as a speaker, his coaching programs, trainings or seminars, use the following contact information:

Jack Canfield
The Canfield Companies
P.O. Box 30880 • Santa Barbara, CA 93130
phone: 805-563-2935 • fax: 805-563-2945
E-mail: info@jackcanfield.com
www.jackcanfield.com

Who Is
Mark Victor Hansen?

*M*ark Victor Hansen is the co-founder of *Chicken Soup for the Soul*, along with Jack Canfield. He is also a sought-after keynote speaker, bestselling author, and marketing maven.

For more than thirty years, Mark has focused solely on helping people from all walks of life reshape their personal vision of what's possible. His powerful messages of possibility, opportunity, and action have created powerful change in thousands of organizations and millions of individuals worldwide.

Mark's credentials include a lifetime of entrepreneurial success. He is a prolific writer with many bestselling books, such as *The One Minute Millionaire*, *Cracking the Millionaire Code*, *How to Make the Rest of Your Life the Best of Your Life*, *The Power of Focus*, *The Aladdin Factor*, and *Dare to Win*, in addition to the *Chicken Soup for the Soul* series. Mark has had a profound influence in the field of human potential through his library of audios, videos, and articles in the areas of big thinking, sales achievement, wealth building, publishing success, and personal and professional development.

Mark is the founder of the *MEGA Seminar Series*. *MEGA Book Marketing University* and *Building Your MEGA Speaking Empire* are annual conferences where Mark coaches and teaches new and aspiring authors, speakers, and experts on building lucrative publishing and speaking careers. Other MEGA events include *MEGA Info-Marketing* and *My MEGA Life*.

He has appeared on *Oprah*, *CNN*, and *The Today Show*. He has been quoted in *Time*, *U.S. News & World Report*, *USA Today*, *New York Times*, and *Entrepreneur* and has had countless radio interviews, assuring our planet's people that "You can easily create the life you deserve."

As a philanthropist and humanitarian, Mark works tirelessly for organizations such as Habitat for Humanity, American Red Cross, March of Dimes, Childhelp USA, and many others. He is the recipient of numerous awards that honor his entrepreneurial spirit, philanthropic heart, and business acumen. He is a lifetime member of the Horatio Alger Association of Distinguished Americans, an organization that honored Mark with the prestigious Horatio Alger Award for his extraordinary life achievements.

Mark Victor Hansen is an enthusiastic crusader of what's possible and is driven to make the world a better place.

Mark Victor Hansen & Associates, Inc.
P.O. Box 7665 • Newport Beach, CA 92658
phone: 949-764-2640 • fax: 949-722-6912
www.markvictorhansen.com

Who Is
Carol McAdoo Rehme?

*C*arol's earliest publishing credits were three-inch columns detailing her weekly Camp Fire Girl meetings for the local newspaper—she was eight years old and held the coveted position of Scribe. Today, the power of words still holds her captive.

Her writing career began more than thirty years ago, when she agreed to exercise her journalism degree in a public relations capacity for her church. Soon, Carol was submitting stories to magazines, competitions, and anthologies.

In 1996, she submitted her first story to the publishing phenomenon, *Chicken Soup for the Soul*. Now an editor, ghost writer, and one of Soup's most prolific contributors, Carol has stories in more than four dozen books in the series. She is the coauthor of *Chicken Soup for the Soul The Book of Christmas Virtues*.

A freelance editor and award-winning author, Carol has 600 articles and stories in various magazines and anthologies. She is the coauthor of five gift books for Publications International, Ltd.

As a professional speaker, Carol entertains and educates the same way she writes—through stories. She workshops her word-craft at storytelling and writing conferences. She offers keynotes and classes to guilds, businesses, associations, and professional organizations.

Carol lives in a stately, historic home rooted to the Front Range of the Colorado Rockies with her husband, Norman, and writes from a sprawling, window-banked sanctuary. They have four married children and five grandkids who call them Grammy and Pops. Contact Carol at:

Carol McAdoo Rehme
1127 Garfield Ave.
Loveland, CO 80537
970-669-5791
carol@rehme.com; www.rehme.com

Who Is
Patricia Cena Evans?

*P*rofessionally, Patricia is a Women's Healthcare Nurse Practitioner and Certified Nurse-Midwife, freelance author, speaker, ministry leader, and mentor. On a personal level, she is most proud of her career as mother and wife, experiencing first-hand her own precious children growing into adults and leaving.

Appreciative of their multiple roles and life-stages, she mentors other women through their life passages from one season to the next, especially those who feel an empty nest is often over-looked and under-realized as a traumatic time. Most importantly, she embodies this pearl of wisdom: You are never alone on your journey.

Patricia lives with her husband and best friend Jack Hankins in Huntington Beach, California. Beginning twenty-three years ago with a blended family — her two children and his three — they now enjoy an empty nest. Although, it seems when they settle in for a quiet weekend, with only peaceful walks and naps on the agenda, the phone rings.

"Are you guys busy?"

"Not really." Their answer is semi-truthful.

And, suddenly, the house is full of adult kids and grandkids raiding the fridge, wrestling on the floor, and enjoying "just being home." Patricia and Jack really wouldn't have it any other way.

Patricia's sincere hope is that this book's collection of parenting experiences brings you joy and inspiration. If you would like to share how these stories affect your life, please contact her at:

Patricia Cena Evans
311 21st Street
Huntington Beach, CA 92648
714-345-4743
pattevans@gmail.com

Acknowledgments

Thank You!

*W*e wish to express our heartfelt gratitude to the following people who helped make this book possible, especially our families, who have been chicken soup for our souls!

- Carol's Family: To my partner-in-crime, Norm, for the thirty-five years of time—and patience... and love... and effort—you've invested in our marriage. Now it's just us again, Sweetheart! To my children Kyle, Katrina, Kayla, and Koy, my lasting appreciation for all the fodder you provide me, enough stories to last a lifetime of writing. Now that you've added mates and grandbabies to the mix, the possibilities are endless! And to my dear friends, Jean and Vic, for sharing my parenting years and the hereafter.

- Patricia's Family: my husband and soulmate for twenty-two wonderful years, Jack Hankins. Thank you for your love, support, encouragement, the new laptop and the ink cartridges. I can't imagine spending my empty nest with anyone but you. To all my children and stepchildren—Dustin, Ryan, Meredith, Kristin and Jonathan. If you hadn't left me with an empty nest, this book wouldn't have been necessary. To my sister Pam Guevara; thanks for your wisdom about what happens when the kids leave home. To my dearest girlfriend, DeeAnn Gray, for doing life with me in the corner, and for taking me to a writer's conference.

- And our gratitude also goes to Maria Nickless for introducing Carol and Patricia and for her love and support throughout this project. We love you Maria!

- Barbara LoMonaco, Chicken Soup's Webmaster and Editor, for nourishing us with truly wonderful stories and cartoons.

- D'ette Corona, our Assistant Publisher, who seamlessly manages twenty to thirty projects at a time and keeps us focused and on schedule.

- Amy Newmark, our Publisher, and a recent empty nester herself, for wholeheartedly embracing this book concept, and for her creative vision and expert editing.

- Patty Hansen, for her thorough and competent handling of the legal and licensing aspects of the *Chicken Soup for the Soul* books. You are magnificent at the challenge!

- Book producer Brian Taylor of Pneuma Books, for his creative direction and the fabulous design for the cover and interior.

- Our glorious panel of readers who helped us with the final selections and made invaluable suggestions on how to improve the book: Janice Alcala, Neva Anderson, Ruth Bartlett, Peggy Bolinsky, Marsha Buccambuso, Denise Carr, Joan Clayton, Edie Cutler, Chris Dahl, Jennifer L. Dale, Michele Edelstein, Vic Elliot, Sally Engeman, Pam Goldstein, Pam Guevara, Anne Guevara, Jack Hankins, Lynn Hansen, Joyce Harmell, Renee King, Cathy McAdoo, Peggy McMillen, Maria Nickless, Joan Parr, Lavada Patterson, Wanda Quist,

Sallie Rodman, Jodi Schnitker, Dorothy Smith, Sherri Torelli, Joann Tyler, Beth Vanderpool, Jeanie Winstrom, and Deb Zika.

- To everyone who submitted a story, we deeply appreciate your letting us into your lives and sharing your experiences with us. For those whose stories were not chosen for publication, we hope the stories you are about to enjoy convey what was in your heart.

- Because of the size of this project, we may have left out the names of some people who contributed along the way. If so, we are sorry, but please know that we really do appreciate you very much.

We are truly grateful and love you all!

~Chicken Soup for the Soul

More Chicken Soup

Chicken Soup for the Soul: Divorce and Recovery

101 Stories about Surviving and Thriving after Divorce

**Jack Canfield,
Mark Victor Hansen,
Patty Hansen**

Chicken Soup's first book on divorce is wonderfully uplifting and filled with stories and poems from men and women who have been there and successfully navigated the divorce and recovery process. Heartfelt stories provide support, inspiration, and humor on all the phases of divorce, including the initial shock of the decision, the logistics of living through it, the inevitable self-discovery, and the new world of dating and even remarriage.

978-1-935096-21-4

*C*heck out our great books about

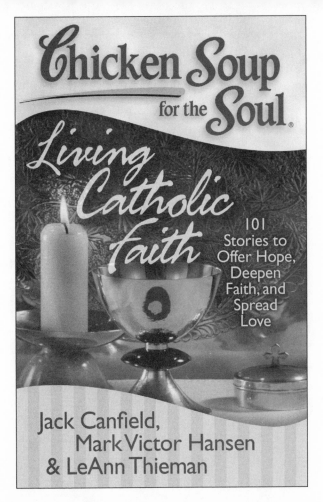

Chicken Soup for the Soul

Living Catholic Faith

101 Stories to Offer Hope, Deepen Faith, and Spread Love

Jack Canfield,
Mark Victor Hansen
& LeAnn Thieman

This is Chicken Soup for the Soul's first book written just for Catholics. From the once-a-year attendee at Christmas Mass, to the devout church volunteer and daily worshipper, 101 poignant and spirit-filled stories written by Catholics of all ages, this book cover the gamut, including fun stories about growing up Catholic to serious stories about sacraments and miracles. Whether the reader is a cradle Catholic, a convert, simply curious or struggling, these stories describe what it means to be a Catholic. They bring happiness, hope, and healing to everyone in all stages of life and faith.

978-1-935096-23-8

Life Changes

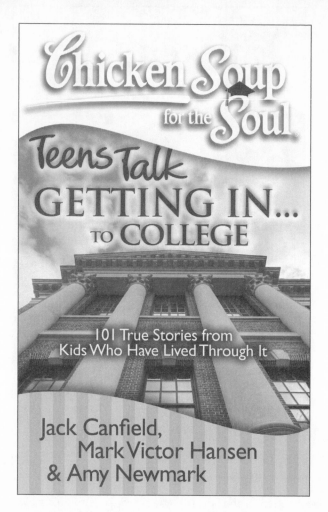

Chicken Soup for the Soul
for the
Teens Talk
GETTING IN...
TO COLLEGE

101 True Stories from
Kids Who Have Lived Through It

Jack Canfield,
Mark Victor Hansen
& Amy Newmark

This book isn't about how to get into college — it's about providing emotional, support. The stories in this book are written by kids who have been there and want to pass on their words of support to the kids about to go through the whole ordeal. Story topics include parental and peer pressure, the stress of grades and standardized tests, applications and interviews, recruiting, disappointments, and successes. Parents and students alike will find it a great source of inspiration.
978-1-935096-27-6

ollege-bound kids?
Teens Talk Getting In...

On Being a Parent

Inspirational, Humorous, and Heartwarming
Stories about Parenthood
978-1-935096-20-7

Parenting is the hardest and most rewarding job in the world. This upbeat and compelling new book includes the best selections on parenting from Chicken Soup's rich history, with 101 stories carefully selected to appeal to both mothers and fathers. This is a great book for couples to share, whether they are just embarking on their new adventure as parents or reflecting on their lifetime experience.

Grand and Great

Grandparents and Grandchildren Share Their
Stories of Love and Wisdom
978-1-935096-09-2

A parent becomes a new person the day the first grandchild is born. Formerly serious and responsible adults go on shopping sprees for toys and baby clothing, smile incessantly, pull out photo albums that they "just happen to have" with them, and proudly display baby seats in their cars. Grandparents dote on their grandchildren, and grandchildren love them back with all their hearts. This new book includes the best stories on being a grandparent from 33 past Chicken Soup books, representing a new reading experience for even the most devoted Chicken Soup fan.

Books
for Families

Inside Basketball

Chicken Soup has a slam dunk with its first sports book in years, and its first on basketball, with the Orlando Magic's very own Pat Williams, well-known author and motivational speaker. Pat has drawn on his basketball industry connections to compile great stories from on and off the court. Fans will be inspired, surprised, and amused by inside stories from well-known coaches and players, fascinating looks behind the scenes, and anecdotes from the fans.

Tales of Golf & Sport

Golfers are a special breed. They endure bad weather, early wake up calls, great expense, and "interesting" clothing to engage in their favorite sport. This book contains Chicken Soup's 101 best stories about golfers, golfing, and other sports. Chicken Soup's approach to sports books has always been unique — professional and amateur athletes contribute stories from the heart, yielding a book about the human side of golf and other sports, not a how-to book.

The Golf Book

Chicken Soup and Golf Digest magazine's Max Adler and team have put together a great collection of personal stories that will inspire, amuse, and surprise golfers. Celebrity golfers, weekend golfers, beginners, and pros all share the best stories they've told at the 19th hole about good times on and off the course. Chicken Soup's golf books have always been very successful — with the addition of Golf Digest's industry connections, this book should hit a hole in one.

Books for Men!

Moms Know Best

"Mom will know where it is...what to say...how to fix it." This Chicken Soup book focuses on the pervasive wisdom of mothers everywhere, and includes the best 101 stories from Chicken Soup's library on our perceptive, understanding, and insightful mothers. These stories celebrate the special bond between mothers and children, our mothers' unerring wisdom about everything from the mundane to the life-changing, and the hard work that goes into being a mother every day.

Like Mother, Like Daughter

Fathers, brothers, and friends sometimes shake their head in wonder as girls "turn into their mothers." This new collection from Chicken Soup represents the best 101 stories from Chicken Soup's library on the special bond between mothers and daughters, and the magical, mysterious similarities between them. Mothers and daughters of all ages will laugh, cry, and find inspiration in these stories that remind them how much they appreciate each other.

Moms & Sons

There is a special bond between mothers and their sons and it never goes away. This new book contains the 101 best stories and poems from Chicken Soup's library honoring that lifelong relationship between mothers and their male offspring. These heartfelt and loving stories written by mothers, grandmothers, and sons, about each other, span generations and show how the mother-son bond transcends time.

Books for Mom!

Enjoy these additional fine books for Women:

Chicken Soup for the Woman's Soul
Chicken Soup for the Mother's Soul
A Second Chicken Soup for the Woman's Soul
Chicken Soup for the Parent's Soul
Chicken Soup for the Expectant Mother's Soul
Chicken Soup for the Christian Family Soul
Chicken Soup for the Mother's Soul 2
Chicken Soup for the Grandparent's Soul
Chicken Soup for the Christian Woman's Soul
Chicken Soup for the Mother & Daughter Soul
Chicken Soup for Every Mom's Soul
Chicken Soup for the Grandma's Soul
Chicken Soup for the Single Parent's Soul
Chicken Soup for the Mother and Son Soul
Chicken Soup for the Working Mom's Soul
Chicken Soup for the Soul: Celebrating Mothers and Daughters
Chicken Soup for the New Mom's Soul
Chicken Soup for the Soul: A Tribute to Moms

More books for Men

Chicken Soup for the Veteran's Soul   1-55874-937-3
Chicken Soup for the Baseball Fan's Soul   1-55874-965-9
Chicken Soup for the Gardener's Soul   1-55874-966-7
Chicken Soup for the Fisherman's Soul   0-7573-0145-2
Chicken Soup for the Golfer's Soul   1-55874-658-7
Chicken Soup for the Golfer's Soul,
The Second Round   1-55874-982-9
Chicken Soup for the NASCAR Soul   0-7573-0100-2
Chicken Soup for the Father's Soul   1-55874-894-6
Chicken Soup for the Grandparent's Soul   1-55874-974-8
Chicken Soup for the Father & Daughter Soul   0-7573-0252-1
Chicken Soup for the Single Parent's Soul   0-7573-0241-6

Books for Teens

Chicken Soup for the Soul: Preteens Talk
Inspiration and Support for Preteens from Kids Just Like Them
978-1-935096-00-9
Chicken Soup for the Soul: Teens Talk Growing Up
Stories about Growing Up, Meeting Challenges, and
Learning from Life 978-1-935096-01-6
Chicken Soup for the Soul: Teens Talk Tough Times
Stories about the Hardest Parts of Being a Teenager
978-1-935096-03-0
Chicken Soup for the Soul: Teens Talk Relationships
Stories about Family, Friends, and Love
978-1-935096-06-1
Chicken Soup for the Soul: Christian Teen Talk
Christian Teens Share Their Stories of Support, Inspiration and Growing Up
978-1-935096-12-2
Chicken Soup for the Soul: Christian Kids
Stories to Inspire, Amuse, and Warm the Hearts of Christian Kids and Their
Parents
978-1-935096-13-9

Chicken Soup for the Soul.

Older & Wiser

Our 101 BEST STORIES

Stories of
Inspiration,
Humor,
and Wisdom
about
Life at a
Certain
Age

Jack Canfield
& Mark Victor Hansen
edited by Amy Newmark

We know how it is to cross the magic 60-year mark and feel young at heart despite a few new wrinkles. We wouldn't trade away a bit of our wisdom and experience to get rid of all those life markers. This is the first Chicken Soup book to focus on the wonders of getting older, with many stories focusing on dynamic older singles and couples finding new careers, new sports, new love, and new meaning to their lives. Includes the best 101 stories for today's young seniors from Chicken Soup's library.

978-1-935096-17-7

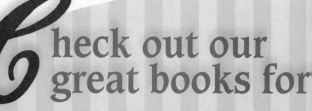

Check out our great books for

Chicken Soup for the Soul.

Our **101** BEST STORIES

Grand and **Great**

Grandparents and Grandchildren Share Their Stories of Love and Wisdom

Jack Canfield & Mark Victor Hansen
edited by Amy Newmark

A parent becomes a new person the day the first grandchild is born. Formerly serious adults become grandparents who dote on their grandchildren. This new book includes the best stories on being a grandparent from past Chicken soup books, representing a new reading experience for even the most devoted Chicken Soup fan. Everyone can understand the special ties between grandparents and grandchildren—the unlimited love, the mutual admiration and unqualified acceptance.

978-1-935096-09-2

Seniors!

Loving Our Cats

Heartwarming and Humorous Stories about
Our Feline Family Members
978-1-935096-08-5

We are all crazy about our mysterious cats. Sometimes they are our best friends; sometimes they are aloof. They are fun to watch and often surprise us. These true stories, the best from Chicken Soup's library, will make readers appreciate their own cats and see them with a new eye. Readers will revel in the heartwarming, amusing, inspirational, and occasionally tearful stories about our best friends and faithful companions — our cats.

Loving Our Dogs

Heartwarming and Humorous Stories about
Our Companions and Best Friends
978-1-935096-05-4

We are all crazy about our dogs and can't read enough about them, whether they're misbehaving and giving us big, innocent looks, or loyally standing by us in times of need. This new book from Chicken Soup for the Soul contains the 101 best dog stories from the company's extensive library. Readers will revel in the heartwarming, amusing, inspirational, and occasionally tearful stories about our best friends and faithful companions — our dogs.

Check out our books for Pet Lovers

Chicken Soup for the Soul: Woman to Woman

Women Sharing Their Stories of Hope, Humor, and Inspiration

Women have always been wonderful sources of inspiration and support for each other. They are willing to lay bare their souls and share their experiences, even with perfect strangers. This new volume includes the 101 best stories and poems in Chicken Soup's library for women of all ages, written by women just like them.

978-1-935096-04-7

*Just for
Women by Women!*

Everyone loves Christmas and the holiday season. We reunite scattered family members, watch the wonder in a child's eyes, and feel the joy of giving gifts. The rituals of the holiday season give a rhythm to the years and create a foundation for our lives, as we gather with family, with our communities at church, at school, and even at the mall, to share the special spirit of the season, brightening those long winter days.

978-1-935096-15-3

Check out our

Dating and courtship, romance, love, and marriage are favorite Chicken Soup topics. Women, and even men, love to read true stories about how it happened for other people. This book includes the 101 best stories on love and marriage chosen from a wide variety of past Chicken Soup books. These heartwarming stories will inspire and amuse readers, whether they are just starting to date, are newly wed, or are veterans of a long marriage.

978-1-935096-10-8

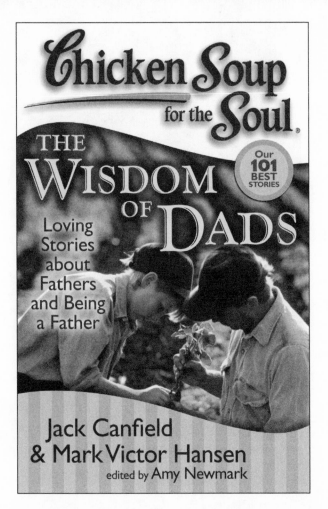

Chicken Soup for the Soul®

THE WISDOM OF DADS

Our 101 BEST STORIES

Loving Stories about Fathers and Being a Father

Jack Canfield
& Mark Victor Hansen
edited by Amy Newmark

Children view their fathers with awe from the day they are born. Fathers are big and strong and seem to know everything, except for a few teenage years when fathers are perceived to know nothing! This book represents a new theme for Chicken Soup—101 stories selected from 35 past books, all stories focusing on the wisdom of dads. Stories are written by sons and daughters about their fathers, and by fathers relating stories about their children.

978-1-935096-18-4

*C*heck out our
great books for

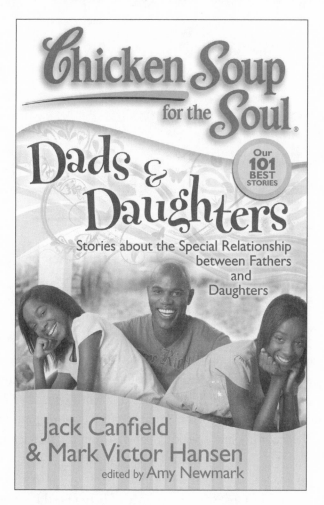

Chicken Soup for the Soul

for the Soul®

Dads & Daughters

Stories about the Special Relationship between Fathers and Daughters

Our **101** BEST STORIES

Jack Canfield & Mark Victor Hansen

edited by Amy Newmark

Whether she is ten years old or fifty — she will always be his little girl. And daughters take care of their dads too, whether it is a tea party for two at age five or loving care fifty years later. This wide-ranging exploration of the relationship between fathers and daughters contains selections from forty past Chicken Soup books. Stories were written by fathers about their daughters and by daughters about their fathers, celebrating the special bond between fathers and daughters.

978-1-935096-19-1

Dads

Chicken Soup for the Soul

Share with Us

We would like to know how these stories affected you and which ones were your favorites. Please e-mail us and let us know.

We also would like to share your stories with future readers. You may be able to help another reader, and become a published author at the same time. Please send us your own stories and poems for our future books. Some of our past contributors have launched writing and speaking careers from the publication of their stories in our books!

Your stories have the best chance of being used if you submit them through our web site, at:

www.chickensoup.com

If you do not have access to the Internet, you may submit your stories by mail or by facsimile. Please do not send us any book manuscripts, unless through a literary agent, as these will be automatically discarded.

Chicken Soup for the Soul
P.O. Box 700
Cos Cob, CT 06807-0700
Fax 203-861-7194